INSIDE THE PRIMARY CLASSROOM: 20 YEARS ON

Maurice Galton, Linda Hargreaves, Chris Comber and Debbie Wall with Anthony Pell

ROUTLEDGE

London and New York

First published 1999
by Routledge
11 New Fetter Lane, London EC4P 4EE

Simultaneously published in the USA and Canada
by Routledge
29 West 35th Street, New York, NY 10001

© 1999 Maurice Galton, Linda Hargreaves, Chris Comber,
Debbie Wall and Anthony Pell

Typeset in Sabon by Puretech India Ltd, Pondicherry
http://www.puretech.com
Printed and bound in Great Britain by Clays Ltd, St. Ives PLC

British Library Cataloguing in Publication Data
A catalogue record for this book is available from the British Library

Library of Congress Cataloging in Publication Data
Inside the primary classroom: 20 years on / Maurice Galton . . . [*et al.*].
    p.   cm.
Includes bibliographical references and index.
1. Education, Elementary–Great Britain. 2. Elementary school teaching–Great Britain.
    3. Educational change–Great Britain. 4. Observation (Educational method)
I. Galton, Maurice J.
    LA633.I57   1999
    372.941–dc21
                                            98–21898
                                            CIP

ISBN 0–415–17019–2 (hbk)
ISBN 0–415–17020–6 (pbk)

This book is respectfully dedicated to Professor Brian Simon, who began these studies of primary classroom practice over twenty years ago. His determination to portray the reality of the lives of children and their teachers with intellectual honesty has been a continuing inspiration to us all.

CONTENTS

FIGURES

TABLES

ABBREVIATIONS

AMMA	Assistant Masters and Mistresses Association
APU	Assessment of Performance Unit
AT	Attainment Target within National Curriculum subject
CATE	Council for the Accreditation of Teacher Education
ICL	International Computers Ltd
DES	Department of Education and Science
Df EE	Department for Education and Employment
EDSI	Education Department's Superhighways Initiative
EOC	Equal Opportunities Commission
ERA	Education Reform Act
HMI	Her Majesty's Inspectorate
ILEA	Inner London Education Authority
INCSS	Implementation of the National Curriculum in Small Schools (project)
KS1	Key Stage 1 of the National Curriculum, relating to children aged 5–7
KS2	Key Stage 2 of the National Curriculum, relating to children aged 8–11
LEA	Local Education Authority
LMS	Local Management of Schools
NC	National Curriculum
NCC	National Curriculum Council
NFER	National Foundation for Educational Research
NVQ	National Vocational Qualification
OFSTED	Office for Standards in Education
OMR	Optical Mark Reader
PACE	Primary Assessment, Curriculum and Experience (project)
PRINDEP	Primary Needs Independent Evaluation Project
PRISMS	Curriculum Provision in Small Schools (project)
RTBS	Richmond Tests of Basic Skills
SATs	Standard Assessment Tasks
SCAA	School Curriculum & Assessment Authority

SCENE   The Rural Schools Curriculum Enhancement Evaluation
          (project)
SEAC   Schools' Examination and Assessment Council
SEN   Special Educational Needs
SENCO   Special Educational Needs Co-ordinator
TGAT   Task Group on Assessment and Testing
TVEI   Technical and Vocational Education Initiative

CONTRIBUTORS

Chris Comber read psychology and sociology at the University of Leicester as a mature student. Following graduation, he taught developmental psychology in Further and Higher Education for three years before becoming a researcher in Education at Leicester in 1993. He has been involved in a number of research projects that have examined gender, assessment and the impact of new technologies in education. He is currently researching for a Ph.D. on the development of masculinity, and the effects of transition from primary to secondary schooling on boys' self-image and achievement.

Maurice Galton is Professor of Education at the University of Leicester and former Dean of the Faculty. He co-directed the original ORACLE project with Professor Brian Simon and directed the recent replication study reported in this volume. He is author of numerous publications dealing with aspects of primary classroom practice, including some that concern small rural schools and the effects of class size. He has acted as a consultant to the Council of Europe and is also involved in a number of international studies comparing practice in the UK with that in countries around the Pacific Rim.

Linda Hargreaves was a lecturer in Education at Leicester University before moving to Durham in 1998. After graduating in psychology from Durham University, she taught in primary schools in Leicestershire. She was a classroom observer in the first ORACLE project, and, after more primary teaching, gained a Ph.D. on assessment at primary level. She has worked with Professor Maurice Galton on research on small schools, primary science, class size and the national evaluation of the Education Department's Superhighways Initiative.

Anthony Pell studied for an M.Sc. in Research Methods at Lancaster University and a Ph.D. at Leicester after taking his first degree at Birmingham University. He was for eight years Science Education Consultant to the Gazankulu Government of South Africa. His main interests are curriculum development, educational research, physics education, and science and society studies. After many years working in schools and a further education college, he is at present a research analyst at the University of Leicester and an educational consultant.

Debbie Wall has been a research associate in the Leicester University School of Education since 1993. She qualified as a secondary school teacher before taking a Masters degree in Sociology of Education and working as a researcher at Lancashire Polytechnic (now the University of Central Lancashire) and the University of Edinburgh. She has worked on numerous projects at the University of Leicester School of Education, mostly concerned with aspects of training, including both ITT and Continuing Professional Development.

INTRODUCTION

This book reports the findings of an observational study of primary class-rooms. There has, of course, been other similar research in recent years. What makes this study unique, however, is that the present observations have been carried out in some of the same schools which were visited twenty years ago when the ORACLE project, the first large scale observational study of primary school classrooms to be carried out in this country, was undertaken. The ORACLE study (Observational Research and Classroom Learning Evaluation) was completed over five years and followed what are now called 'Key Stage 2' pupils, over the last two years of their primary schooling and into their first year after transfer. At the time, the results were of great significance and have continued to be so. Among its most important findings, ORACLE highlighted the consequences of children sitting together in groups while working individually. A number of teaching styles were also identified and were shown to be linked closely to different types of pupil behaviour. The relationship between these patterns was remarkably stable across the two years of observation. ORACLE also demonstrated that certain pedagogic styles, including one associated with individual teaching, were more effective than others. Studies conducted in the following decade have largely confirmed these findings.

My co-director at the time, Professor Brian Simon, and I ended the first-volume of the five-volume ORACLE series, *Inside the Primary Classroom*, by expressing the hope that the findings 'would make a modest contri-bution to the debate on primary education which should now be carried out in a more conciliatory and informed manner, with less conviction on either side that they hold a monopoly of truth'. Sadly, particularly for primary teachers and their pupils, this has not happened. In particular, since the coming of the National Curriculum, there has been an endless campaign of denigration of primary teachers and their methods in the media and elsewhere which has led one commentator to refer to the period as 'a reign of terror'. According to these critics, standards are continuing to fall, because teachers are teaching badly as a result of 'slavish adherence' to harmful ideologies. These are the same old shibboleths that were current some twenty years ago when the first ORACLE study was undertaken.

What better, therefore, than to return to many of the same schools that were used in the original ORACLE study, to carry out the same kinds of observation on teachers and pupils, and to give pupils the same tests of attainment? Armed with these findings, it then becomes feasible to examine, in as careful a way as possible, what has happened to primary teaching over the two decades, particularly in the light of the changes brought about by the National Curriculum. It may be, as Professor Brian Simon once said, that to have a serious debate about primary teaching of this kind would be like 'crying for the moon', but at least studies such as the present one can provide the evidence whereby those wishing to engage seriously with the subject have the means to do so.

The writing of this book has not been an easy task, partly because there is still a mass of data available that would allow us to explore our findings in more detail. We intend to do this through a further series of published research papers. Here, we have tried to bring together our most important findings that relate specifically to the current debate about primary pedagogy. The mode of working was for each of us to take responsibility for the first draft and then for others to work on those drafts until a final version was completed. In particular, I must take responsibility for the first and final chapters. These are more to do with policy matters than the middle five, which deal specifically with the research. I make no apology for expressing my feelings at the way in which primary teachers have been unfairly portrayed during the last decade. As a classroom researcher for more than twenty years, I think I may claim to have seen a wider sample of primary teaching than those who criticise these teachers. I retain nothing but admiration for the vast number of men and women who spend long hours, both inside and outside the classroom, educating young children. In Chapter 1, therefore, I examine the way in which this criticism of primary teachers has developed over the last two decades and in the final chapter, having summarised our findings, I attempt to look forward positively to the future, a future which should take account of what is happening elsewhere in the world and not focus on a rather narrow vision of primary classroom practice.

Chapter 2 examines whether the National Curriculum has brought about changes in the structure of primary classrooms and observes that little appears to have altered. Chapter 3 examines how far the overall pattern of teaching has changed and notes, in particular, the consequences of the increased shift to whole-class teaching, the result of pressure from critics and the media. Chapter 4 then looks at the primary classroom from the typical pupil's point of view. Here again, we find that, although children are working harder, the way in which they receive attention from the teacher is very similar to that of twenty years ago. One positive outcome has been the increase in task-related activity within groups. Twenty years ago most talk in groups was social; now it has much more to do with the task in hand. Chapter 5 explores how far teaching styles have changed and ways in which these styles influence pupil behaviour. Finally, in Chapter 6 we compare the performance of today's pupils with those of two decades ago in standardised tests of reading, mathematics and language. This has a bearing on the current debate about falling standards, and we consider this in Chapter 7.

This book could not have been completed without the help of a number of people. First, we should like to record a debt of gratitude to the primary teachers and to the pupils who generously gave of their time and allowed us open access to their classrooms. Our thanks are also due to our families and friends, who have been very tolerant of our obsessive concern to turn the ticks recorded during our observation of classrooms into a meaningful analysis of contemporary primary practice. Dr Tony Pell painstakingly carried out the statistical analysis on our behalf. We also have to thank both Chris Rouse and Lynn Smolinski, who have prepared the manuscript and kept track of successive drafts, and also Roy Kirk, our librarian, for hunting down some of the more obscure references. Lastly, we acknowledge the help of the Economic and Social Research Council (ESRC) who provided a grant for the study.

Our story begins with Donna, who was one of our original ORACLE pupils but who now has a child of her own in the same school where she was observed two decades ago. Her daughter, Hayley, and her classmates represent the future. We hope that this book is a small contribution to making it a better one.

Maurice Galton

1

TWO DECADES OF PRIMARY EDUCATION

Donna Leason was born in October 1965. She now lives on a council estate on the edge of an east Midlands city, the same one where she spent her early childhood.[1] She began school in April 1971 when she was five years and six months old. Her friend Allison, who lived next door, had started school the previous September because she had her fifth birthday two weeks before the school year began. During those first two terms of the school year before Donna started school, there were only twenty children in the reception class, and Mrs Cooper, the teacher, had been able to devote extra time to helping each pupil with their reading and number work.[2] After the April intake, however, the number increased by fifteen and it became more difficult to give each child sufficient attention.

Donna didn't do particularly well at school and left in April 1982 without bothering to turn up for her Certificate of Secondary Education (CSE) examinations. In the following September she applied and was accepted for a training course at the local Further Education College, and found a job as a care assistant in a local authority home for the elderly. There she met Neal, who was working as a Community Volunteer, and moved into his bedsit. Hayley was born in November 1985. The couple were given a council house on the same estate as Donna's parents, but Neal moved out and Glen, an unemployed labourer, took his place. Two other children, Jason and Kristen, were born in 1987 and 1990. When Glen also left, shortly after the birth of the third child, Donna decided to 'give up on men and better herself', and in 1992, when Jason had started school, she began a GCSE course at the local community school where there was a 'toddlers' club' for Kristen. She surprised herself by getting an A for English and a B for Mathematics and is now studying A level Biology, and Health and Social Care for an NVQ with a view to taking a degree in social work at one of the local universities.

It is now the 1995–96 school year, and Donna's eldest child, Hayley, has entered year 6 in the same primary school that her mother went to. Donna is a frequent visitor to the school and comes in whenever she has time to help with the poor readers. Unlike her mother, Hayley had the advantage of a full

1

year in the reception class and is doing very well. She will take the Key Stage 2 tests at the end of the year and move to the local high school next to the community college where Donna is finishing her 'A' levels. Although neither of these two schools has done well in the published league tables, Donna has decided to let her eldest daughter go on to the high school because her own experience suggests that the teachers care about the pupils and also because most of Hayley's friends will move with her. There is also another reason. It would cost money to bus Hayley to another school and Donna already finds it difficult to manage on her family allowance and what she gets from Social Security.

This brief biography of Donna offers a useful reference point for our study of *Inside the Primary Classroom: 20 Years On*. What then does this parent notice about her daughter's classroom compared to how it was when she sat there as a child in the 1970s? Is her first impression one of 'busyness', as it was all those years ago when visitors entered the classroom?[3] Are the children still seated in groups, either around flat topped tables or desks drawn together to form working surfaces? Will the children still be talking intermittently to each other as they go about their tasks as Donna herself did twenty years ago? Are pupils still free to move around the room when seeking help or a resource? Do some children find ways of slowing down their work rate despite the prevailing air of busyness? In Donna's time a favoured dodge was to move to the back of the queue just before reaching the teacher's desk to have your book marked.

A more detailed examination of this busy classroom may reveal distinct differences between Donna's own experience as a pupil and that of her daughter. In 1976, typically, the teacher would have been moving around the room for most of the time, talking first to one group of children and then another, or to an individual child within the group. Such exchanges would in all likelihood have been very brief, variously concerned with giving information or directions, suggesting how to tackle a problem, asking someone how they were getting on, telling another pupil how to spell a word, correcting a sum, or occasionally giving a cautionary reprimand for disruptive or antisocial behaviour. At other times there may have been quiet periods when Donna was expected to work on her own, either colouring a picture, completing a mathematics worksheet or doing a comprehension exercise from her English book. During these quiet periods, various pupils might be called out to the teacher's desk to have their work marked. One consequence of this teaching strategy was that a different picture of the classroom emerged if a visitor decided to concentrate their attention on one of the pupils rather than on the teacher. Because the teacher's exchanges were for the most part with individual pupils, and with typically between thirty and thirty-five pupils in the class, the proportion of time devoted to each child during a day was necessarily limited. Thus when asked by the visitor to comment on a typical day the teacher might respond, 'I'm exhausted, I've been talking with children all day', while a pupil might say 'I just got on with it. I only talked with the teacher for a few minutes when she either marked my work, said "well done" or "do it again" or told me when I'd finished I should get on with my picture.'

This kind of analysis, based upon observation of moment-by-moment exchanges between teachers and pupils, has been one of the major strands of research in primary education. It generally involves an observer selecting a sample of 'target' pupils, either randomly or matched by ability and gender, and carrying out several rounds of observation in which each target is observed according to a predetermined pattern at fixed time intervals. In some studies the observation of pupils is also interspersed by extended observation of the teacher in order to give both the adult's and child's view of the classroom.

One of the first British studies to make use of this style of observation was the ORACLE study (Observational Research and Classroom Learning Evaluation). This programme commenced in 1975, and over three years, beginning in September 1976, carried out observations in fifty-eight primary classrooms, distributed across three local authorities. In the third year of the observation, the children were followed as they transferred out of their primary or first school into their next phase of education. During each of the three years of observation the children's academic progress was also measured, using standardised tests of reading, language and mathematics. The study was able to identify a number of different teaching styles and to describe the effects of these styles on pupils' behaviour and on the pupils' attainment. Over the three-year period during which the fieldwork took place, a mass of information was acquired. There were, for example, 47,000 observations of the fifty-eight teachers, and 84,000 observations of 489 pupils (Galton *et al.*, 1980; Galton and Simon 1980).

Turning the progressive tide?

The ORACLE study was completed in 1980. In the intervening period up to the present time, there have been a number of other studies either using the same or similar systems of observation. In the early 1980s the Curriculum Provision in Small Schools (PRISMS) Project (Galton and Patrick 1990) used a version of the ORACLE observation system in which the observation categories were extended to include more details about the curriculum. The study involved sixty-eight small schools (schools with less than a hundred pupils on roll) drawn from nine local authorities, during which 188 teachers and their classes were observed. During the same period there was also a study that used observation to examine the problems associated with the one in five pupils who were designated as having special needs (Croll and Moses 1985) and in the mid-1980s, two studies of London schools, one which studied the early years (Tizard *et al.* 1988) and one in the junior age range (Mortimore *et al.* 1988). Following on from this work there was a study of primary classrooms in Leeds (Alexander *et al.* 1989; Alexander 1995). Taking us into the 1990s, there have been two further studies which have coincided with the introduction of the National Curriculum. One of these was located in small schools (Galton *et al.* 1998). The other, the PACE (Primary Assessment Curriculum and Experience) project, which began in 1989, was designed to track the impact of the 1988 Education Reform Act on primary school practice. PACE has reported its findings on early years classrooms (Pollard *et al.* 1994) and on the junior years in Croll (1996a).

Despite this almost continuous scrutiny of primary practice, there has been continued disagreement about the changes that have taken place over the last two decades. One popular view within media and political circles is that back in the 1970s, 'progressivism' ruled, and it was 'the wild men', although not in those days women, who were bent on destroying our education system.[4] Depending on party allegiance, it was either the brave intervention of the then Labour Prime Minister, James Callaghan (1976) in his Ruskin speech, or else his replacement by a Conservative, Margaret Thatcher, following her party's victory in the 1979 General Election, which halted this progressive tide. Eighteen years of Conservative rule saw the 'new right' gain increasing control of education policy (Ball 1990). Beginning with a series of 'position' papers emanating from the Centre for Policy Studies, the right wing 'think tank', this faction in the Conservative party played a key role in the design of the 1988 Education Reform Act and the introduction of a National Curriculum by the then Secretary of State for Education, Kenneth Baker (Baker 1993).

However, a decade after these reforms were introduced there are those who argue that this tide of progressivism has yet to be stemmed. Chief among those expressing this view is the current HM Chief Inspector of Schools, Chris Woodhead, who argues that progressive ideology still dominates primary practice and that the greatest barrier to raising standards is the progressive's contempt for the study of 'all the matters which most concern us, the best which has been thought and said in the world' (Woodhead 1995a; 1995b).[5] A more extreme view has been expressed by the journalist Melanie Phillips (1996), who not only agrees with the Chief Inspector that these progressive trends have brought about a decline in academic standards, but also argues that they are the cause of serious moral turpitude within contemporary society.

Part of the cause of this continued uncertainty about the extent of change in primary schooling over the last two decades, despite the apparent wealth of observational data, stems from the fact that many political and media activists choose to fit the facts around their theories rather than the other way round when they write on such matters. Journalists, by the nature of the profession, tend to oversimplify and generally focus on the negative features of any incident since, to paraphrase the late Lord Rothermere, 'If the reader feels angry, disgusted or worried that's news but if they are merely better informed that's public relations.' More controversially, however, Colin Richards (1997), a former senior inspector in the Office of Standards in Education (OFSTED), commenting on the Chief Inspector's annual reports, has argued that OFSTED inspection data have been manipulated for political reasons.

Uncertainty in the interpretation of the research among some academics has, it must be admitted, fuelled this media debate. Differences in interpretation have arisen either because the observations of primary practice have had different emphases, or because different sampling techniques were used, or because the research was carried out in different parts of the country where it could be argued that pupil performance in multi-cultural inner city schools could not be equated with that recorded by pupils from small schools in rural areas. The strength of the study reported in the following chapters is that it represents both the beginning and end of an era, marked respectively by the defeat of one Labour government and the election of another. New Labour now offers educational prescriptions which are almost identical to those emanating from the previous Conservative regimes. Indeed, recent pronouncements have perhaps gone further than the previous government would have dared. For example, the first act of the new Labour government's Secretary of State for Education and Employment, David Blunkett, was to 'name and shame' eighteen failing schools.[6]

Throughout this debate, with its charge and counter charge, the original ORACLE research, although based on observations carried out twenty years ago, still retains a pre-eminent position. While critics such as Scarth and Hammersley (1986; 1987) and Edwards and Westgate (1987) have doubted whether an observer can reliably categorise teachers' questions without knowledge of their intentions, the central findings appear to have stood the test of time, and have been admired for their 'growing sophistication at both policy and methodological level' (Hargreaves 1997). Furthermore, in a review on the lessons to be learnt from primary research, Caroline Gipps (1992) devotes nearly a third of her twenty-seven pages to the ORACLE findings. The research has also been cited by critics of primary practice such as Melanie Phillips (1996) and Chris Woodhead (1995a) as well as by supporters. Moreover, since many of the other studies referred to in the previous paragraphs have tended to confirm many of its findings, ORACLE has remained the most authoritative source of data on primary practice, until, perhaps, the recent PACE studies (Pollard *et al.* 1994).

What better, therefore, than to repeat the original ORACLE study, using exactly the same instruments, the same attainment tests and the same schools? For if ORACLE findings have, by and large, been accepted as one of the most authoritative statements on primary classroom practice in the pre-National Curriculum period, then it should be difficult for either present critics or supporters of primary education to dispute its replication using the same methodology and the same schools. Some minor changes in the research design have been necessary; for example the observation schedules have been expanded to provide more detailed information, attainment tests have been modified to replace words which were commonplace in the 1970s but have now either changed their meaning or have become politically incorrect, and some of the secondary-phase schools have changed their age of entry. At present-day values, the full 1975 ORACLE programme would cost over a million pounds. The grant for this replication study was just over £50,000. Not every school in the 1975 sample could, therefore, be included, and six rather than eight target pupils were observed during each teaching session. However, before describing these changes in more detail and setting out the main purposes of this research, it may prove useful to place primary schooling in a contemporary context. This includes, in particular, the effects of 'globalisation' associated with the growth of the 'Tiger' economies around the Pacific Rim and the resulting changes to our personal lives in this post-traditional society (Giddens 1994). Primary schools not only have to reflect and interpret existing societal characteristics, but also have to anticipate future trends, since children now entering school are being educated for work and leisure well beyond the millennium. Given that the period between 1975 and the present has been one of rapid change politically, educationally, economically and socially, this is not an easy task. In reading the remaining chapters of this book, which deal specifically with changes in primary practice, these varying contexts need to be continually borne in mind.

The 1975 version of primary education

When ORACLE began, English primary education was still thought by many people to be the 'best in the world'. It was also assumed to have had a stable and uniform structure, the result of the reforms enacted some thirty years previously following the passing of the 1944 Education Act. Then, in the mid-1960s, the post-war consensus that had sustained this stability started to break down as more radical ideas began to dominate educational debate. In primary education the key event was the publication of the Plowden Committee's Report (1967) which critics described as 'a progressive's charter'.[7]

A more accurate picture, as described by Brian Simon in the first volume of the ORACLE research output, *Inside the Primary Classroom*, was that after the 1944 Act and into the 1970s, periods of change were followed by yet more periods of change, 'a state of almost continuous transition' (Galton *et al.* 1980: 42). In the 1950s separate infant and junior schools were merged into 'all through' primary schools.[8] Then in the late 1960s, as the comprehensive movement expanded, a three-tier system catering for five to eight and five to nine year-old children was created to feed eight to twelve and nine to thirteen middle schools as a way of utilising existing accommodation. These new structures ensured that the primary curriculum was subject to frequent if largely uncoordinated review. The greatest issue, however, was the continuing debate throughout the 1960s on the virtues of selection and of the 11+ examination which was a consequence of this selection process. Following the Plowden (1967) report, which set out a blueprint for the future of primary education (based in part on the optimistic view of that time, that more education for more children equalled greater national prosperity), the shift to comprehensive education and the demise of the 11+ consequent on the end of selection, led to a rapid de-streaming in primary schools. This was sharply illustrated in the work of Joan Barker Lunn (1970), who in the late 1960s began an evaluation study with a countrywide sample of primary schools in which she compared streamed junior classes with unstreamed ones, only to find that by 1970 her streamed sample had been reduced to a point where it was no longer possible to make any valid comparisons.

Throughout this period concerns were expressed by both the media and politicians concerning this rapid shift to comprehensive education and the effects upon primary schools. The debate centred around the publication of a series of 'Black Papers' in which academics and well-known writers such as Kingsley Amis argued, amongst other things, for retaining the grammar schools and the reintroduction of streaming. At the centre of the debate about primary schooling was a concerted attack upon methods such as discovery learning, which it was claimed was widely used by teachers, some of whom were 'taking to an extreme the belief that children must not be told anything, but must find out for themselves'. According to one Black Paper writer, this *laissez-faire* approach,

> now favoured in infant and primary education encourages a regrettable laxity in systematic work: the modern child is encouraged to read fluently and talk glibly in terms commensurate with his tender years; but his introduction to the hard process of learning and mastering what might be called the mechanics of this subject, is put off too long.
>
> (A. Hardie in Cox and Dyson 1969: 57)

Black Paper authors were not in favour of group activity since, according to these critics this pernicious doctrine led to the teacher acting as a kind of 'peripatetic adviser'. Taking his criticism further, Hardie (Cox and Dyson 1969: 58) claimed,

> A conscientious young teacher faced with several groups of children all engaged in different activities (and probably one or two unable

to read) finds herself [*sic*] helpless in a chaotic situation, and eventually seeks refuge in a nervous breakdown.

Referring to this situation as 'progressive collapse', a phrase used by the editorial writer of *The Times* (27 September 1968) to describe the disintegration of a tower block of council flats at Ronan Point, Cox and Dyson (1969) refer to an education college lecturer who claimed that students wrote *his* for *is*, did not know the difference between *their* and *there* or *where* and *were* and could neither punctuate nor spell.

Initiating reform: a great debate?

These claims and counter claims will sound very familiar to readers of today's popular press. What can be said of the debate at the time, although as with the current one it was often characterised by ignorance and prejudice, was that it was generally conducted in good humour, respect for each other's views and a degree of give and take. Perhaps nothing illustrated this state of affairs so well as the situation at the University of Leicester where in the School of Education, a leading Black Paper writer, Professor Geoffrey Bantock, worked alongside Professor Brian Simon, founding editor of the progressive journal *Forum* and a strong advocate of comprehensive education. This atmosphere of reasoned debate pervaded not only the world of academia but also that of the leading broadsheet newspapers, where the writings of educational correspondents such as Peter Wilby and Virginia Makins were both highly respected and frequently quoted. At the core of the debate, as described elsewhere by Galton (1989) and more recently by Alexander (1995; 1997), was a clash of ideologies which could be traced back to the eighteenth century. Then, the elementary school curriculum had been principally designed to meet the economic and labour needs of an expanding industrial society. In contrast, reformers arguing for an experiential and developmental curriculum placed greater emphasis on allowing each child to realise his or her full potential. At one extreme this curriculum was to be open and negotiable, while at the other it was to be structured to accommodate children's psychological and physiological development (Blyth 1984). Opposed to the 'progressive' approach were the classical humanists, whose prime aim was to induct children into the best of the cultural past, usually through the study of discrete subject disciplines. It was this latter approach that the Black Paper writers were concerned to defend.

Evaluation studies during the 1970s, however, showed that it was hard to find examples of a curriculum based exclusively upon either of these contrasting ideologies. Rather, through a process of hybridisation (or mixing) these contrasting strands of primary education became interwoven, with certain strands gaining prominence in different schools (Kliebard 1986). Only in a few isolated examples, as in the case of the William Tyndale School in

8

London, which became something of a *cause célèbre*, were attempts made to put a more extreme version of progressive ideology into practice, that is until inspectors from the Inner London Education Authority were called in, and the headteacher and his deputy dismissed (Auld 1976). Despite the claims that intermittently surface, often as a justification for more repressive legislation, the evidence would suggest that there never was a primary revolution (Simon 1981a).

Support for this view emerged during the 1970s with the publication of an educational report entitled *Teaching Styles and Pupil Progress* by Neville Bennett (1976). Taking schools in Cumbria and Lancashire, Bennett sent questionnaires to 871 primary schools, to which 468 'top junior' teachers responded. Bennett grouped their responses into twelve distinct teaching styles along a continuum from formal to informal. At the extreme informal end were teachers who favoured integration of the subject matter, allowed pupils choice of work and in many cases a choice of seating. Intrinsic motivation was favoured and tests, grading and homework 'appeared to be discouraged' Bennett (1976: 45).

At the other extreme in the most formal group, no teacher favoured an integrated approach, subjects were taught separately to the whole class and followed up with individual seat work. No pupil was allowed a choice of seat and every teacher curbed movement and talk. The most formal teachers were above average on the use of all assessment procedures, and systems of reward such as stars and grades were common. However, of the 468 teachers included in the clustering, only 14 per cent were located in the two most extreme informal groups, and even within these groups there was considerable variation. For example, only two-thirds of these informal teachers allowed children to sit where they wished, a fifth gave weekly spelling tests, and only just over half allowed pupils an element of choice in what work they could do. The main factor which defined the informal category was 'above average' use of integrated subject teaching (Bennett 1975). Over the years the words, 'above average' have tended to be forgotten and 'trendy' or 'woolly' primary teachers have frequently been accused of believing that 'knowledge is unimportant and subjects are artificial impositions' (*Daily Telegraph* 27 January 1995).[9] In Bennett's study, however, to become an 'above average' user of integrated subject teaching you would only have had to devote just over 19 per cent of the time (four and three-quarter hours of a twenty-five hour school week) to project and topic work. Typically, over two-thirds of the time was devoted to single-subject teaching. If these descriptions of teaching, collected during the early 1970s, constitute the evidence that a revolution was taking place in English primary schools, then the claims are not very convincing.

Bennett then went on to take a smaller group of teachers from the extremes of the continuum and also from the middle to enable comparisons to be made between the effectiveness of the formal, mixed and informal

9

teaching approaches. His conclusion (Bennett 1976: 96–7) was that, overall, pupils in the formal classroom made significantly better progress in English than those in mixed and informal classrooms, and that those in mixed classrooms also made significantly better progress than pupils in informal classrooms. In mathematics, it was the formal teaching styles which again were most successful, except with the lowest achieving boys.

On re-analysis however, some of these results were less clear-cut, because a number of additional variables from the teacher attitude scale were added to the clustering (Aitken *et al.* 1981). Teachers who had been in either the formal or informal groups moved to other clusters. The least effective group of teachers were now those who had 'above average' discipline problems, something one might have surmised was a consequence and not a characteristic of a teacher's style. In the interim period attention had focused on the case of an informal teacher from the original analysis who achieved results comparable with teachers using more formal approaches. This became a key element in the then Labour government's call for a 'Great Debate', made during a speech at Ruskin College, Oxford, by the Prime Minister, James Callaghan (1976). According to the (by now Lord) Callaghan (1992), 'of all the countless speeches I have delivered in a long political life, the Ruskin speech is the one best remembered, even today.' In the 1976 speech the Prime Minister asked why there was so much criticism among parents and employers about educational standards, and suggested that it could be that child-centred informal instruction was being misunderstood, or misused. In a clear reference to Bennett's successful informal teacher he pointed to the unease 'felt by parents and others about the new and informal methods of teaching, which seemed to produce excellent results when they are in well qualified hands, and much more dubious ones when they are not'.

The 1980s and the emergence of the New Right[10]

The Labour government under James Callaghan was defeated in 1979 following the 'winter of discontent'.[11] However, given what was to follow during the 1990s, the years preceding the passing of the 1988 Education Reform Act were relatively settled ones for the educational system. The new Conservative government had bigger concerns to do with the development of its new monetarist policies, the implementation of the market forces philosophy in the public sector and, most importantly, the reform of the trade union movement culminating in the bitter battles fought during the miners' strike of 1984. In this same period, there was a war in the Falkland Islands and the privatisation of the nationalised utilities, a policy which a former Conservative Prime Minister, Harold Macmillan, likened to 'selling off the family silver'.[12]

The education debate during this period shifted to questions that were less concerned with teaching methods and more with curriculum entitlement.

Survey work by Bassey (1978) and Bennett *et al.* (1980) had shown that there were wide variations in the amounts of time given to different subjects in different schools. The argument about the need for breadth and balance within this entitlement curriculum was developed by social reconstructionists such as Dennis Lawton (1975). Although Lawton agreed with the classical humanists that education was mainly concerned with the transmission of culture, for him culture implied 'the whole way of life' of a society and not simply its finest literature, art, music and scientific discoveries. Lawton accepted that the curriculum should include the study of these disciplines, but argued that this subject knowledge should be integrated within a wider study of changes within society, particularly ideas about the nature of social relationships and the creation of the new political democratic movements, which had arisen in response to the less positive aspects of industrialism (Williams 1961). For Lawton the idea of a common culture led naturally to the notion of a common curriculum in which every pupil had an entitlement to a central core consisting of both academic and practical options.

The first half of the 1980s saw the publication of a series of documents on curriculum matters, mostly written by Her Majesty's Inspectors (DES 1980a; 1980b; 1983; 1985a; 1985b). Meanwhile in the primary phase, researchers switched from the study of teaching styles to that of pupil learning and began to challenge the application of Piaget's ideas as reflected in the emphasis given to individualisation within the primary classroom (Brown and Desforges 1979; Desforges 1982). In keeping with the views of the curriculum reconstructionists, increasing emphasis was also placed on the idea of learning as a social as well as a cognitive activity as, for example, in the contrast between children attempting to construct the world as social beings and as lone scientists (Bruner and Haste 1987). Doubts about the value of individualisation in learning were reinforced by studies of time spent by pupils on-task (Denham and Lieberman 1980) and of the quality of pupils' learning (Bennett *et al.* 1984).

However, there was a marked contrast in the philosophy of the 'New Right' that had set the agenda for the new Conservative government and the social democratic ideas which underpinned the reconstructionist curriculum reformers. Reconstructionism was based upon an assumption that the individual can best realise his or her full potential within the framework and value system of democratic society. The common curriculum should therefore include themes such as citizenship and community education. Learning through co-operation should be encouraged during teaching. However, according to the Prime Minister, Margaret Thatcher,[13] there was 'no such thing as society' in the sense that the community had a collective responsibility to nurture its members. Society was simply reflected in the uncoordinated actions of millions of individuals. The reconstructionist advocacy of a common curriculum as a means of empowering the

economi'
Thatcher
socuts

underprivileged was no longer in keeping with contemporary political orthodoxy. The main argument for curriculum reform was once more an economic one, to enable the next generation of workers to compete effectively in the 'market-places' of the future (Lawlor 1988).

This period when the new agenda for schools began to be drawn up is charted by John Tomlinson, at the time a Chief Education Officer. Commenting on the new government's educational policy initiatives, he argues that during the period from 1979 to 1985, 'it was the methods, not the objectives that were new' (Tomlinson 1992: 47). According to Tomlinson, 'consultative bodies were disbanded and procedures compressed.' Consultations were often undertaken over the summer holiday period, 'to the intended discomfort of teachers and local authority associations'. Tomlinson further argues that underlying these processes were deeper objectives of a

> neo-liberal programme, namely removing or neutralising institutions and power groupings which intervene between the state and the individual, notably the breaking of the power of the teachers' trade unions (over pay, conditions of service and the curriculum), a significant reduction in the powers of local government and its re-alignment towards being an agency of central government, together with an orchestrated denigration of the teaching profession.
>
> (Tomlinson 1992: 47–8)

LEAs were also marginalised, in that a great deal of work in schools was subject to earmarked grants from central government, thereby forging the tools of direct central control of schools. Some initiatives were no longer controlled by the DES (Department of Education and Science) as, for example, the Technical and Vocational Education Initiative (TVEI), which was funded through the Department of Employment. By 1986, according to Tomlinson, a system which for thirty-five years

> had been run through broad legislative objectives convention and consensus had been replaced by one based on contract and management... The stage had been set for a radical phase of neo-conservative educational policy. Although there were some deliberate leaks, the manifesto of 1987, which provided the mandate for the 1988 Reform Act, was prepared in secret in the previous nine months under the general direction of the Prime Minister's policy unit. The aim was to make an irreversible change in the public education system similar to that already achieved in other aspects of social economic policy, such as trade union legislation, the sale of council houses and the privatisation of the national industries.
>
> (Tomlinson 1992: 48)

The 1988 Education Reform Act – and all that followed

The Education Reform Act of 1988 in many ways represented an uneasy compromise between those advocating a free market approach and those arguing for a greater degree of centralisation in education. Although not going so far as to recreate grammar schools, under Mrs Thatcher's leadership, schools were encouraged to break away from local authority control and to become 'grant maintained', city technology colleges were created, and more assisted places at independent schools provided. Conservative dominated councils, such as Wandsworth, were encouraged to develop 'magnet schools', which would be noted for excellence in particular aspects of the curriculum. Schools that remained under LEA control now had delegated budgets and relative financial independence. Since the size of the budget depended on the number of pupils on roll, an element of competition was introduced between neighbouring schools. Free market conditions were simulated by no longer requiring schools to fill their quota of places from within their catchment area. Schools were now free to enrol as many pupils as they felt able to cope with.

In a totally free market, however, schools would also have been free to create their own curriculum. Then, as with the private sector, parents would choose a particular school because the curriculum and the teaching methods met the talents and needs of their child. However, those favouring greater centralisation argued that there was a need for tighter control on the subject matter taught in schools, and also for formal procedures by which the outcomes of this teaching could be assessed. Those advocating a market approach also supported an extension of the assessment process, since it provided the means whereby competition between schools could be regulated. In theory, at least, the test scores for each school could be published, allowing parents to make more informed decisions as to which education was the 'best buy'. Over time, therefore, test scores which were originally designed to assess whether certain educational criteria had been met were now also called into service as a measure of the overall standard. This went ahead despite the experience of the United States, which indicated that when tests were used for a multiplicity of purposes then the validity and reliability of the instruments suffered (Burstall and Kay 1978).

Nevertheless, none of the ministers involved, nor the officials who were set up to run the two new agencies, the National Curriculum Council (NCC), in charge of curriculum, and the Schools' Examination and Assessment Council (SEAC), appeared willing to listen to any reservations from the educational experts, seeing their concerns as a manifestation of a desire to delay the introduction of the new measures for as long as possible. Within two years of the passing into law of the Education Reform Act there were new assessments in place at 7+ and trials underway at 11+, and a statutory national curriculum had been designed and introduced into primary schools.

13

New agencies were established under government control for determining the initial teacher training curriculum, and teachers' pay and conditions. Levels of capitation for building and repairs and determination of the formula for fixing school budgets were taken away from the LEA and placed under central government control (Tomlinson 1992).

Criticism of the magnitude or the speed of these changes was viewed as ideological rather than as a genuine expression of practical concern. It has been alleged, for example, that at a reception to mark the completion of one National Curriculum subject panel's task, a government minister asked for advice on 'how things might be improved next time'. When the answer 'give us more time' was offered the minister allegedly rounded on his unfortunate informant and asked her, 'How do you think we would have won in the Falklands with such an attitude?'

If the above account was accurate, then what was glossed over in this trite remark was the fact that, on the way to the retaking of Port Stanley, there were several disasters, such as those at Goose Green and Bluff Cove, not to mention the damage to a sizeable part of Her Majesty's naval task force. In a similar way, although with less fatal consequences, the battle to impose the National Curriculum and its related assessments on a sceptical teaching profession did considerable damage. In particular, the lack of genuine consultation appears to have created a sense of confusion, frustration and bitterness among the 'foot soldiers' who were required to teach and assess the new programmes of study; this, in turn, has led to a spate of stress- related illness and an increase in early retirements. Initially, an Interim Primary Committee was established, which was disbanded after a year with its work incomplete. As Galton (1995) recounts, the writing of the report was taken over by officials of the National Curriculum Council, so that the advice given was bland, too general and restricted to uncontroversial issues. Teachers were encouraged to create development plans, and to reduce the amount of 'evaporated time' (i.e. the transition time between lessons, or non-contact time during lessons) with the aim of increasing the proportion of intellectually demanding teacher-and-pupil conversations. At its final meeting, the committee suggested that an advisory group dedicated solely to consideration of the primary curriculum should be retained. However, this view was rejected by the then Chief Executive, Duncan Graham, appointed by Kenneth Baker because 'he was not in thrall to the prejudices of academics' (Baker 1993: 198). Planning of the primary curriculum was to be left to the subject committees, which were dominated by representatives from the secondary and tertiary levels.

The new programmes of study were fed into the schools after only cursory trials. The new assessment procedures, though subject to a more extended evaluation, proved to be extremely time-consuming, often taking the class teacher over a week to implement at Key Stage 1. Most teachers felt this time could be better spent since the SATs scores 'didn't tell them anything they didn't know already' (Shorrocks *et al.* 1992). Three crucial surveys, carried out for the Assistant Masters and Mistresses Association (AMMA), showed that there was massive overloading in the primary curriculum (Campbell 1993). The pressure felt by teachers was not, as National Curriculum officials argued, just a feature of getting used to the new arrangements. Teachers complained that the introduction of both core and the foundation subjects, particularly at Key Stage 1, left little time for teaching children to read, and there were warnings that standards of literacy would fall. Eventually, the National Union of Teachers successfully brought teachers out on strike to protest against the introduction of the new assessment procedures, on top of the new national curriculum orders. Kenneth Baker now departed from education to become Home Secretary.

1992 and all that[14]

There was a brief interregnum before another cabinet reshuffle brought Kenneth Clarke to the Education Department in 1990. From the outset, in keeping with his reputation while Minister of Health, his approach appeared to be more confrontational than Kenneth Baker's. Having shaken up first the police and then the doctors, he now set about doing the same thing to the teachers. Appearing to work on the assumption that when people complain about change, they usually do so because they wish to preserve the status quo, there was no shortage of 'scare stories' about poor teaching which the new Secretary of State for Education could use to justify further reform of primary pedagogy. Among the selected examples of poor teaching was Culloden Primary School, the 1990 equivalent of William Tyndale, which was heavily criticised in an HMI report for its 'progressive practices', particularly its use of 'real books' for teaching reading (Alexander 1997: 187). The new Prime Minister, John Major, struggling to meet criticism from the right wing of the Tory party that he was seeking to 'dilute' Thatcherism, was on several occasions forced to over-react when faced with various educational incidents.

Typical was the case at Nene College in Northampton (Alexander 1997: 187–8), where a candidate with a good Cambridge honours degree in Classics was rejected for entry to the teacher training course, mainly because she failed the selection criteria administered by the Council for the Accreditation of Teacher Education (CATE). The CATE criteria required intending primary teachers to have studied, at least as the main part of their degree, one of the subject specialisms of the National Curriculum. It was also thought preferable that applicants had already gained some experience working with young children. Having been rejected on both counts, the unsuccessful candidate then penned a second, deliberately mis-spelt, application claiming to be an Afro-Caribbean student with a third-class sociology degree, with a penchant for active participation in various protests, such as the animal rights campaign. This time the college, acting in accordance with a government-sponsored campaign to increase the number of people from ethnic minorities within the teaching profession, particularly those from Afro-Caribbean backgrounds, offered a place on the basis of the second application. To make matters worse, according to Mrs Garfield, the author of both applications, she had originally been advised by the admissions tutor to consider employment as a dinner lady! This advice she took to indicate a contempt for her Cambridge classics qualification, although the tutor was merely suggesting a way in which Mrs Garfield could gain some experience with primary age children, since dinner ladies in small rural schools often performed similar tasks to that of classroom assistants in larger suburban institutions.[15] However, to the right wing of the Conservative Party, this episode typified all that was wrong with the English education system, which according to these critics was riddled from top to bottom with left-wing fanatics (Lawlor 1990). After an outcry in the popular press, Prime Minister Major sent inspectors into the college. Subsequently little further was heard concerning these events, and the investigation was quietly dropped.

According to Alexander (1997: 186), when Kenneth Clarke took over the Department of Education a departmental memorandum concerned with ways of improving primary education was already in existence. One of its main suggestions was for a specific initiative directed at changing the way teachers taught. At the time, there was an emerging view among senior officials and some junior ministers that, despite the assumptions inherent in the construction of the National Curriculum and its related assessments, the emphasis given to content in the core and foundation subjects had not led to increased use of more formal direct teaching approaches. Inner-city schools were thought to be most resistant to change. Whereas the Chief Executive of the National Curriculum Council, Duncan Graham, had enjoyed a close relationship with Kenneth Baker, these other ministers held that by making the curriculum too complicated, the Council under Graham's leadership was partially responsible for failing to 'sort out the way that teachers teach' (Graham 1993: 111). When, after a series of increasingly sharp disagreements, Duncan Graham resigned, Kenneth Clarke approved the appointment of an insider, Chris Woodhead, as the new Chief Executive. Although a surprise appointment to many outside the National Curriculum Council, it was not unexpected by some within the organisation who regarded their new boss as a 'low profile appointment', a member of a team 'prepared to work with increasingly right-wing councils' (Watkins 1993: 66). His manner was said, at times, to be somewhat abrasive rather than conciliatory.[16] Whatever view is taken about the reason for Woodhead's advancement, subsequent events quickly showed that he was at one with the government in regarding the 'problems' of primary education as mainly the result of poor teaching.

Just as in 1976, when Neville Bennett's book, *Teaching Styles and Pupil Progress* provided the launching pad for James Callaghan's Ruskin speech and the inauguration of a great debate on education, so too in the 1990s another research study was to be used to focus concern on current primary teaching methods. In 1985, the Leeds Local Education Authority inaugurated its Primary Needs Programme. Over a five-year period the Authority allocated nearly £14 million to school improvement, of which £11 million was spent on enhanced staffing. The aim of the project was to identify the needs of all children, and in particular those experiencing learning difficulties. A team of researchers from Leeds University under Robin Alexander was appointed to evaluate the project, and the final report was delivered at the end of July 1991 (Alexander 1991). The Primary Needs Independent Evaluation Project (PRINDEP) produced fifty-five specific recommendations, and listed over twenty positive achievements of the LEA's initiative. Few of the listed achievements, however, concerned the key areas of teaching and learning, apart from the positive effects of improving the physical environment and the development of greater co-operation between teachers. What made the newspaper headlines were the findings dealing with the apparent lack of major improvements in reading standards, the tendency of some headteachers to defend ineffective practice in terms of progressive ideology, and the perceived views among teachers that the Leeds Authority wished to promote a specific model of 'good practice'. This model emphasised children working in groups, with different groups involved in different areas of the curriculum at any one time, and encouraged an enquiry or exploratory approach. The conclusion in the right-wing press that this had been a very expensive demonstration of the failure of progressive teaching, provided the justification for the Secretary of State for Education and other ministers to act. The results of these deliberations was to commission a discussion paper from Robin Alexander and the Chief Inspector for primary education, Jim Rose. Its purpose was to

> review available evidence about the delivery of education in primary schools and to make recommendations about curriculum organisation, teaching methods and classroom practice appropriate for the successful implementation of the National Curriculum, particularly at key Stage 2.
>
> (Alexander *et al.* 1992: 1, para 1)

A full account of the writing and subsequent publication of this discussion paper, together with the review of the various criticisms made at the time can be found in Alexander (1997). According to this account, subsequent events were largely determined by two late interventions by the Education Secretary, Kenneth Clarke. First, apparently without prior discussion with fellow ministers, he announced that he would add to the two-man team the Chief Executive of the National Curriculum Council, the same Chris Woodhead mentioned previously. Alexander and others argued without success against this move because it would prejudice their impartiality in reporting the impact of National Curriculum on practice, since its Chief Executive could hardly be regarded as neutral.

The second intervention came just as work on the discussion paper began. In the same way that the BBC 'Horizon' programme featuring Bennett's 1976 research had released a backlash against modern primary methods, so now 'Panorama' featured a report on the PRINDEP evaluation. Pre-recorded comments by LEA representatives, Alexander and some of the headteachers were incorporated into the programme and interlinked with interviews from both Kenneth Clarke and his opposition shadow, who at the time was Jack Straw. The BBC received a large number of complaints about what was perceived as biased reporting. In a subsequent programme objectors were allowed to have their say, but Alexander's own reservations were not included. Committed to writing the discussion paper with Rose and Woodhead, he was unable to appear live on the second programme; instead he wrote a letter setting out his views. He then came under pressure from a member of the 'Panorama' team, threatening legal action if he did not withdraw his written comments for the programme, which he subsequently did (Alexander 1997: 202)

Nine days after the 'Panorama' programme, Kenneth Clarke issued a press release announcing the Alexander, Rose and Woodhead initiative, but he chose to do so in terms which seemed to anticipate the discussion paper's conclusions, so that the next day press headlines announced that 'Clarke frees pupils from the groups of the 60s' and that 'Clarke shuts the classroom door on 25 years of trendy teaching.' Other versions, such as 'Back to Basics' and 'Clarke backs return to formal lessons', appeared to be giving a strong 'steer' to the authors of what, since it was published in the period of Epiphany, the press eventually dubbed as 'The Three Wise Men's' Report (Alexander 1997: 204).

It is not the intention here to go over the detailed academic arguments concerning the merits or otherwise of the discussion paper (Alexander *et al.* 1992), since a very full and balanced account is given by Alexander (1997). He accuses his critics of failing to give sufficient weight to the educational arguments that were enshrined in the document, and in this he is supported by Simon (1992), who argued that the views expressed in the discussion paper deserved 'a serious response'. Alexander directs much of his fire at Hammersley and Scarth (1993), whom he argues misinterpret key paragraphs and make statements which are 'neither correct nor legitimate'. He also makes a strong case when he accuses both Dadds (1992) and Galton (1995) among others of failing to read key paragraphs sufficiently carefully 'perhaps' because of their 'understandable desire to defend a profession and a set of beliefs under strong attack by politicians and the press' (Alexander 1997: 241), so that the discussion paper's argument for *some* specialist or semi-specialist teaching at Key Stage 2 was not, as Galton (1995: 92) suggests, an endorsement of media calls for 'a *move* to specialised teaching in the Junior school'.

Galton's (1995) main criticism, namely that the discussion paper's statements about classroom practice were too broad to be of use to the practitioner, is also echoed by Simon (1994: 155), who argues that 'the question as to how pedagogical means, designed to facilitate mental, or cognitive development of *all* children are to be elaborated, nor what implications these might have for classroom organisation and teaching techniques' are not entered into and yet '*it is this issue which lies at the heart of the matter*'. In making a similar point, Galton (1995), for example contrasts the report's rather hesitant attempt to point out the limitations of methods such as direct instruction, where the research findings are very clear, with the more forthright statements condemning aspects of progressive practice, and deduces from this that, under pressure from certain members of the team, the educational purposes were sometimes relegated to a minor role in comparison to political ones. In the light of Alexander's (1997) detailed account, however, Galton's suspicions are unfounded, and the explanation for the lack of any detailed discussion of the circumstances governing the appropriate use of specific teaching strategies is more likely that of Simon (1994: 155), who argues that detailed discussion of pedagogy was 'not in the English tradition' and that, therefore, it would have been asking too much of Alexander that 'he should tangle with these questions' when his two colleagues 'could hardly, perhaps, be expected to chance their arms in this field'.

The discussion paper was launched by Kenneth Clarke at a special press conference some six weeks before its contents were available to teachers and other educational bodies. A specially prepared list of bullet points was presented to the journalists with a recommendation to read the briefing paper rather than the full document (Simon 1993). The result was a further wave of headlines criticising progressive practice and praising the Secretary of State for finally laying the Plowden report to rest after nearly thirty years. For the purposes of this review, however, which aims to separate fact from fiction in the events occurring during the intervening two decades between the first and second ORACLE study, the crucial and fascinating part of the 'Three Wise Men' episode is the detailed account of the final drafting process (Alexander 1997: 209–12). Readers of the discussion paper might have been expected to assume that normal practice would be for one of the team to draft a section, for the others to comment, and for the author then to undertake revisions in the light of the ensuing discussion. In this case, however, a decision was taken – Alexander does not say how or why or by whom – whereby a section drafted by one of the three team members was to be redrafted by another, so that in effect the author of the first draft lost editorial control.

In the light of what had happened at the earlier December press conference at which Clarke launched the initiative, the crucial section was the one on primary classroom practice. Alexander (1997) acknowledges that Galton's (1995) speculations as to 'who wrote what' were reasonably accurate, so we can conclude with confidence that the initial draft on classroom practice was the work of Alexander. The likelihood is that it was then redrafted by Chris Woodhead. Although Alexander does not name him directly, a subsequent article in the *Guardian* (11 February 1992) under Chris Woodhead's name, uses identical phrases to those that appeared in the published version of the report. We can surmise, therefore, that the initial draft, in keeping with standards of academic scholarship, tried to balance arguments for and against various positions. These statements were then either amended or removed in the editing to give a more robust presentation which was supportive of Kenneth Clarke's original steer during his December press conference. During subsequent discussion Alexander then tried to retrieve the situation but could do so only by managing to insert conditional or qualifying clauses into the text. In this way an initial emphasis on the limited use of whole class teaching is turned into a positive affirmation. One example, taken from Alexander's (1997) account of the drafting process serves to make the point. Alexander's second draft on the merits of whole class teaching is a balanced and accurate representation. The opening sentences read (our italics):

> Commentators look wistfully across the Channel, or back into their own childhood, and see in whole class teaching the order, control, purpose and concentration which they find lacking in many primary classrooms. To *some* extent the evidence from HMI, Galton, Mortimore ... Osborne and others supports them.
>
> (Alexander 1997: 245)

The editor of the final draft then gives these sentences a positive 'spin' in favour of whole class teaching,

> Whole class teaching appears to provide the order, control, purpose and concentration which many critics believe are lacking in modern primary classrooms. To a *significant* extent, the evidence supports this view of whole class teaching.
>
> (Alexander *et al.* 1992: para 89–90)

When the discussion paper was finally made available to the schools, the divergence of view between Alexander and Woodhead was clearly exposed by the simultaneous publication of articles by the two authors in the *Education Guardian* (11 February 1992). In the light of what we now know about the redrafting process, Alexander's piece would appear to be an attempt to redress and refashion the argument along the lines of his original draft while, if anything, Woodhead appears to harden his position. Finally dispensing with the need for research evidence, he bases his case on a tele-phone conversation involving a friend whose child is under-achieving at school. Woodhead then rounds off his piece with an emotional appeal for schools to provide this young victim with her entitlement, by reintroducing a sound dose of traditional teaching. This episode was subsequently rein-forced by an attack on Professor Alexander's independence in both the edi-torial pages of the *Guardian* and in an article by Melanie Phillips, who claimed that the Leeds professor had backtracked on what he originally wrote under pressure from the educational establishment (*Guardian*, 14 February 1992).

This rather extended account of the so called 'Three Wise Men' episode is important in the recent history of primary education for two main reasons. First, Alexander's account (1997) stresses the parallels between the above events and the 1970 Black Paper period and tends to see the episode as a recycling of events in which the PRINDEP report acted as the catalyst in much the same way as Bennett's book (1976) did. There are, however, important differences. As argued in an earlier section of this chapter, the 1976 debate was less extreme and better balanced. Unlike public reaction to the 'Panorama' programme, few complained of bias in the 'Horizon' report of Bennett's *Teaching Styles and Pupil Progress*. The programme, for example, faded out with Professor Bennett voicing his opinion that pro-gressive teaching was not all bad but that there needed to be a better balance with more formal approaches. Although Simon's argument (1981a) that there was no progressive revolution can also be found in the Three Wise Men's report, and although, like Bennett, the discussion paper also calls for a balance between different organisational strategies in accordance with 'fitness for purpose' (para. 101), these messages do not come across as strongly in the final draft as the case in favour of the virtues of whole class teaching. In the prepared press handouts it was largely the negative aspects of existing practice which were stressed. As a result of this 'steer', both the broadsheet and tabloid press, with the possible exception of the *Independent*, was uniformly hostile to primary teachers and virtually un-animous in calling for a 'back to basics' policy and a return to traditional whole class teaching.

Second, this media pressure and hype led to a closing of ranks between the politicians. The Labour opposition, sensing that education could become a major election issue, began to compete strongly with the Conservative gov-ernment to show that it would not be soft on 'trendy teachers'. By the time that David Blunkett assumed the role of opposition spokesman for educa-tion, Labour were promising to 'weed out' weak teachers using the appraisal system, to close failing schools within an even shorter period of time than that proposed by the government, and to exert even tighter control on the inspection process, not only in schools but also in LEAs, universities and teacher training institutions. In the following years, various 'task forces' on literacy and eventually numeracy were set up.[17] There have been recommendations on homework and on the amounts of time to be devoted to the 'basics'. New Labour's modern-day version of 'puritanism' stresses parental *duties* not *rights*. Now entry of one's child into a school may be conditional on signing a contract pledging the son or daughter's good conduct in matters such as timekeeping and behaviour, and agreeing to enforce the school's homework policy. Furthermore, this reform of primary education has to be achieved without any major increase in resources, since New Labour, when in opposition, pledged itself to retain the monetary targets of the previous government. This despite a clear identification of considerable underfunding of primary education by all 'Three Wise Men' (Alexander *et al.*, 1992: 5–6, 44, 54).

When James Callaghan delivered his Ruskin Speech in 1976, there was a genuine divergence of views among the political parties which increased even further after the election of Mrs Thatcher to the premiership. Indeed, the now Lord Callaghan, reflecting later on the speech, observed that it was thought by some 'to be an unseemly intrusion of a Prime Minister to poke his nose into educational matters and stir up trouble on matters best left to those who know most' (Callaghan 1992: 9). Now, it would appear, both major political parties are united in the view that in education they have every right to 'poke their noses' where they please since the popular view, as expressed by the media, is that teachers are no longer 'those who know most' but those who 'cling to outdated practices'.

John Patten appoints a Chief Inspector: 'The Reign of Terror' begins?

For a brief period after the publication of the 'Three Wise Men's' Report, education dropped out of the public arena in the wake of 'Black Wednesday', when the pound sterling 'crashed', and a greater part of the United Kingdom's reserves were used in an unsuccessful attempt to shore it up. Although the then Chancellor, Normal Lamont, hung on in office, an alleged lack of confidence in his management of the nation's financial affairs by the bankers in the City of London eventually led to his forced resignation and to his replacement by Kenneth Clarke, who in turn was replaced at the Department of Education by John Patten.[18] Patten, a committed market advocate from the right wing of the Conservative party, was also something of a moral crusader with strongly held religious convictions.

One of Kenneth Clarke's last tasks as Education Secretary had been to oversee the passage of yet another education bill through parliament. The 1992 Act abolished HMI, Her Majesty's Inspectorate, and transferred the resources used by LEAs for local inspections to a specially created body, the Office for Standards in Education (OFSTED). HMI was abolished partly because it was felt to be too sympathetic to the educational establishment; in the past, several of the senior staff had taken up professorial or senior administrative posts in universities immediately upon retirement. Furthermore, the measured and balanced tone of its reporting appeared out of step with the current preference for 'blunt' speaking characterised by Kenneth Clarke. Under the new privatised system of school inspection, OFSTED invited consortia of trained inspectors to bid for contracts to inspect schools. Initially, training was conducted by OFSTED, although later this function also was contracted to an outside body. All inspection reports were to be published to inform parents in their choice of schools. Some £130 million was set aside for the enterprise which visualised a four-year cycle of inspections. Not surprisingly, most of the new consortia consisted of local inspectors as LEAs desperately attempted to 'claw back' the money which they had lost to OFSTED, although a sizeable proportion of this money would have been used to administer a system which required contracts to be issued for each school.

Accountability for OFSTED's activities remained in the hands of the Chief Inspector of Schools but the post was made a part-time one. Besides inspections, OFSTED also took on the HMI role of conducting regular reviews on aspects of schooling and in subsequent years carried out a number of surveys of primary practice (OFSTED 1993; 1994a; 1995), which were specifically commissioned as follow-ups to the 'Three Wise Men's' Report. The themes addressed in these documents were, therefore, identical to those set out in the 1992 discussion paper Alexander *et al.* 1992, but now the advice was expressed in such general terms as to be virtually useless to teachers seeking practical solutions to their problems. In the 1995 document, *Teaching Quality: The Primary Debate*, for example, teachers were told that to be successful they needed to plan carefully, to use time and resources effectively and to set high expectations. Pupils were to be challenged and, as a consequence, deepen their knowledge and understanding. The more difficult question of how such high ideals were to be translated into practice in a situation of diminishing resources was left unanswered.

John Patten's brief reign at the Department for Education ended in 1994, partly as a result of a number of political gaffes, not least impugning the integrity and sanity of Birmingham City's Director of Education in an ill-considered aside to the press.[19] Invited to resign by Prime Minister John Major, almost his last act, seemingly a defiant one, was to appoint Chris Woodhead, the Chief Executive of SCAA (School Curriculum and Assessment Authority) as Her Majesty's Chief Inspector and full-time head of OFSTED. Woodhead, who had moved to SCAA when the National Curriculum Council and the Schools' Examinations and Assessment Council were recombined, immediately adopted a more direct and challenging style from that of his predecessors. Beginning with a series of conferences, with the declared purpose of discussing with primary headteachers the implication of the 1992 discussion paper (Alexander *et al.* 1992) and the first two

Woodhead

OFSTED follow-up reports, he sought to structure the debate around a sharp polarisation between traditional and progressive practice – the one associated with whole class teaching of specialist subject matter and the other with integrated topics and an emphasis on individualisation. This despite the twenty years of research evidence, which he had reviewed along with Professor Alexander in 1992 and which, if it had done nothing else, had demonstrated that the traditional–progressive dichotomy was over-simplistic and was of little value in representing the complexity of primary practice. Where evidence was presented, it seems to have been chosen to support the Chief Inspector's own views as expressed, for example, in the OFSTED publication *Primary Matters* (1994a) as well as the *1993–1994 Annual Report* and in his lecture given to the Royal Society of Arts (Woodhead 1995b). Typical of the press reaction was the *Daily Telegraph*'s report (27 January 1995) of the Royal Society Lecture under the headline, 'Inspector Attacks Woolly Teachers.' The newspaper went on to report the lecture as 'an outspoken attack on progressive methods'. According to the newspaper account, the Inspector saw the threat to educational standards arising in particular from,

 child-centred teaching that relied on impulse and inclination and a commitment to discovery learning in place of formal instruction. Teachers acting as facilitators rather than moral and intellectual authorities. The practice of dividing classes into groups instead of teaching them as a whole and the view that knowledge such as English and History were arcane and irrelevant to the needs of industry and commerce.

Throughout 1995 the message was repeated and the pressure maintained. For example, *The Times* (17 November 1995) reported that the Chief Inspector had called for a return 'to traditional teaching methods to try to reduce one third of lessons consistently judged to be poor'. In the following year (*Evening Standard*, 5 February 1996), the attack had become more focused. The headline now read 'Sack These Failed Teachers Now', and the piece featured the Chief Inspector's claim that pupils were badly taught in nearly half of all our schools and his demand for a purge of inadequate staff, an end to trendy teaching methods and a concerted drive against endemic mediocrity and plunging standards of literacy.

The impact of this pressure on schools, together with the aggressively 'hostile' attitude of some inspection teams, has recently been described as a 'reign of terror',[20] during which 'primary teachers and their headteachers have had the confidence and self-esteem challenged at every turn' (Brighouse 1997: 106–7). Despite denials by OFSTED, there are also financial implications in the Chief Inspector's demands for more whole class specialist subject teaching in the National Curriculum, since this makes it less important to

24

give heed to the teaching unions' call to reduce class size, at least at KS2 (Galton and Hargreaves 1996). The Chief Inspector's message has been reinforced by a report commissioned by OFSTED from Professor David Reynolds (Reynolds and Farrell, 1996).[21] Reynolds, who has limited experience of primary education either as a teacher or as a researcher, nevertheless concludes, on the basis of statistical analysis and a short visit to Taiwan for a BBC 'Panorama' programme (3 June 1996), that it is mainly interactive whole class teaching that makes the difference. Alexander (1996) tends to see the subsequent media treatment of Reynolds' and Farrell's report as another example of the way that serious academic research is distorted for political ends, as with his PRINDEP study. It can be argued, however, that researchers such as Professor Reynolds were more 'streetwise' than previous generations and understood exactly the implications of making the television programme. Alexander (1996) refers to Reynolds and others, such as the former Professor of New Initiatives at the London Institute, Michael Barber (now a Director of the Government's Standards in Education Unit), as the 'Essex men of educational research'.[22] Associated with an International School Effectiveness Research Project (ISERP), this strand of educational research began in the 1970s when data collected by the statistics branch of the Inner London Education Authority showed that, on average, pupils in schools from similar catchment areas achieved very different examination results. The movement has published numerous books and articles on the six key determinants of school effectiveness (Rutter *et al.* 1979; Sammons *et al.* 1995), based partly on the analysis of international comparisons of mathematics and science performance. Transferring from one conference to another throughout the globe, these 'jet-setting, high-tech intellectual sharp dressers' (Alexander 1996) often appear to recycle similar material under titles such as *School Effectiveness: Research, Policy and Practice* (Reynolds and Cuttance 1992) and *Advances in School Effectiveness Research and Practice* (Reynolds *et al.* 1994), which creates an impression that the movement's members are operating at the frontiers of educational research.

Only recently have some of these researchers began to consider and discuss the processes of learning, surely a central issue in any debate about school improvement. Others who have studied such matters in countries around the Pacific Rim such as Taiwan and Hong Kong, notably Professor John Biggs (1994), stress the importance of distinguishing between teaching pupils to acquire *surface* and *deep* learning strategies and dispute the simplistic solutions put forward by the school improvers to account for the relatively poor performance of English pupils. While Reynolds and Farrell (1996) do acknowledge that cultural differences influence performance, they have a much more limited view of culture than, for example, Biggs (1994) in that they appear to think it possible and desirable to partition school, cultural and social effects and to attribute a proportion of pupil performance to each factor, a viewpoint which Alexander (1996: 17) reasonably argues seems 'conceptually untenable'. Elsewhere, Alexander also asks why, if interactive whole class teaching (as yet not very well defined by its proponents) is the key to school improvements, it doesn't also work in other Pacific Rim countries whose scores on international tests are of the same order as those of the United Kingdom and the United States (Alexander 1996: 21). Despite such reservations, however, the Chief Inspector insisted, in the same 'Panorama' programme that described Professor Reynolds' Taiwan experiences, that teachers should now use whole class teaching for 60 per cent of mathematics lessons.

Returning nearer home, OFSTED's own data, which have been used to support the Chief Inspector's view, namely the annual report (OFSTED 1996a) and a study of reading in the Inner London primary schools (OFSTED 1996b), have been criticised by Colin Richards (1997).[23] A former primary teacher, university lecturer, and long time Senior Inspector, Richards left OFSTED and took early retirement partly, it would now appear, because of concerns about the methods used to present data collected during school inspections. However, the fact that Richards' attack on OFSTED's methodology coincided with his early retirement from the organisation provided the opportunity for several 'Chinese whispers' to circulate. Some were open to the interpretation that his departure from OFSTED was not altogether voluntary and that his criticisms could, therefore, be regarded as 'sour grapes' over the manner of his treatment.[24]

Richards' criticisms, however, are substantial. His detailed knowledge of the inspection process, of which he was one of the architects, and his familiarity with the schools' data, to which he had access as one of the team responsible for drafting the annual reports, allow him to present a detailed and convincing case which has never been answered satisfactorily. Richards' main concerns relate to statements in the *1996 Annual Report* to the effect that 'the proportion of good lessons in Key Stage 1 is around 1 in 4 while in Key Stage 2 there are fewer lessons with good standards and about 1 in 5 are unsatisfactory.' This then leads to the conclusion that, 'standards taken across all subjects require improvement in about half the primary schools' (OFSTED 1996a: paras 36–7). Richards points out that these figures can only be arrived at by adding the neutral point of the scale to the unsatisfactory totals. This, of course, leaves open the option of adding the neutral point to the satisfactory end of the scale in subsequent years and then claming that OFSTED inspections have played a crucial part in improving the quality of primary education.

Richards' account of drafting the report of OFSTED's reading survey (1996b) tells a similarly depressing story to that recounted by Alexander (1997) in the writing of the 1992 discussion paper (Alexander *et al.* 1992). Like Alexander, Richards quotes directly from the original drafts (which, presumably, he helped to write) and then from the final published version (given in italics). Compare, for example, the following extracts:

The quality of teaching in reading was satisfactory or better in approximately two thirds of the lessons observed in Year 2 and just over half the lessons in Year 6.

Good teaching was found in about a quarter of the lessons observed in each Year group (i.e. Years 2 and 6).

There was a small number of schools where the teaching was part-icularly good. In a few it was poor; these schools are in urgent need of help and support.

Weaknesses in teaching hampered pupils' progress and attainment in reading in 1 in 3 lessons in Year 2 and nearly half the lessons in Year 6.

The unevenness in teaching quality as pupils move from class to class, seriously weakens progress in these schools.

Far too many children were found not to be making the progress which they should, the main reason for this was weak teaching.

(Richards 1996: 11–12)

This provides striking confirmation of what is hinted at in Alexander's account (1997) of the editing process during the writing of the 'Three Wise Men's Report': namely that from someone, somewhere, there has been a concerted attempt to impart the maximum amount of 'spin' on any findings implying that teachers were less than satisfactory, or that vestiges of informal teaching approaches were in use, in an attempt to pressurise headteachers to bring about desired changes in practice. These changes were not to be based on research but, it would seem from Richards' account, upon ideological bias.[25] The effect of these negative messages on teacher morale can easily be judged and is documented in research that suggests the job is now much more stressful and less enjoyable (Galton and Fogelman 1998). Clearly, whichever hand penned the final draft, the Chief Inspector must have been the principal decision maker and must therefore accept much of the responsibility for bringing about a situation which 'for the majority of primary teachers...has become almost intolerable' (Brighouse 1997: 107).

Surprisingly, given this record of events and the criticisms made by the likes of Birmingham's Director of Education, Professor Brighouse, the Labour Party while in opposition committed itself to retaining the services of Chris Woodhead as the Chief Inspector.[26] At times, the new government has appeared to commit itself to a similarly threatening approach, for ex-ample, recently advising parents to report teachers who do not teach their children satisfactorily, particularly if they refused to use phonics as part of their reading programme. Parents were told that if they did not get satisfaction from their own Local Education Authority they should phone the Department for Education. Non-cooperating schools could ultimately face inspection! Subsequently, a different spin was placed on this story to the effect that the 'hotline' was an advisory service, not an invitation for parents to 'sneak on teachers' (*Times Educational Supplement*, 19 September 1997). However, the teachers' leaders continue to express concerns that the very detailed prescriptions associated with the task force recommendations for literacy and numeracy hours smack of authoritarianism, particularly when coupled with the threat of an inspection for those not following the 'letter of the law'.

Situating the new ORACLE study

The previous paragraphs have traced the education debate over two decades and concentrated, in particular, on the claims of critics that 'trendy teaching methods' imposed on schools by an ideologically prejudiced educational establishment have failed the nation's children. How might Donna Leason, whom we met in the opening paragraphs of the chapter, react to such claims? Certainly, during her schooldays, the education system appeared to fail her, although she cheerfully admits now that some of her problems were of her own making. If she had worked harder while at school she might had done better. Now school is not quite the informal place it once was. For security reasons it is no longer possible for parents to come and go as they please. Donna now needs to enter her name in the log book and wear an identity badge. When she goes into Hayley's class, she also notices some changes but there is much that, on the surface, remains the same. The tables and desks are still arranged rather similarly, but there are now more pupils with different ethnic backgrounds than there were in 1976. The parents of these children came to the city around the same time as Donna entered the junior phase of primary school. She knows from her conversations with Hayley's teacher and her own work with poor readers that there are special learning needs when only the mother tongue is spoken in the home. These children get very little experience of using English outside school, often spending most of their leisure time within their own community. The teachers, therefore, do their best to compensate by increasing the amounts of time the devote to language work. Many of these children now attend extra religious or mother tongue classes after school, so their day is extended.[27]

Another difference is that Donna sees little of the school principal, Mrs Vain, whereas when she attended the school, Mr Pride, the headteacher, was a frequent visitor to her classroom and often did some teaching. Now headteachers seem to her to be involved in endless meetings and overwhelmed by administrative matters to do with running the school (Webb and Vulliamy 1996).[28] When Mrs Vain visits Hayley's classroom, she is more likely to talk about financial issues to do with repairing leaking windows, buying books or replacing apparatus than about curriculum matters. Often she will be accompanied by parents who are contemplating sending their child to the school or by one of the governors on a tour of inspection. Hayley's teacher often looks stressed and there seems less time for the relaxing periods in class which she remembers, when, for example, a friend would bring in a treasured object and they would spend some time talking about it. Now they seem to be always engaged in studying mathematics or English, or preparing for the SAT examinations. Donna is pleased that Hayley is working hard, but she does sometimes wish that her daughter could have a little fun.[29]

From her own work experience, Donna understands the need for her children to receive a good grounding in the basics of reading, writing and arithmetic, but she doesn't see any signs that today's teachers are less concerned about these things than teachers were when she went to school. Donna voted New Labour because they were in favour of *education, education, education,*[30] but when it rains heavily the water still leaks through the ceiling and around the windows in Hayley's classroom. Donna doesn't understand the repeated calls to sack teachers because they are not teaching children properly. She supposes that the people who make these criticisms know a lot more about education than she does; they must do, otherwise they wouldn't make life so difficult for Hayley's class teacher and the rest of the staff. Donna finds it hard, sometimes, to make sense of what the politicians and the papers say when this is set against her own experience of daily living.[31] Things seemed much simpler for her parents when she was growing up. There was a much clearer understanding of right and wrong. Some of the parents with children in Hayley's class send them for religious instruction after school and want to set up their own schools, like those of the Church of England and the Roman Catholic Church. Donna doesn't know whether to think this is a good thing, particularly when she looks at the effects of religion in Northern Ireland (the son of a friend of her mother was killed by the IRA when serving in the army in Belfast). She would like to believe that all children, if they are living in Britain, should have the same education, but she also appreciates that children need to learn about their own cultural background.

Donna often worries about Hayley's future. A friend in a local bank is losing her job because more and more of the work is being done by computers. There is work, but it is very low paid and many people on the estate prefer to live on social security and pick up casual work when they can without declaring it.[32] Donna, of course, hopes to do better but now there are fees to pay for going to university and maintenance grants have been abolished. Child benefits have also been cut and this will make it more difficult to manage. Now that the Conservatives are no longer in power, it seems strange to Donna that people on low incomes, like her, are asked to make these sacrifices, yet the government says it is wrong to take more tax off the very rich, even if it was used for improving schools and hospitals. Often Donna gets so angry that she gives up reading the newspapers and just concentrates on her studies and coping with the demands of bringing up her three children.

Education in the post-modern world

Donna, of course, is trying to make sense of her personal circumstances in a world of rapid change that is creating what social scientists such as Giddens (1994) and others term a 'post-traditional society'. The collapse of communism has led to the creation of numerous small nation states with endless disputes over borders and ownership of scarce resources. This, in turn, has given rise to extreme forms of nationalism,[33] with periodic bouts of 'ethnic cleansing'. Perhaps of more significance in the long term is the growth of technology, particularly for controlling the financial markets. This has produced a degree of uncertainty and anxiety concerning the stability of national currencies. What happens on the stock markets of Tokyo and Hong Kong while most of us in Britain are asleep then has 'knock on' effects the next morning in London. At the same time, individual actions may also have global consequences. Buying this product rather than that in a supermarket may not only affect the livelihood of someone living thousands of miles away but may also affect the world's ecology. The result of this process of 'globalisation' is that our security, not only of employment, is often dependent on remote organisations about which we have little awareness, so that we live in a state of 'manufactured uncertainty'. As a consequence society is in the process of 'de-traditionalising' which means that values are no longer accepted unquestioningly but need to be explained and argued for.[34]

The uncertainties and anxiety that this process generates can lead to conflict and strong disagreements about how best to cope. There are gaps between generations, between the haves and have-nots, between the developed and the undeveloped worlds. As an unemployed lone parent with no capital assets, Donna is not directly affected by the various financial crises which have regularly occurred throughout the 1980s and 1990s, any more than her parents were by the oil crisis in the 1970s when she was a child. Her main concern is to pay the rent and her electric bill and to have enough benefit left to cover the weekend without having to borrow from her mother. But she is, of course, aware that Hayley's generation faces an uncertain future. As we approach the millennium, the future prosperity of Britain may well depend on the ability of a small group of entrepreneurs to maintain our foreign investment earnings. Work for those with relatively modest educational achievements may largely be in the retail, hotel, catering and caring sectors of the economy. While these young adults will need basic literacy and numeracy skills and a capacity to think for themselves, there will also be a requirement to learn skills of co-operation, reliability and responsibility, perhaps through the study of citizenship education and personal and social studies. What future citizens may not require is a common curriculum based on a need 'to acquire the best that is known about our culture', where culture is narrowly defined in terms of specialised subject knowledge as argued for by Chris Woodhead.[35]

Giddens (1994) and others suggest that there are two main ways of attempting to control this complex environment, thereby reducing the level of uncertainty in the lives of families like Donna's. One solution is to bolster up the nation state by fanning nationalistic feeling. We achieve a sense of comfort by sticking to 'old ways' and leaving it to leaders 'wiser than ourselves' to stand firm against the demands of the foreigners about whose intentions we are always naturally suspicious. The alternative solution, supported by Giddens (1994: 116) is to 'create active trust through appreciation of the integrity of others' since nation states are 'power containers... and of declining significance because of the processes of globalisation'. One response, therefore, to the threat of nationalism is to create larger supranational organisations to regulate not only economic but also political and social order and to mitigate the effects of size by devolving as much decision making as possible to regions. In this country this polarisation of view is best seen in the current debate about the United Kingdom's role in the European Union as reflected in the issue of a single currency. But it also manifests itself in education between those, like the Chief Inspector, who call for a return to traditional practices and those seeking to shift the debate away from 'unresolved dichotomies' such as 'progressive' and 'traditional', 'child centred' and 'subject centred' teaching, or more generally between the 'informal' and the 'formal' curriculum (Simon 1981b). Those attempting to escape from the sterile debate about primary practice that has dominated education over two decades seek, instead, a pedagogy that begins by asking what young Hayley and her classmates need to know to cope in a post-traditional world and how this knowledge can best be taught. In the light of the strong criticisms of contemporary primary teaching by Chris Woodhead and others, as set out in this chapter, Simon's utterances at the beginning of the 1980s have taken on a prophetic ring, particularly when he goes on to argue that such terms as 'progressive' and 'traditional',

> are basically meaningless but expressed in this form deflect attention from the real problems of teaching and learning. Indeed so disparate are the views expressed that to resuscitate the concept of a science of teaching that underlines that of 'pedagogy' may seem to be crying for the moon.
>
> (Simon 1981b: 125)

While there are obvious signs that at least some in 'New Labour' are persuaded by Giddens' analysis (1994), this does not appear, at present, to extend to education where, as in the 1980s, the concept of pedagogy is still 'alien to our experience and way of thinking' (Simon 1981b).

Reaching for the moon: the contribution of the present research

If, therefore, we are to reach Simon's 'moon' and meet the educational needs of children in today's primary schools, in ways which equip them to pursue useful and contented lives as adults, we need to base the educational analysis not only on a clear understanding of what the future may bring but also on what the past has brought about. In this, the ORACLE research can prove invaluable. As Campbell (1997) has argued, the debate about standards has largely been a futile exercise. Because of England's failure, unlike many other countries, to have a regular programme of testing which is reliable and valid, we have been unable to monitor changes within primary education from decade to decade. This replication of the original ORACLE study is unique in this respect, in that it has data from tests which were administered during the 1970s and which now, twenty years later, have again been administered in the same schools, providing a direct comparison of attainment over two decades. This provides a baseline from which the other studies carried out in the intervening period, using different tests, can be interpreted. More important, however, is the power of the ORACLE replication to inform the debate about pedagogy. Since the original study was carried out in the late 1970s, there has been, as documented in the previous pages, a sustained attack upon primary teachers who have allegedly embraced, mainly for ideological reasons, progressive methods to the detriment of more traditional forms of practice such as whole class teaching. In making these criticisms of primary teaching, commentators such as Chris Woodhead and Melanie Phillips have both cited this original ORACLE data.[36] Hence one is led to believe that these critics accept its validity and reliability. When, therefore, the findings of this present study, using the same observation methods are presented, it is to be hoped that they will be equally acceptable.

The research team has gone back to many of the same primary schools visited in 1976. We have excluded one of the original catchment areas situated some seventy miles from Leicester and replaced it with another some fifteen miles distant.[37] Unlike the original ORACLE study, we took a sample rather than included all primary schools in each of the three catchment areas. This was, as explained earlier, because our limited budget restricted the amount of observation we could carry out. Within each of these sample schools, however, we have used the same research methodology, using the Teacher Record (Boydell 1974) to observe the class teacher, and then switching to the use of the Pupil Record (Boydell 1975) in a predetermined order to observe a group of six 'target' pupils, matched by sex.[38] In the 1976 study eight target pupils were matched not only by sex but also by their reading test scores. We chose two 'above average', four 'average' and two 'below average' readers. This time, for reasons of strategy as well as economy, we made a random selection of boys and girls from the class list, omitting any who were 'statemented' or who the teacher identified as having special needs.[39] Subsequently, when test data became available, pupils could then be differentiated by ability to compare the behaviour of low and high achieving pupils in a similar manner to the analysis carried out in the 1976–77 ORACLE study. The analysis set out in the following chapters is based upon 6663 observations of twenty-nine teachers and 8562 observations of around 600 pupils from twenty-eight classes in fourteen primary schools. Observations were carried out every twenty-five seconds in a pre-determined sequence.

Restating the aim of this research

Given the same schools, the same research instruments and the same methods of analysis, has practice changed? Is there still resistance to the use of whole class teaching, as alleged by Chris Woodhead? Have literacy and numeracy levels when measured using standardised tests fallen? Has the National Curriculum brought about improvements either in entitlement or in the balance between subjects? In the following chapters we explore these issues in an attempt to provide a definitive comparative analysis. However, before beginning to examine in greater detail what changes have taken place in classroom practice and then going on to look at changes in pupil performance, we will begin by looking at the more general picture of life in primary schools. Is the classroom organised in similar ways? Is the curriculum similar or very different? To what extent is the curriculum now more concerned with teaching children to think for themselves rather than treating them as mere receptacles for information? The next chapter, therefore, provides the context in which to examine current teaching strategies and their impact upon pupils.

This subsequent analysis will seek to penetrate classroom life to a level which is not, perhaps, perceived by Donna and other parents who spend time in their children's classrooms. But the questions we hope to raise by means of this analysis should have an impact on the future of her daughter, Hayley, and the thousands of pupils like her who must learn to cope with our post-traditional society. These and other issues will be addressed in the final chapter when we will return to the question of Hayley's future prospects.

Notes

1 Donna was the pseudonym of one of the pupils who took part in an observation study of primary classrooms during the period 1975–80. The account presented here is part truth and part fiction.

2 The practice of accepting new pupils in the September or April after they had reached their fifth birthday persisted into the 1970s despite growing evidence that the summer born children who spent an extra six months in a smaller reception class were advantaged throughout their schooling. The main factor in bringing about the change was a declining birth rate forcing some schools to take 'rising fives' to maintain numbers on roll.

3 The following description of a visitor's impression is based upon Chapter 4 of the original *Inside the Primary Classroom*, first published in 1980 but using classroom observations made during 1976–78.

4 The headline 'The Wild Men of the Classroom' appeared in a *Times* editorial and referred to events at the William Tyndale Primary School where teachers had formed a co-operative in which all staff, including the headteacher, received the same remuneration. The school was subject to adverse publicity following a complaint by one teacher and subsequent inspection by the ILEA (Inner London Education Authority).

5 This, of course, is the Chief Inspector's version of the definition of culture and is taken from the introduction of Matthew Arnold's *Culture and Anarchy*.

6 It was subsequently reported in the press that several of these schools had been judged after reinspection by OFSTED to be on the way to recovery and the DfEE was unable to provide the rationale which governed Mr Blunkett's original selection (see *The Daily Telegraph* 16 and 23 May 1997).

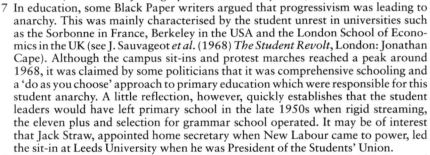

7 In education, some Black Paper writers argued that progressivism was leading to anarchy. This was mainly characterised by the student unrest in universities such as the Sorbonne in France, Berkeley in the USA and the London School of Economics in the UK (see J. Sauvageot *et al.* (1968) *The Student Revolt*, London: Jonathan Cape). Although the campus sit-ins and protest marches reached a peak around 1968, it was claimed by some politicians that it was comprehensive schooling and a 'do as you choose' approach to primary education which were responsible for this student anarchy. A little reflection, however, quickly establishes that the student leaders would have left primary school in the late 1950s when rigid streaming, the eleven plus and selection for grammar school operated. It may be of interest that Jack Straw, appointed home secretary when New Labour came to power, led the sit-in at Leeds University when he was President of the Students' Union.

8 Such mergers are, of course, still taking place. For example some infant and junior schools in south London were only merged in September 1997.

9 The quote is from the report of a lecture to the Royal Society of Arts by the Chief Inspector, Chris Woodhead (1995b), in the *Daily Telegraph*, Friday, 27 January 1995.

10 The main source of evidence for the political sequence of events described in the next section is the autobiography of Kenneth Baker, *The Turbulent Years*, published by Faber and Faber in 1993.

11 In the winter of 1978–9 the then Labour Government introduced a voluntary 'pay norm' which was quickly broken in the private sector, initially by the Ford Motor company. This led to a series of strikes by 1.5 million workers in the low-paid public sector service industries, resulting in the closure of schools and hospital wards. Ambulance 999 calls went unanswered while dustbins and refuse bags piled up in town centres. Newspapers and TV contrasted the situation of the elderly and the sick with Prime Minister Callaghan's tanned appearance on his return from a conference in the Caribbean where he had stayed on for extra days of relaxation. A crucial episode was a strike of Liverpool grave-diggers which left departed loved ones unburied. A full account of these events can be found in Kenneth Morgan's *Callaghan: A Life* (Oxford University Press, 1997).

12 Macmillan actually used the phrase, 'First of all the Georgian silver'. 'Family sil-
    ver' was substituted by the media when describing the gist of his speech given to
    the Tory Reform Group on 8 November 1985 (see the *Oxford Dictionary of
    Famous Misquotations*).

13 The statement is said to have originally come from *Woman's Own* (31 October
    1987), where Mrs Thatcher expressed the view that, 'There is no such thing as
    society. There are individual men and women, and there are families' (see Phillips
    1996: 289).

14 Much of the material for this section is derived from the very detailed account by
    Robin Alexander of his encounters with Kenneth Clarke and his junior ministers
    during 1991–92 in Chapter 10 of *Policy and Practice in Primary Education* (2nd
    edition) published by Routledge in 1997.

15 Annis Garfield told her story in *The Times* (30 April 1990). Two years previously,
    she had been rejected by Oxford Polytechnic 'by a woman whose qualifications
    were considerably less than mine'. According to her account, when she rang the
    tutor at the Midlands college (Nene) to ask how her application was progressing,
    she was told that it was not, 'because her degree course was not relevant to the
    primary curriculum', but that she could compensate for its inappropriateness
    'by a year's hands-on experience in a primary school'. When Mrs Garfield
    pointed out that, without a teaching qualification, she was not allowed to teach
    in such a school, the tutor explained that he had meant 'experience as a play-
    ground assistant or dinner lady'. Mrs Garfield told *The Times*' readers, 'I was
    affronted to be told that a year as a dinner lady might compensate for the inade-
    quacies of my Cambridge Classics degree.'

16 During the evaluation of a Rural Schools Project at Leicester between 1985 and
    1990 a young fieldworker had occasion to attend a meeting of Advisers in Corn-
    wall. The fieldnote remarks on the confrontational tone adopted throughout the
    meeting by a Mr Woodhead, one of the LEA's senior officers, in particular with
    his junior colleagues. The note ends with the summary, 'a very unpleasant atmo-
    sphere'.

17 The term 'task force' came into popular use after Mrs Thatcher used it when
    announcing the campaign to retake the Falkland Islands. Military or aggressive
    metaphors have been a persistent feature of New Labour 'sound bites'. There
    has been the *campaign/battle* to improve standards, an *attack* against trendy tea-
    chers and *zero tolerance* of failing schools etc.

18 One of John Patten's first acts was to produce a White Paper entitled *Choice and
    Diversity* (DfEE 1992). The first chapter, a passionate restatement of a market-
    driven education system, was written by Patten himself (see Hunter 1997: 42).

19 In yet another twist in this tale, the alleged 'nutter' Tim Brighouse is now the
    Vice-Chair of New Labour's task force on Raising Educational Standards.
    Although the city of Oxford had no responsibility for education when John Pat-
    ten was a councillor, his reference to Brighouse's mental state must have reflected
    his views on the period when Brighouse was Oxfordshire's Chief Education Offi-
    cer and was involved in a number of disagreements with the Conservative major-
    ity on the County Council.

20 This is, of course, not an isolated view. The former deputy leader of the Labour
    party, Roy (now Lord) Hattersley, in the *Guardian* (12 March 1997) described
    Chris Woodhead as 'the apostle of improvement by confrontation', going on to
    claim that 'in pursuit of that point of view, he has dismissed his own inspectors
    as unacceptably sympathetic, rewritten OFSTED reports to exclude passages of
    support for struggling education authorities, and blithely misinterpreted serious
    research.'

21 Another academic subsequently to find favour with the New Labour Government in the role of Chair of the Mathematics Task Force. In addition to his lack of primary expertise, he is also without experience of mathematics teaching.

22 Essex men and women were said to portray the typical 'blue collar' families who switched their allegiance from the Labour to the Conservative party to support Mrs Thatcher. It was argued by pundits that Basildon, one of the first seats to declare its result, and a key marginal, was a barometer of feelings in the country at large. Many of these younger voters had left school at sixteen but were upwardly mobile. There were lots of 'Essex' jokes, mainly about the sexual habits of these young people and also about their limited intelligence. Typical of the latter was the following: *Question: What is the difference between an Essex man/woman and a supermarket trolley? Answer: The supermarket trolley has a mind of its own.*

23 Colin Richards was originally seconded to Her Majesty's Inspectorate to help write the 1983 Middle Schools Survey. Thereafter, because of his academic background and excellent drafting skills, he rose rapidly through the ranks to become the Inspectorate's leading expert on primary curriculum matters. Within OFSTED it can be surmised that he played a leading role in drafting the primary sections of the annual report.

24 Thus a report in the *Guardian* (20 April 1996), under the headline 'Poor Schools Report Branded Political', begins its account of Richards' main criticisms with the sentence, 'Mr Richards, who was passed over for a post heading OFSTED's primary team, said ... '

25 Indeed, the Chief Inspector is on record as having commented that no further research on school improvement is needed. It is noticeable how most of his public pronouncements focus on failure, as for example in the *Guardian* pre-election debate with Professor Ted Wragg (4 February 1997) on the motion, 'The current approach to Inspection, league tables and testing is detrimental to raising educational standards.' The Chief Inspector in his opening address spoke about teachers who were 'simply in the wrong job', of facing up to 'the inadequacy of incompetent colleagues', of never solving our problems until we 'face up to failure and inefficiency', of requiring a system which 'clearly states what teachers do and fail to do'. In turn, Professor Wragg claimed that this 'Me Tarzan, You scum' approach had constantly undermined the teaching profession and was based on the belief that 'professional people are best motivated by threat and criticism' (*Guardian*, 3 March 1997).

26 The negative messages in respect of teacher competence in recent OFSTED reports now extend to LEA inspections. The *Observer* (18 January 1998) claimed that Professor Brighouse was in dispute with the Chief Inspector over the editing of the Inspection team's draft report on LEA provision in Birmingham.

27 The point being made here is not that these are 'problem children' but that they perhaps require a different kind of curriculum from the statutory one laid down under the 1988 Education Reform Act. Nor is it fair to judge the performance of children in such schools on culturally biased assessments which favour pupils from more affluent suburban, mainly white middle-class areas. Although the Labour government will publish future league tables with an added value component, this analysis will include pre-test scores but not social class measures nor such factors as mother tongue, which are clearly significant in schools such as the one Hayley attends. Cynics might argue that, by leaving out these latter variables, the government avoids a possible conclusion that increased resources to deal with such factors, rather than low-cost school improvement measures, are the major determinant in raising standards.

28 Comparisons of roles in large and small schools by Webb (1993a) shows that in the bigger schools headteachers find it difficult to keep up with the details of the National Curriculum as a consequence of delegation of budgets, part of the Local Management of Schools (LMS) reform. In small rural schools headteachers have to teach as well as manage so have a working knowledge of the curriculum. A further consequence of delegating curriculum responsibility to subject co-ordinators has been a decline in the 'collegial' ethos in primary schools (Webb and Vulliamy 1996). Decisions are now taken in committee or by planning groups and not through informal networks as in the past. According to the results of the PACE research the situation has worsened since Webb's study (1993a).

29 A recent survey, again backed up by the PACE research, shows that many teachers feel under considerable stress and don't think primary teaching is fun any more (Galton and Fogelman 1998). School inspections, the SAT scores and league tables drive teachers to increase the amounts of time devoted to mathematics and literacy beyond that recommended by the task forces. Consequently some areas of the curriculum are becoming squeezed out or offered as optional lunchtime or after-school activities.

30 This was one of the oft repeated 'soundbites' used by the then opposition leader, Tony Blair, during the 1997 General Election campaign and was the main theme of his 1996 Party Conference speech.

31 Donna's experience of the teaching at Hayley's school appears to conflict with the claims by political leaders, OFSTED, etc., that standards in primary school are poor. She is, however, not alone in her confusion, since according to Hughes *et al.* (1994) over 80 per cent of parents, when asked about their own child's school, are 'happy' or 'very happy' with progress in literacy and numeracy and think the teachers are doing a good job. Less than 2 per cent are 'seriously concerned'. Parents 'were more concerned about standards in general than they were about their own child's school' (Hughes *et al.* 1994: 119). Clearly, if these results were aggregated over all schools, there would be a national endorsement of primary education. As it is, parents, although feeling their own child's school is OK, are persuaded by these press criticisms that the one down the road may have problems. Meanwhile, the parents who send their children to the school down the road think they are doing fine but that the pupils at the other school up the road may not be doing as well. Hence the overall confusion.

32 The assumption that the better educated the population the more prosperous the nation state will become has also been challenged in the home of capitalism, the United States (Berliner and Biddle 1995). As not only manufacturing but also servicing jobs move to countries around the Pacific Rim and to South America where labour is cheaper, surveys of American employers show they rate 'freedom from drug abuse', 'ability to cooperate with others' and 'responsible attitudes' more highly than academic attainment when recruiting for their workforce.

33 Giddens makes a distinction between the nation state and nationalism. The former is an institution whereas the latter is a psychological phenomenon (Best 1996: 10). Everyday life is built upon routine. When these safe routines break down, as happened when the old Soviet bloc disintegrated, people seek the security which nationalist symbols provide, in particular with the myths surrounding the strong leader.

34 For a reasonably straightforward explanation of terms such as globalisation, manufactured uncertainty etc. see Shaun Best's article for sixth-form teachers in *Social Science Teacher*, Vol. 25, Summer 1996, pp. 9–13.

35 The Chief Inspector would, of course, have no truck with this argument for less instruction in a traditional classroom with strong subject boundaries. Indeed,

according to John Clare in the *Daily Telegraph* (14 December 1995), when Professor Caroline Gipps advanced the same view and expressed a preference for learners who could 'think critically, synthesise and transform, experiment and create', Mr Woodhead dismissed her views as '*siren half-truths*' giving as his opinion that children 'should suspend their eagerness to criticise and learn something first'.

36 In her book *All Must Have Prizes*, Phillips (1996: 58) selectively quotes from Galton (1995) *Crisis in the Primary Classroom*. Whereas the meaning attached to the full passage was that whole class teaching was not the answer to the problems of individualisation in large classes, Phillips manages to suggest that it was to be taken as a wholesale condemnation of individual instruction.

37 Another reason for the change was to provide the opportunity to study transfer at 10+ and 11+ and to look at the effects of Key Stage 2 SATs before and after moving to the secondary school. This will be reported in a second volume, provisionally entitled *Moving from the Primary School: 20 Years On*.

38 For those interested, full details of both observation systems and their use can be found in Chapter 1 (pp. 11–21) in the first ORACLE volume, *Inside the Primary Classroom*, by Galton, Simon and Croll (1980) and a summary is provided in Appendix 2 of this book.

39 In the 1976 ORACLE study, observing the same eight pupils throughout made it very difficult to find sufficient numbers of our 'target' pupils in any one post-transfer class to make valid comparisons about the influence of teaching style on pupil behaviour. By choosing pupils at random on each observation visit to the primary classroom we had a larger sample to follow in post-transfer classes.

2

THE CLASSROOM ENVIRONMENT
A framework for learning[1]

Introduction

Primary classrooms are remarkably crowded places. This much has always been true, but in recent years the pressure on space has increased. Pupil numbers, having dipped in the 1980s, gradually rose again during the 1990s,[2] so that earnest debates about 'class size' have once more entered the educational and political arenas.[3]

It is not simply a matter of numbers which determines the level of congestion, however, it is also one of the physical space in which teacher and pupils are obliged to work. Both the dimensions of the room in which learning takes place and its overall design have implications for the way in which teachers organise its layout. Some have the luxury of spacious rooms, which allow for adaptation and movement, while others are obliged to work in confined or awkwardly shaped spaces which place particular constraints on the degree of flexibility available. While the dimensions and design of a classroom are fixed, and therefore largely beyond the control of the teacher, the challenge is, and has always been, to make the optimum use of what space and resources are available. In the following pages, we examine the ways in which teachers went about this task, and the impact of curricular reform and shifts in educational philosophy since the first ORACLE studies.

The 1976 classroom

By the time of the first ORACLE studies, the pre-war image of the primary classroom as a place where children sat behind serried rows of desks had virtually disappeared.[4] Children mostly sat together in groups around desks or tables brought together to form larger working areas. The teacher, meanwhile, no longer stood in front of a blackboard, or instructed the pupils from behind a centrally positioned desk, but instead moved around the room interacting with pupils as individuals or as members of their group.

This form of organisation reflected the philosophy of the time which emphasised the child as being at the 'heart of education' (Plowden 1967, para. 1) and which extolled the principle of individualisation, while recognising the educational and social virtues of collaborative learning. As the ORACLE research established, however, this proposition was never seriously tested, and the surface appearance in these classrooms of activity, discovery and interaction – the Plowden ideal – was somewhat illusory. Pupils spent most of the time at their working base rather than moving around the class, and communicated only infrequently either with their teacher or with others in their group. In this situation levels of distraction were relatively high, interaction between pupils was relatively low, and such communication as there was rarely had much to do with the task in hand. This discovery led to a refinement of the original ORACLE observation schedule to take account not only of where and how children were seated, the pupil's 'base', but also of who they worked with, their 'team'. Subsequent research which used these categories confirmed that, while children mainly *sat* together in groups, they *worked* on their own for most of the time (e.g. Hargreaves 1990).[5]

Classroom organisation and attention to task

In the light of such findings, there followed a growing interest among researchers in the relationship between seating arrangements and time on-task (e.g. Wheldall and Lam 1987; Yeomans 1989; Hastings *et al.* 1996).[6] Given that, in most primary schools, a single classroom has to serve multiple functions, requiring flexibility on the part of both teacher and children, the goal of such research was to examine the impact of varying the physical classroom organisation on the level and nature of communication. The general but consistent finding from these kinds of studies was that, where children were required to be sitting down and engaged in individual work, the level of on-task work was substantially higher when seated in rows than when grouped around tables.

Furthermore, the research suggests that the greatest beneficiaries of such arrangements may be those who are most likely to be distracted in a group situation (Wheldall and Congreve 1981). Nevertheless, as Hastings *et al.* (1995) point out, to use these findings to support a return to 'rows with everything' position would be to 'miss the point entirely', which is that, in order to encourage effective learning, teachers need to use a variety of organisational approaches to ensure that 'seating organisation reflects teaching intentions and task demands.'

There is, therefore, a considerable body of research, from ORACLE 1976 onwards, which indicates a clear relationship between classroom seating arrangements and the pupils' involvement in the task. The recent shifts in thinking about the nature and purpose of primary education, described in detail in Chapter 1, and the policy changes which have followed, have further emphasised the importance of this link. The National Curriculum, with its clearly delineated subject areas, programmes of study, attainment targets and assessment procedures, was designed to provided a common curricular structure which had hitherto been absent in the primary classroom (Bennett *et al.* 1980). Later pronouncements concerning the most appropriate teaching methods and classroom organisation for its successful implementation (Alexander *et al.* 1992), coupled with the introduction of more exacting inspection procedures and compulsory end-of-Key Stage testing, have brought considerable pressure to bear on primary teachers to alter their practice. How, then, have teachers in these various environments responded to demands placed upon them by this period of policy-led reform? In particular, what has been the impact of these changes upon the way that teachers make use of the classroom environment they find themselves in?

The 1996 classroom

The schools in the present study ranged from the very old to the relatively new. The oldest was a cramped, high windowed early Victorián building, designed at a time when teachers lectured from the front, and pupils were seated shoulder to shoulder behind rows of fixed desks, which were often bolted to the floor (Boydell 1978).[7] The most recently built schools were, on the other hand, spacious, light and modern open-plan units, the design of which is variously claimed to be influenced by the so-called progressive ideology of the 1970s (Brogden 1986), the result of financial necessity (Bennett *et al.* 1980),[8] or a practical response to the move towards de-streaming of the primary classroom (Simon 1966).

Of the twenty-eight classrooms observed, twenty-two were of the type generally referred to as 'box like', the key characteristics of which were that they were discrete rooms defined by walls and a door which closed them off from the rest of the school. As we shall see, however, this term should not be taken to indicate a uniformity of shape or size. The remaining six classrooms, or more accurately 'home units'[9] were part of open-plan teaching spaces.

Given this diversity, what was remarkable was that, regardless of the shape, size or original purpose of the classrooms observed, the organisation within them had hardly changed in twenty years. Children were still mainly to be found 'seated in groups around flat-topped tables or desks drawn together to form working surfaces',[10] just as they were in 1976. Moreover, a number of studies during the 1980s found that this model of classroom organisation described in the 1976 ORACLE study had remained remarkably stable throughout that period (e.g. Mortimore *et al.* 1988; Alexander *et al.* 1989). More recently, the PACE project also reported the continuing existence of this kind of arrangement (Pollard *et al.* 1994).

It would appear, therefore, that two decades of classroom research, curriculum reform on an unprecedented scale, and a shift in educational thinking

which has produced calls for a return to whole class teaching and more subject specialisation has had almost no impact on the way in which teachers organise the pupils. Within this general picture of stability, however, there have been some variations beyond the arrangement of the pupils' working surfaces, and in the following section we briefly examine three features of the primary classroom and their effects on the organisation of the classroom: the teacher's desk, the 'carpet area' and the computer.

The teacher's desk

What of the teachers themselves? How do they organise their 'space' in the primary classroom, and how do they operate within it? In earlier times, it was the teacher's desk which dominated the class, symbolising both the authority of the teacher and a pedagogic style of teaching. Positioned at the front, and often in the centre of a raised platform, it afforded an uninterrupted view of the class, so that the pupils, like the inmates of Bentham's panopticon,[11] were acutely aware that their activities could be observed at all times.

By the 1970s, however, the central positioning of the desk, and its powerful symbolism, had all but disappeared; it was often to be found instead placed in a corner of the room. Although the majority of teachers still preferred to situate it in such a way as to be able to monitor the class when necessary, the 1976 ORACLE study showed that teachers spent most of their time moving around the class, going from pupil to pupil, monitoring children's activities or 'housekeeping'. The desk therefore became something akin to a 'base' to which the teacher returned periodically to collect or replace materials, to mark or plan work, to register the class, or occasionally served as a place for children to come to read to the teacher, or to queue for information or clarification of instruction.[12]

In some ways, little appears to have changed since that time. In only a quarter of all observed classrooms in the present study did the teacher's desk occupy a traditional centre-front position, and even here teachers were rarely observed 'teaching-from-the-front'. Occasionally, children were brought out to gather around the desk for a demonstration of some kind, reflecting to some extent the increasing importance of science and technology in the curriculum, but in general the teacher's desk appears to have much the same function in the modern primary classroom as it did twenty years ago, irrespective of its location.

However, although teachers were still mobile for much of the time, they were less likely than their ORACLE 1976 counterparts to interact with individual pupils, or to be silently monitoring the class or organising materials, and they were much more likely to be addressing the whole class. We have seen that in the main teachers have not been busy rearranging the children's desks into rows, neither have they returned to a front of class style of delivery. What then, is the context in which this increase in whole class interaction is taking place?

The answer to this question is a complex one, and these findings, and their implication for teaching and learning, are discussed in considerable detail in the following chapters. In the context of the present discussion, however, one clue lies in the use of communal spaces in the primary classroom, the 'carpet area'.

The carpet area

The carpet area or reading corner represent spaces which have traditionally been marked off as a place for shared activities which often involve the whole class and the teacher (see Figure 2.1). In the 1970s these areas were often used by teachers when they wanted to talk to the whole class, particularly first thing in the morning to take the register, outline the morning's activities and so on. The children would often gather again at the end of the day to sit and listen to a story read by the teacher. Beyond these shared events with the teacher, a carpet area was also used spontaneously by children who required additional work space, or as a place for silent reading.

In 1996, these carpeted areas continued to be an important part of classroom life, and even in the case of some modern classrooms that were carpeted throughout, a space was often marked out in some way. What was particularly interesting, especially in the light of the shift towards the use of whole class teaching discussed above, was that in many classrooms this area was used more frequently than in ORACLE 1976 times, so that children were sometimes brought out from their desks to 'sit on the carpet' mid-way through lessons for whole class instruction or discussion.

One possible cost of increasing class-based activity is a rise in the kind of behaviour defined as 'partially co-operating and partially distracted'.[13] Where a discussion or instruction is relatively lengthy, for example, it becomes difficult for the teacher (and indeed the observer) to determine whether or not the children are fully engaged or not, allowing some pupils to 'melt into the crowd'.[14] However, teachers reported that bringing the children out to the carpet area so that the children were close to them allowed a greater degree of control over the pupils' behaviour and attention.[15]

The strategy can also can be seen as pragmatic. Since pupils are still mainly seated in groups around tables, addressing the whole class in this situation necessarily involves a measure of 'talking to the back of children's heads', making it difficult for the teacher to engage directly with all of the pupils, or to monitor behaviour. The alternative would be to ask some of the children to twist around so that they all faced the front. Bringing them out to the carpet obviates the need for either tactic. Having said this, seating children in groups is, of course, a strategy in itself, so that the argument for the practicality of one arrangement over the other becomes rather circular.

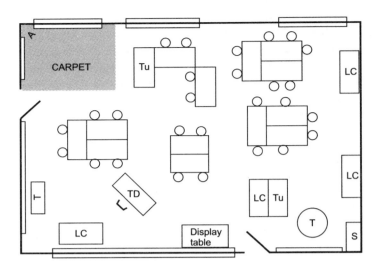

Figure 2.1 Typical classroom layout
Source: adapted from Moyles (1995: 14), figure 1.1.

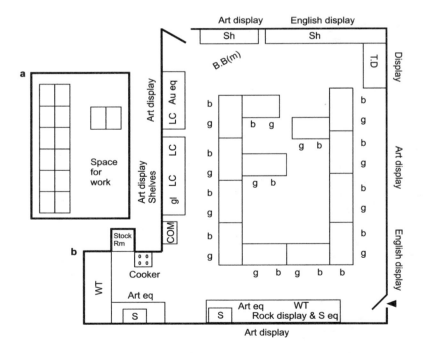

Figure 2.2 'Horseshoe' layout

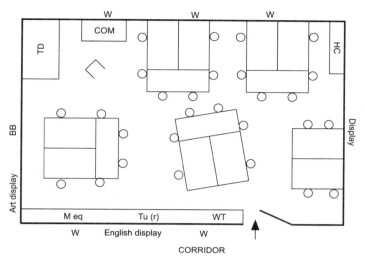

Figure 2.3 'Shoebox' layout

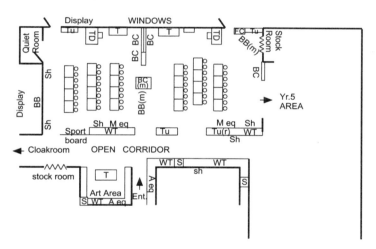

Figure 2.4 Open-plan layout

Key to figures 2.1–2.4

A	Arm Chair	HC	High cupboard	Tu	Tray units
A eq	Art equipment	LC	Low cupboard	Tu(r)	Tray units (resources)
Au eq	Audio equipment	M eq	Maths equipment	W	Windows
BB	Black/White board	O	Pupils' seating	WT	Worktop
BB(m)	as above(mobile)	S eq	Science equipment	∧∧	Folding door
BC	Bookcase	Sh	Shelves	Ⓢ	Sink
COM	Computer	TD	Teacher's desk	⊓	Teacher's chair
gl	globe(s)	T	Table	▬	Wall

Source of key: adapted from Alexander *et al.* 1989: 248.

45

There is, however, another, perhaps more powerful purpose behind these communal gatherings. The relationship between teacher and pupil in the primary classroom develops over the period of a whole year, and in some instances longer, which allows for a more intimate, relational style than is possible in the secondary classroom, where a teacher might interact with the class for no more than an hour or two per week. In other words, teachers are able to retain what Moyles (1995) calls the 'cosy togetherness' of sitting together, while still meeting the demand for more whole class interaction.

Information Technology

One major development since the 1976 study was conducted is the increasing importance of Information Technology (IT),[16] and much has been written about its potential impact on the organisation of learning and the implications that the increasing use of computer-mediated activities have for the role of the teacher (e.g. Somekh and Davis 1997). What effects has this had on organisation within the primary classroom?

In most of our sample schools the answer is very little. Most of the primary classrooms in our sample confirmed the general findings of the McKinsey survey of IT provision in the UK (McKinsey & Co. 1997) which showed a national average of one computer for every seventeen pupils, and that in 40 per cent of primary schools the ratio was 1:20 – that is about one per class. What is more, many of the computers that schools did have were obsolete.[17] In the present study, although there was often a dedicated space for a computer, occasionally accompanied by a printer, much of the equipment was relatively old, of varying make, of low specification, and rarely used, so that out of almost 1,000 records of curriculum activity, just twelve recorded the use of IT.[18] Indeed, in a number of classrooms, IT had seemingly taken the place of science, which, according to an account by Ridley and Trembath (1986: 110), 'was lost somewhere in the detritus of a nature table and fishtank.' It would seem, therefore, that primary schools may have a little time to wait yet before the 'Information Age' significantly affects the organisation of most primary classrooms.[19]

Despite the tremendous changes in primary education in the previous decade, then, we see that, with a few general exceptions, the layout and use of the primary classroom of the 1990s is remarkably similar to that of the 1970s and 1980s. We are not suggesting, however, that teachers have somehow failed to deliver the National Curriculum, or that practice has not changed at all in two decades. There has clearly been a reluctance to make major changes in the geography or utilisation of the classroom environment, however, and such shifts as we have so far identified represent a rather subtle movement.

Some explanations for this position are offered later in this chapter, but in the mean time, we move beyond the general picture to examine in a little more detail three of the classrooms in the present study. These examples demonstrate the flexibility of teachers when presented with particular organisational challenges, and we examine the different ways in which each teacher went about meeting them.[20]

As we have already said, all but six of the classrooms in the present study conformed to one of the four types of 'box' classrooms described by Alexander *et al.* (1989), the chief variation between which was the number and location of workbays (a 'typical' box primary classroom, an amalgam of these four, is depicted in Figure 2.1). Nevertheless, classrooms come in all shapes and sizes, and some of those in the sample were much more conducive to flexible organisation than others.

The first example is of an L-shaped room (see Figure 2.2). The smaller part of the 'L' was unsuitable for teaching purposes, and was therefore used as a storage area. This left a rectangular teaching area of about 9 by 6 metres. The presence of fixed storage cupboards down the longer side of the room further reduced the space available, resulting in a fairly awkwardly shaped area to accommodate twenty-eight Year 6 pupils. Because of the teacher's approach to this situation, we call this classroom the 'horseshoe'.

Classroom 1: the 'horseshoe'

Largely in response to the restrictions imposed by the dimensions of the room, the teacher decided to experiment with a 'U' shaped, or horseshoe, arrangement of the children's tables. As an alternative to isolating pupils with behavioural difficulties by placing them next to the teacher's desk, children who required additional monitoring, in some cases for a temporary period, were seated at tables arranged at right angles to the 'U' formation and thus facing the front of the classroom. The same arrangement pertained for children with certain learning difficulties. As far as possible, boys and girls were seated next to each other, the pairings carefully selected, and regularly changed, as part of a deliberate policy to encourage interaction, a strategy which has been found to be particularly effective in raising the level of time on-task (Wheldall and Olds 1987).

McNamara and Waugh (1993) suggest that this U-shaped arrangement, commonly found in further and higher education (Hartley 1997), but unique among the primary classrooms observed in the present study, is the most effective for allowing the three main working styles, individual, group and whole class, with a minimum of modification. The horseshoe pattern was indeed maintained for many activities, for example class discussions and for most written work, and it also facilitated working in pairs. However, the teacher also used other arrangements according to the demands of the curriculum, exemplifying the 'fitness for purpose' ethic advocated by Hastings (1995), particularly when the task required or was designed around small-group work. The tables were rearranged in smaller blocks for these

47

purposes, as well as a variety of other arrangements for particular curriculum activities. For example, one task required several pairs or small groups to collaborate with one another to design and make a large mural. The tables in the classroom were pushed together to form one long 'boardroom table' for the main sections of the artwork, with separate areas for the organisation and distribution of materials, and for designing the border for the mural (see Figure 2.2a). Working for about an hour a day over several days, the children had become adept at quickly breaking down the horseshoe to construct this and a variety of other arrangements and at reforming it just as efficiently.

This 'flexible horseshoe' strategy thus proved to be an extremely effective means of making the most of a fairly unpromising situation. Interestingly, having moved in the year following the observational study, to a larger classroom in which the seating layout initially conformed to the more typical group style, the teacher in question reported difficulties in getting the class to work together. Mid-way through the second term, having reverted to the horseshoe arrangement, she found an almost immediate improvement in the level of collaboration between the children, and in her ability to communicate effectively with the pupils. The somewhat anecdotal nature of this evidence makes it difficult to separate cause and effect – for example the confidence developed with using the U-shape may have been temporarily lost when the teacher transferred to the new room. Nevertheless, the strategy was clearly successful in the observed classroom.

In the second example, the limitations of space were even more extreme, imposing severe restrictions on the scope for flexibility, and for this reason, we call the room the 'shoebox'.

Classroom 2: the 'shoebox'

The Key Stage 2 classrooms were located in an early Victorian building, constructed in an era when pupils were taught but not heard, and which retained most of the features of the original design. If conditions were cramped at the time of its construction, then the variety of teaching approaches demanded by the modern curriculum rendered the situation in the school even more difficult. The building was divided by a narrow corridor which also served as a makeshift cloakroom, and breaktimes were staggered in order to cope safely with the number of pupils who used the small playground. A recent OFSTED inspection report acknowledged that the cramped nature of the classrooms restricted opportunities for teaching and learning, drawing attention to the lack of adequate storage space and the fact that a lack of water supply to most classrooms adversely affected practical activities.[21]

The observed classroom measured just over 7 by 6 metres. As in the previous example, there were twenty-eight pupils in the class, and as Figure 2.3 shows, the scope for reorganising furniture under these conditions was extremely limited with space at such a premium. There was no sink in the room and very little storage space in which to put materials and resources, much of which was stacked on top of a worktop which ran along one side of the class, the only surface in the room available, apart from the children's tables. Underneath the worktop was stored a variety of mathematics equipment, cubes, blocks, scales, measuring equipment and so on. The only other storage space was a high 'wardrobe' style cupboard positioned in a corner of the room, directly behind two pupils' seats. The high Victorian window ledges were used to shelve extra books and National Curriculum documentation.[22] The only area dedicated to a specific activity was a small space against the wall where the computer was located. Much of the wall space was uneven white painted brick, which had proved to be less than suitable for displaying work.

The teacher's plight was similar to that of a group of teachers who, having attended a LEA in-service course on 'model' classroom layouts, found themselves unable to effect change because of unsuitable conditions (cited by Alexander *et al.* 1989). The response of this teacher was to use the space efficiently and, in some cases, ingeniously, so that, although the size of the room meant that it was impossible to create work bays for different activities, the teacher successfully taught all curriculum activities in the space available.

The strategy for achieving this involved a high level of organisation. In order to save space, personal equipment trays were integral to the pupils' tables, which meant that they did not have to move around the classroom to collect materials. The children were assigned to specific groups for each activity. A sign affixed to the board indicated the seating arrangements for each successive task. Some flexibility was built into this system depending upon the nature of the task. In science, geography, history and technology, for example, pupils were often given choices as to where they sat, whereas they had set places for the core areas of maths and English.

The teacher had contrived to find a small 'carpet space' for whole class activities. However, since there was not enough room for the whole class to sit on it together, for example when the teacher was reading a story, those children with seats nearest to the front of the class stayed where they were. For tasks such as spelling, groups of pupils interacted with the teacher on a rotating basis, each coming in turn to sit on the limited open carpet area. By using these various devices, the teacher had been able to introduce, in a severely restricted space, a level of flexibility which allowed for individual, group and classwork, and which could be tailored to different curriculum activities, without any rearrangement of the furniture.

This account and the preceding one demonstrate a high degree of flexibility on the part of the teachers in question. Both cases represent a considered and deliberate response to a difficult situation, overcoming the constraints of an inadequate or difficult classroom environment. In each class, a kind of partnership developed, an understanding between teacher and learners that co-operation and organisation were required, which was fundamental to the success of the strategy. This is not to say, of course, that such understandings cannot develop in classrooms where conditions are rather more suitable, but in the case of an inadequate or difficult classroom environment, it would seem to be a prerequisite if the teacher is successfully to deliver the full curriculum.

Our final example is of quite a different environment, an open-plan area. Three of the schools in the sample were built on open-plan principles, and most, like the Victorian school described above, had retained the major features of their original layout. Open-plan schools were mainly constructed during the 1970s, and although the origin of their design is contested (see p. 4) the series of spaces of different shapes, sizes and purposes were clearly created to encourage the use of space and resources 'leading to co-operation between teachers and flexible grouping of children' (Bennett 1976), that is, team teaching and the integrated day. At the time of the ORACLE research in 1976, about 10 per cent of all primary classrooms could be described as being open-plan (Bennett *et al.* 1980).

Detractors of open education saw these schools as the repositories of an extreme and damaging form of progressive practice. However, as Brogden (1986) argues, the reality rarely matched the rhetoric: a number of studies showed that there were wide variations in pedagogy that were little different from those found across primary education in general.

Nevertheless, the requirement to deliver a 'broad and balanced' curriculum in the 1990s, and the calls for more whole class teaching and for greater subject specialisation in the upper years of KS2, creates considerable logistical problems for teachers in schools that have retained an open-plan design. How did teachers in our example cope with these new demands in an environment designed for a quite different approach to teaching and learning?

Classroom 3: the open-plan

Figure 2.4 depicts the home-unit for two Year 6 classes in one of these open-plan schools. This unit was part of a larger L-shaped space which served four classes altogether (two Year 5 and two Year 6). Furniture served as space-dividers between the four units, with bookshelves and a mobile blackboard also arranged as a partition and demarcation line. Low cupboards and worktops further separated the Year 6 from the Year 5 areas, and helped to define a corridor which ran around one side of the whole area, allowing access to each of the home units. On one side of this corridor was a practical art area, which was shared by Year 6 pupils, with worktops, sinks and shelving for materials. There was also a well-equipped technology room at the end of the Year 5 unit which was suitable for small group activity.[23]

In the basic seating plan, the children all faced the same way behind three long rows of tables with seven or eight children to each row, an apparently contradictory and somewhat inefficient use of a space designed for flexibility. However, this seating arrangement was used for specific activities requiring individual work, and the layout was frequently reorganised, for example for art and craft, or for activities which involved collaborative group work. On some occasions, the whole year group worked together on a single project, for example in technology sessions, where children organised themselves into working groups. The tables were also rearranged when the Year 6 children divided into ability groups for mathematics.

This interesting combination of open-plan flexibility and traditional structure was also to be found in the approach to teaching. The teachers in the school described their arrangement as 'team teaching', and while this may not have conformed to a purist definition of the term, there was considerable evidence of a genuine collegial approach within and between year groups, in contrast with what Hargreaves and Dawe (1990) term 'contrived collegiality', which is largely a forced response to external bureaucratic pressures. The teachers planned together and worked on a two-year rolling programme for Levels 2–5 of the National Curriculum so that, for example, a teacher would take a class in Year 5 and continue to work with that class throughout Year 6. Moreover, the pupils sometimes moved to the teacher rather than the other way round; this was deliberately introduced as part of a strategy for transition to secondary school, which also allowed a particular unit to concentrate resources for different curriculum areas. Thus, for example, a Year 6 class went to a Year 5 teacher's home-unit for all science lessons, while their own teacher taught a Year 5 class.

Similar exchanges were observed between geography and PSE, while in history each teacher taught their own class but shared resources across the whole year group. In Years 5 and 6, for example, four teachers taught subject-based work in history, geography, science and technology, allowing each teacher, in the words of the KS2 Co-ordinator, 'to teach one thing four times, instead of four things once'. This system of 'teaching swaps' crossed year groups and extended downwards as far as Year 3.

The 'quiet room', a common feature of most open-plan schools built in the 1970s, was a place where groups of children could work away from distractions when necessary. In the present example, this area tended to be mainly used for SEN support. On one observed occasion, however, the whole class squeezed into this small room to listen to the end of a story which had been disturbed by a Year 5 class returning from a different activity. This episode, although rare, demonstrates one of the problems associated with the use of open-plan areas for more structured teaching of the kind now demanded by the National Curriculum, namely the maintenance of an appropriate noise level in which children can work without distraction.

Nevertheless, it would appear that, in general, the open nature of the classroom units did facilitate 'team arrangements' which teachers found both flexible and effective. Although open-plan areas were designed for the sharing of resources and working spaces, and to enable classes to move easily to common areas, or for teachers to move to classes, an early criticism of this system was that it increased the amount of 'evaporated time', the time lost during in transitional activities (DES 1972). Ironically, therefore, the school designed originally to facilitate an open educational approach enabled a flexible response to the changing demands of a much more prescriptive curriculum.

A conservative culture?

Earlier in this chapter we raised the issue of teachers' apparent resistance to changing their practice, despite public exhortation to do so, and in the wake of a completely restructured primary curriculum. We have presented three examples of classroom organisational strategy, each of which demonstrates considerable flexibility and, in the case of the open-plan classroom, a high level of collaboration. While these were the exceptions rather than the rule, we do not intend to imply that flexible approaches were not to be found elsewhere. Variants of many of the approaches described above could be found, to varying degrees, in a number of the classrooms in the sample. Nevertheless, it is an inescapable fact that for most of the time, in most of the classrooms, children sat together in groups, and that despite some rather general modifications, the typical layout of the primary classroom has hardly altered in twenty years.

Are we to conclude, therefore, that teachers are as conservative in matters of classroom organisation and layout as Cuban (1984) suggests they are in their teaching strategies? Some, like Alexander (1997), argue that the grouping principle has such a 'powerful doctrinal status' for primary teachers that they refuse, or are unable, to consider any other arrangement, and if we accept this proposition, it would appear to be a strong enough force to override a considerable rise in whole class teaching. An alternative, and more cautious view, is that unless teachers feel that they have some sense of ownership over the process of change they will operate according to what Doyle and Ponder (1977) call the 'practicality ethic', where the benefits of introducing an innovation are weighed against the personal cost. Only when teachers see a clear sense of the usefulness and purpose of the new curriculum will there be a shift towards its adoption at anything other than a utilitarian level. Beyond this, when teachers have begun to feel that they have some control over the direction of the innovation, will they move towards fully integrating it into their professional practice.

This model presupposes some element of choice, however, whereas the National Curriculum was, in effect, a technical innovation that was imposed on teachers, with little or no guidance as to how to implement it. In this situation, it is hardly surprising that teachers draw upon familiar, tried-and-tested practice. Although, as Simon argues, 'tinkering' with the primary curriculum has continued more or less unchecked since the 1940s (Galton *et al.* 1980), the pace of educational reform in the past decade has been rapid and continuous (Campbell 1993a). Teachers simply have not had the time or opportunity to get accustomed to one demand before a new requirement is upon them, let alone begin to feel that they have a real stake in the process. The first response in such situations is to 'bolt on' each new development to existing (and familiar) practice. The idea that teachers would, in the face of relentless change, dismantle the traditional and familiar framework in which they work is deeply unrealistic. This is not conservatism, therefore, but basic survival.

In the previous chapter, we met Donna, a part fictional pupil from the ORACLE era, now an adult, and her daughter Hayley, now the same age as her mother was then and attending the same school. When we ask, on the basis of the evidence we have looked at so far, how different Hayley's experience is from Donna's in 1976, the answer would seem to be, with a few exceptions, 'not much'. The picture we have of Hayley's classroom appears very similar to that of her mother twenty years ago. But so far we only have the rough sketches. In the next two chapters, we fill in the finer details, the minutiae of classroom life based on moment-by-moment observations of classroom interaction. Only then will we be able to see how much really has changed, and how much has remained the same. We begin with the teacher.

Notes

1 We borrow this phrase from Cohen *et al.* (1996: 242).
2 1996 Department for Education and Employment figures (DfEE 1996). The figures used for this calculation are based upon Form 7 returns. Schools are asked to list on a particular day in January the way a class is timetabled and taught on the 'census day'. No account is taken of sickness such as flu epidemics, nor of bad weather which could seriously affect attendance. All qualified staff are listed and only classes taught by one teacher are counted. The return might not, for example, include a class where a special educational needs co-ordinator (SENCO) was in attendance on that day helping a small number of 'statemented' pupils. A study by Plunkett (1996) showed that, in a number of schools, choosing a different day over the month of January returned an average class size between twenty-six and thirty-six.
3 The Conservative governments of the 1980s and early 1990s consistently refuted arguments that linked the quality of learning to class size, claiming that it was the quality of the teacher that was the essential ingredient. The intention to reduce class sizes to under thirty in all KS1 classes, within a parliamentary term, was one of the 'Five Key Pledges' of the Labour Party, which came to power in May 1997.
4 Children still sat in rows in just four (7 per cent) of the fifty-eight classrooms observed in the 1976 ORACLE study.
5 The fieldwork for this part of the study was conducted in 1984–85.
6 Much of the material for this discussion derives from a review of research findings by Hastings, Schwieso and Wheldall (1996), Chapter 3 in Croll and Hastings' *Effective Primary Teaching*
7 This approach was not universally accepted, however. For example, early in the twentieth century, Margaret Wroe argued the case that, 'If all the fixed desks

could be removed for a couple of hours each day, or, better still, if a room were provided without them, in which the work not only permitted but demanded free movement of the body, half the difficulties which teachers experience with these children would vanish.' M.A. Wroe (undated: 8) *Thoughts on the Training of Children*, London: National Society's Depository.

8 Bennett *et al.* (1980: 25) cite the *1967 Report* of the Pilkington Research Unit on primary school design, which argued that the building of open-plan schools was driven by the 'usual combination of forces in the world of education . . . necessity, expediency (and) financial pressure'.

9 A number of writers describe the main teaching area in an open-plan area as the 'base'. This term has a specific meaning in the ORACLE observation schedule as the seating arrangements of the pupils (see Chapter 4 and Appendix 2). For that reason we use the alternative term 'home-unit'.

10 This quotation is taken from the opening to Chapter 4 of *Inside the Primary Classroom*, which describes the view that might greet a passing visitor to a typical primary classroom in 1976.

11 Jeremy Bentham's 'Panopticon' was a model for an 'ideal' prison, based around a central surveillance tower which allowed for the observation of all prisoners all of the time. The idea informed the design of many of the penitentiaries of the 1830s and 1840s.

12 This was most often the case with the teacher style identified in the 1976 study as the 'individual monitor', associated with a high level of instruction, marking, and the checking and recording of pupils' progress. Chapter 5 examines the degree to which the 1976 teacher styles still exist.

13 The incidence of recording this behaviour has indeed increased since 1976. The reasons for this are examined more fully in Chapter 4.

14 An increase in this kind of behaviour is discussed in the section on pupil–teacher interaction in Chapter 4, and the relationship between whole class teaching and pupil 'types' in Chapter 5.

15 This strategy was also evidenced by the continuing use, in many classrooms in the present study, of a system where 'one or two children were seated on their own, often close to the teacher'(Galton *et al.* 1980: 68), for example sitting a child on his or her own next to the teacher's desk.

16 The term IT is increasingly being replaced by ICT, Information and *Communications* Technology, which includes developments such as email, the Internet and video-conferencing. At the time of the fieldwork, however, IT was still commonly used in National Curriculum and HMI documentation, and is therefore retained here. See also footnote 19.

17 Stevenson (1997: 18) recommends that computer equipment which is over five years old should be discounted for the purposes of an audit of IT provision.

18 It is possible that the system of observation may have somewhat underestimated the level of use. Given that IT work is usually a solo or paired activity, and since there was often only one computer in a classroom, the chances of the target pupil working on it at the time of observation were relatively low. Nevertheless, observers' fieldnotes confirm that, although IT was used fairly regularly in some classes, it was a low priority area in most.

19 At the time of the fieldwork for the present study, the then Conservative government had launched its 'Educational Superhighways' initiative, while the Labour opposition were announcing ground-breaking plans to give all schools high-speed access to the Internet, should it attain office. Shortly before the time of writing, the now Labour government completed a consultation exercise for the establishment of a 'National Grid for Learning', and has made a number of recent pro-

nouncements, including the intention to provide high-speed Internet access for all schools by the year 2002, and to give all school-age children a 'for life' email address. At around the same time, the Synoptic Report of the Superhighways Initiative was published, with a clear call to the government to support and encourage UK schools to prepare for the 'Information Age'.

20 These examples serve as illustrations of different approaches used in particular classrooms, and are not intended to be representative of the full range observed in the sample schools.

21 Four years before this OFSTED inspection, the headteacher of the school had written to the Local Authority highlighting the problems of having to deliver a curriculum for the 1990s in an establishment designed for the 1890s. In 1998, the staff will not have to 'adapt to the problems inherent in the building', as plans are underway to construct a two-storey extension. All classes will have craft areas with water. Figure 2.3 will no longer function as a classroom.

22 In primary school classrooms, where space is a precious commodity, there was evidence of shelves being given over to National Curriculum folders and documents and filing cabinets being used to store an ever-increasing array of records and profiles on individual students. The demands for additional equipment, resources and learning materials for a National Curriculum based on subject specialism has led to chronic storage problems in some schools (Webb 1993a: 36).

23 This example does not appear to represent technology facilities in general. Webb's six-month study of the implementation of the National Curriculum at KS2 in fifty schools across thirteen LEAs (1993a: 35) found that teachers considered technology to be very under-resourced at KS2, and sets of tools and equipment were only suitable for small groups to use.

3

TEACHING IN TODAY'S PRIMARY CLASSROOM

Whatever views one holds about the quality of today's primary education, everyone will recognise that the classrooms are very busy places. Even children in the reception class quickly come to talk about their school as a place of work where 'we all have our jobs', and where play is what you do once 'you've finished your work' (Barrett 1986; Blatchford 1992; Cullingford 1997a). Primary classrooms are also places where there is much coming and going. The headteacher or the school secretary sometimes 'drop in' to report that a mother has phoned to say her child is ill and won't be coming to school. Pupils from another classroom arrive to borrow a piece of equipment or a book. Local advisory teachers and governors may visit to see what is going on. As with Donna in Chapter 1, parents come to give help with reading or other activities (Cullingford 1996). If the school is linked to a local church, the vicar or the priest may call in on the way from taking morning assembly.

For most parents from whatever background, however, it is the particular teacher in whose class their child is placed that is most important. Listening to parents talking to each other while waiting for their child to come out of school at the end of the day, it is not unusual to hear someone say something like, 'My Josie couldn't get on with Mrs Silver last year but now she is in Miss Patterson's class she loves it and is doing really well.' Such statements of course beg the question of what it is that Miss Patterson does that Mrs Silver doesn't. While some would argue that it is a question of personalities, there is abundant evidence to show that the moment by moment contacts between the teacher and the children also affect the pupils' progress (Brophy and Good 1986). In the ORACLE study these incidents were captured by the observer every twenty-five seconds. Typically in the course of the lesson, a teacher's activity would be recorded for twenty minutes, leaving enough time to make ten observations of each of the six target children, some of which may also have involved contacts with the teacher. In this chapter we will examine the results from the teacher observation data.

Classroom organisation 1976–96

In chapter one we saw that the debate about primary education over two decades had largely centred around the perceived need to shift from individualised methods of instruction towards the use of more whole class teaching. Just how far a change in this direction has taken place, particularly since the advent of the National Curriculum, is still a matter of dispute (Galton *et al.* 1998). Alexander, who has analysed audio recordings of classroom discourse (1995), claims there has been little change, while Webb (1993a) and the PACE (Primary Assessment Curriculum and Experience) Project who carried out direct observations (Pollard *et al.* 1994; Croll 1996a) show considerable increases in class teaching when compared with the 1976 ORACLE findings.

Croll (1996b) has summarised the main results of a series of studies involving observation of primary classrooms, mostly at KS2. To his figures in Table 3.1 have been added the results from the PRISMS (Curriculum Provision in Small Primary Schools) Project (Galton and Patrick 1990) and also those from the study of the Implementation of the National Curriculum in Small Schools (INCSS) Project (Galton *et al.* 1998). If these two studies

Table 3.1 Summary: observational studies of teacher–pupil interaction

	Teacher interacts with:		
	Individuals %	Groups %	Whole class %
ORACLE (Galton and Simon 1980), late 1970s			
Junior classes	72*	9	19
PRISMS (small schools), (Galton and Patrick 1990) early 1980s			
Infant classes	61	13	26
Junior classes	58	16	26
One in Five (Croll and Moses 1985), early 1980s			
Junior classes	51	18	30
School Matters (Mortimore *et al.* 1988), mid-1980s			
Junior classes	65	10	25
INCSS (Galton *et al.* 1998), early 1989–90			
Junior classes	59	18	23
PACE (Pollard *et al.* 1994; Croll 1996b),1990–95			
Infant classes	50	19	32
Junior classes	57	14	30

Note
* figures have been rounded to nearest whole number.

and that of Mortimore *et al.* (1988), which span the 1980s and used the original two ORACLE instruments, the Teacher and Pupil Record (Boydell 1974; 1975), are examined, it will be seen that there is a degree of consistency about the proportion of whole class teaching (less than 3 per cent difference) but more variation in the amounts of individual and group interaction. Then, in the aftermath of the introduction of the National Curriculum, the PACE research findings indicate a further fall in individual teacher–pupil interactions and a further increase in whole class teaching. Thus the original ORACLE data were in some respects atypical, unless we assume that the effect of the Great Debate at the end of the 1970s, following on from the then Prime Minister Callaghan's (1976) Ruskin speech, was to shift practice away from individualisation.

However, a word of caution needs to be entered into the discussion at this point. The next table (Table 3.2), for example, shows the same data as reported in the original ORACLE study, of which the second column is included in Croll's (1996b) table. The first column does not add up to 100 but to 78.4. To get the second column we merely convert this data to percentages by dividing the entries for individual group and class by 78.4 and then multiplying by 100. The reason for the discrepancy is that the ORACLE teacher observation instrument, the Teacher Record, had two other major sub-categories, one to do with what were termed 'silent interactions' – where, for example, a teacher was demonstrating, reading a story or marking work without giving spoken feedback. The other category of non-interaction involves such behaviour as a teacher talking with an adult visitor or a visiting pupil, or carrying out housekeeping duties – such as sorting books or tidying up the room. When critics such as Chris Woodhead, therefore, remark upon 'the high proportion of individualisation in primary classrooms' it is usually as a percentage of teacher talk rather than as a proportion of observed activity.

There are further complications when seeking to look for trends in this data on classroom organisation, since different researchers may interpret the same event in different ways or use a different coding system. In the original ORACLE study, for example, if a teacher read to the class, without breaking off from time to time to ask questions of the pupils, it would be coded as a

Table 3.2 Two versions of the audience categories in the 1975–80 ORACLE study

	Version 1 1976–77	Version 2 1976–77
Individual	55.8	71.2
Group	7.5	9.8
Class	15.1	19.0
Total	78.4	100.0

non-conversation or *silent* interaction, as also would demonstrating and would not have been included in the first column of Table 3.2 on which the figures in the second column two are based. But in the PACE studies both categories would be coded as a class activity. Since reading stories usually takes up the last fifteen minutes of the school day in most primary classrooms (approximately 8 per cent of total class time), this would have a significant effect on the totals. The PACE researchers coded the overall classroom context after every six minutes of pupil observation, whereas in ORACLE the same variable was coded every twenty-five seconds and then expressed as a proportion of the total number of observations aggregated across all teachers or pupils depending on the instrument used. Galton *et al.* (1998) have discussed in some detail the different interpretations given to the notion of whole class teaching, depending on whether it is classified in terms of *base* (how the pupils sit), *team* (how the pupils are expected to work), or in terms of *actual interactions* with the teacher (whether, for example, an exchange between one pupil and the teacher is for private or public consumption). Enough has been said here, however, to make the point that interpretation of such data can be somewhat more complex an activity than one might first assume and requires some knowledge of the observation systems being used.

Changes in classroom organisation in ORACLE schools

The next table (Table 3.3) therefore presents the ORACLE data for 1976–77,[1] alongside that collected in the recent study during 1996, in one case as a percentage of the total number of observations and in the other (enclosed in brackets) where it is expressed as a percentage of teacher–pupil interaction. When we look at both data sets together a more detailed picture emerges. In line with the PACE figures, there has been a decline in individual interactions, with corresponding increases of teacher interaction with both groups and class. However, a proportion of this increase in group and class interaction has come about not mainly as a result of decline in the time that teachers spend interacting with individuals, but as a consequence of the drop

Table 3.3 Changes in audience categories 1976–96

	1976–77	1996
Individual	55.8[a] (71.2)[b]	43.1 (48.4)
Group	7.5 (9.8)	14.6 (16.4)
Class	15.1 (19.0)	31.3 (35.2)
Total	78.4 (100.0)	89.0 (100.0)

Notes
a Figures in first column represent the percentage of all interaction.
b Figure in brackets represent the percentage of teacher–pupil interaction.

in the number of observations occurring in the *silent interaction*, and *no interaction* categories. There was less monitoring, less housekeeping and above all less of what, in the ORACLE study, was termed *silent marking*, in which the teacher marked the students' books with the pupil standing there, but without giving any spoken feedback. Because of this decline in those interactions which did not involve speech, the differences in the figures in the two tables for the 1996 replication of the ORACLE study are now far less than in 1976–77. Individual interactions have changed from 43.1 per cent to 48.4 per cent, group interactions from 14.6 per cent to 16.4 per cent and class interactions from 31.3 per cent to 35.2 per cent when we compare the two sets of figures (inside and outside the brackets) for 1996.

Although minor changes have been made to the observation instruments since 1976, these were done to produce a more finely grained analysis, and sub-categories have been amalgamated to give direct comparisons between the 1976–77 and the 1996 findings. For example, in the original ORACLE study only individual, group or class interactions were recorded. Now class interactions have been subdivided into either *whole class* or *boy for class* or *girl for class*, depending on who was the main focus of the teacher's attention when, for example, the teacher asked the class a question. But in arriving at a figure for the class audience, these boy and girl interactions have been combined to match the 1976 audience category.

Changes in interaction patterns in ORACLE schools

In this next section we examine the change in the pattern of classroom interactions over the two decades. Classroom interaction was divided into two main categories where teachers either asked questions or made statements (see Appendix 2, Table 2A1). In the original ORACLE study there were distinct patterns of interaction related to the different organisational teaching styles so that, for example, teachers who engaged in an above average proportion of one-to-one interactions with pupils were characterised by a large number of routine and task supervision statements as well as by the use of silent interactions, chiefly marking and monitoring. In contrast, teachers who engaged in above average interaction with the whole class were more likely to be involved in task-related interactions, including the highest proportion of what were termed 'higher order' or 'challenging questions'. These results have come to be interpreted by critics of current practice, such as those discussed in Chapter 1, as suggesting that whole class teaching is the major vehicle for enquiry. This conclusion overlooks the fact that there was another group of teachers among those preferring an individualised approach, who matched those using 'above average' amounts of whole class teaching in the proportion of time given over to challenging questions. The value of these one-to-one exchanges for promoting 'deep learning', even in very large classes, has been demonstrated by Biggs (1994: 29) in his

Table 3.4 Changes in teacher activity 1976–96

	1976–77	*1996*
Questioning	12.0	16.2
Making statements	44.7	59.2
Silent interaction[a]	22.3	12.2
No interaction	21.0	12.4
Total	100.0	100.0

Note

a The silent interaction, such as listening to a pupil's report, was sometimes accompanied by short comments from the teacher which observers
also recorded. There were forty-five of these occasions, giving rise to a
total number of 'ticks' on the observation schedule of 6,708 compared
to the 6,663 used to compute Table 3.5, and this changes the figures
for the *silent interaction* category from 12.2 per cent to 12.8 per cent
with corresponding small decreases in the *Question* and *Statement* categories. Some of the later tables involving a more detailed analysis of
silent interaction have been based on 6,708 observations so readers
may note small differences in the decimal point.

analysis of teaching in Hong Kong classrooms. Professor Biggs has argued
from his research that effective teaching environments around the 'Pacific
Rim' share common objectives with those in the West, and this leads to explanations as to why students from 'Confucian-heritage cultures' develop 'deep'
as well as 'surface learning' that are very different from those put forward by
Reynolds and Farrell (1996). We shall take up this issue in Chapter 8.

Table 3.4, therefore, shows the changes which have taken place between
1976 and 1996 in the main interaction categories.

In 1976, just as there were variations in the amount of questioning used by
teachers preferring an individualised approach, the same was also true of
those making above average use of whole class teaching. What has often
been overlooked in the comments on ORACLE was that the group identified
as 'whole class enquirers' consisted of only a small minority of the teachers
and that for the total sample the average of around 19 per cent of the time
which was devoted to whole class teaching was mainly taken up in teachers
making either factual or procedural statements or occasionally setting a
problem demanding 'low level' thinking. In 1976, as Table 3.4 (first column)
shows, the structure of discourse in the English primary classroom loosely
followed the first rule discovered by Flanders (1964), that in the United
States *two thirds of classroom activity involved talk*. Now in 1996 (second
column, Table 3.4) around *three quarters* of all classroom activity involved talk, presumably the consequence of the increase in the proportion
of whole class teacher–pupil interaction from 19 per cent in 1976 to 35
per cent in 1996 shown in Table 3.3. When we examine Table 3.4 in more
detail and compare the proportions of different teacher activities, we see
that the result of this shift to whole class teaching has largely been taken

up by an increase in the amount of talking *at* pupils through statements and not in talking *with* pupils by asking questions. Across two decades, the overall proportions of teacher statements and questions have remained remarkably stable. In 1976 an ORACLE teacher typically made use of 3.7 times as many statements as questions. In 1996 the ratio was 3.6. This result appears to be very similar to that found by Alexander in both the Leeds PRINDEP study (Alexander 1991) and in his more recent CICADA analysis of the discourse from sixty lessons (Alexander 1995). In the Leeds study over a third of the interactions were about the content of tasks (in ORACLE terms 'task supervision') and a fifth were involved with monitoring and checking (in part a combination of ORACLE's *silent* and *no interaction* categories). More importantly, as in this present research, most of the questions asked in Alexander's 1991 and 1995 studies were of a low cognitive level, requiring one or two word responses, and many were rhetorical. There were very few cases in which pupils initiated the questioning. Overall, therefore, despite the increase in whole class teaching, the pattern of teacher's discourse at the level of questions and statements has remained relatively stable. In the next section, therefore, we examine the nature of these questions and statements to see how far they are, perhaps, now more intellectually challenging than those uttered by teachers some twenty years ago.

Changes in questions and statenents since ORACLE

The study of teachers' questioning has been the subject of much research. Donneau (1985) reported that teachers' oral questions consumed between 6 per cent and 16 per cent of classroom time and that, furthermore, pupils spent much additional time answering written questions during seat work, homework and quizzes. The ORACLE data in Table 3.4 confirm this finding. In the typical classroom during 1976–77, questioning was 12 per cent of all activity and by 1996 this had risen to 16.2 per cent. Other studies in the United States (Sirotnik 1983), and in eastern Europe and India (Klinzing-Eurich 1987) have demonstrated that in many cultures, most of these questions are almost invariably closed or factual. As a result, there has been a persistent attempt to encourage teachers to increase the proportion of higher order cognitive questioning, even though Samson *et al.* (1987) conclude that the correlations between such questions and student achievement are relatively modest.

One of the reasons for the modest correlations is the way in which such questions have been classified by the researchers. Many studies base their classification on the teachers' apparent intentions so that, for example, if the teacher asks the pupil, 'What do you think is happening when the solution turns blue?' the observer concludes that the student is being asked to speculate and therefore classifies it as an open question designed to encourage the child to hypothesise. However, the pupil, knowing that solutions containing copper ions are often blue, might respond, 'because it's got copper in it', and the teacher might then say, 'yes', thereby confirming the correctness of this information. In these circumstances it is very difficult for the observer to be certain that the teacher had intended the question to be an open speculative one, or whether he or she had been looking for the one correct answer, 'copper'. In the ORACLE research, however, this problem was avoided by defining an open question in terms of the teacher's reaction to the pupils' answers. Only if the teacher accepted more than one answer to the question would it be judged as 'open' rather than 'closed'. In the previous example the teacher would have had to respond to the pupil's answer, 'copper' by, perhaps, turning to the rest of the class and asking, 'What do others think? What else could it be?' before the ORACLE observer would have coded the original question in the *open* category. Defining an open question in this way makes the observer's task an easier one, but it does have consequences in that it does not record the teacher's attempts to encourage pupils to speculate, but only those attempts which are successful. It is for this reason that the relationships between open questions and pupil attainment in ORACLE and other studies using the Teacher Record (Mortimore *et al.* 1988) have proved to be more significant than in cases where the teacher's *intention* was used to categorise the type of question exchange.

That being said, Table 3.5 displays changes in the pattern of questioning between the 1976–77 and 1996 studies. In ORACLE questions could be of five types. First there were task questions, which could be factual or could concern either closed problem solving or open problem solving. There were then questions involving task supervision ('How are you going to measure that?') or of routine ('Why are you out of your place?'). In 1976–77, questions totalled 12 per cent of all observations. Now, in 1996, they amounted to 16.2 per cent (second and fourth columns). As might be expected with the shift in more whole class teaching, there was a greater emphasis on task questions rather than on task supervision but, like the other research reported, it was factual and closed questions which dominated and accounted for the greatest part of the increased proportion of questioning.

Table 3.5 The nature of teachers' questions

Questions	1976–77		1996	
	% of all questions	% of all observation	% of all questions	% of all observation
Of fact	29.2	3.5	24.7	4.0
Closed solution	18.3	2.2	34.6	5.6
Open solution	5.0	0.6	9.9	1.6
Task supervision	32.5	3.9	18.5	3.0
Routine	15.0	1.8	12.3	2.0
Total	100.0	12.0	100.0	16.2

This is perhaps more easily seen by expressing the proportion of questions as a percentage of all questions (first and third columns). As a percentage questions of fact have declined by around 5 per cent, but closed questioning has nearly doubled (up from 18.3 per cent to 34.6 per cent). The same was true of open questions, although they started from a much lower level. The increase in closed and open questions was achieved largely by the decrease in the amount of task supervision questioning (down from 32.5 per cent to 18.5 per cent).

[handwritten margin note: So how does not improve cog skills]

[handwritten note: Q % ↑ but more closed]

Changes in teacher statements 1976–96

Table 3.6 conducts a similar analysis for teacher statements, which were defined as all teacher utterances which do not seek an answer (this category also included rhetorical questions). As in the original ORACLE study, and as Table 3.4 demonstrated, teachers spent most of their time engaging in such utterances. In a similar manner to questions, statements were classified either as task, task supervision or routine. Task statements were further classified into those of facts or of ideas and problems. No attempt was made further to divide these problem statements into either open or closed as with questions. The reason for this decision should follow from the discussion in the previous section dealing with the use of questions, which showed that it was only possible to identify closed or open questions by the pupils' response and teachers' reactions. Here, when only the teacher was speaking, there was usually no way of determining his or her intention at the moment of observation.

Task supervision statements were divided into three sub-groups. There were those which told children what to do, such as telling a pupil to 'Colour in the picture when you have finished the story.' Other task supervision statements either praised work or effort or provided more neutral feedback on work. Thus, 'An excellent story, I particularly liked your ending' would constitute praising work, whereas 'That's the correct answer' would be classified as neutral feedback. In the 1976 version neutral and negative feedback were coded as one category. However, given the 1976 finding that teachers in England appear to use both praise and criticism sparingly, it seemed more logical to keep neutral responses separate. The praise category was therefore extended to include more forceful critical feedback using (+) and (−) signs to record positive and negative responses.

Finally, there were matters of routine where there were four sub-groups. In the first category *providing routine information*, the teacher might tell a child to 'Go and join Jonathan's group', or in the second category might provide either *positive* or *negative feedback* such as, 'Your table is nice and clear' (+ve), or might rebuke a child for behaviour or lack of effort, as when telling a pupil to 'sit down and be quiet' in an aggrieved voice (−ve). The third category consisted of occasions where the feedback was given in a

Table 3.6 The pattern of teachers' statements

	Statements	1976			1996		
		% of all statements (A)	% of all observation (B)	Sub-total (C)	% of all statements (D)	% of all observation (E)	Sub-total (F)
Telling	Fact	15.4	6.9	9.4	13.7	8.1	13.7
	Ideas	5.6	2.5		9.4	5.6	
Task Directions	Telling child what to do	28.1	12.6		22.1	13.1	
	Praise/criticise work	2.5	1.0	23.2	5.0	3.0	27.2
	Feedback on work	21.4	9.6		18.7	11.1	
Routine Directions	Giving information	14.5	6.5		17.4	10.3	
	Feedback	4.5	2.0	12.1	7.6	4.5	18.4
	Critical control	5.1	2.3		3.7	2.2	
	Small talk	2.9	1.3		2.4	1.4	
	Total	100.0	44.7		100.0	59.3	

neutral tone of voice. Here again this marks a change from the 1976 version of the Teacher Record, in which positive and neutral routine feedback were combined and teacher utterances to do with critical control (negative feedback) coded separately. In 1996, on the other hand neutral utterances for both task supervision feedback and routine feedback were coded separately in an attempt to provide consistency. One disadvantage, however, is that direct comparison over the two decades was no longer straightforward. The last category concerned *small talk*, which captured those times when the teacher holds a conversation on matters which have nothing to do with classwork or with school. A teacher might, for example, tell the class where he or she was going on holiday, what he or she did at the weekend or had seen on television the previous night.

As Table 3.6 shows, statements of all kinds have increased since 1976–77. Examining columns (C) and (F) shows that task statements as a proportion of all observations have increased by 4.3 per cent (9.4 per cent to 13.7 per cent), task supervision by 4 per cent (23.2 per cent to 27.2 per cent) and routine by 6.3 per cent (12.1 per cent to 18.4 per cent). However, if we examine columns (A) and (D) where the number of statements is expressed as a percentage of *all* statements, then the extent and the nature of these changes becomes clearer. Task supervision statements still predominate. In 1976–77 they were just over half of all statements uttered (28.1 + 2.5 + 21.4 = 52 per cent). In 1996 there were just under half (45.8 per cent). Telling pupils what to do followed by giving pupils neutral feedback on work were still the most frequently used statements. Interestingly, given the fact that in 1976–77 neutral feedback also included critical statements, the drop of 2.7 per cent in this category almost matched the increase in the combined praise/criticism figure over the two decades. This suggests that the balance between teachers' use of praise and criticism has remained constant. Task statements were slightly up from 21 per cent to 23.1 per cent, but the ratio between statements of facts and statements of ideas was now more balanced. Whereas in 1976–77 there were approximately three times as many factual statements as there were of ideas, the ratio had almost halved to 1.5 per cent.

A total of 17.4 per cent of statements now involved the teacher giving routine directions, a slight increase since 1976–77. Interestingly, however, given the claims that there is more disruption in today's primary classroom, the proportion of critical control fell slightly, even though in the 1996 analysis this category now included positive utterances. Summing up the 1976–77 situation, we wrote that it seemed evident that 'the general pattern of teachers' questions and statements is directed mainly towards ensuring that pupils understand the work in which they are engaged, that they receive feedback on it, that the activity of the class runs smoothly and uninterruptedly' (Galton *et al.* 1980: 90). What was said then now seems even more true of primary teachers in 1996. Whereas two decades ago, questions and statements occupied around 57 per cent of all observations, this figure has now increased by nearly 50 per cent. Today's teachers, therefore devote even more of their time to telling pupils facts and ideas or to giving directions than their counterparts of twenty years ago. What is most significant, however, is that the distribution of statements between task, task supervision and routine is much the same as twenty years ago, despite the increase in the amount of whole class teaching. It would appear that today's primary teachers have responded to the pressures described in the first chapter by increasing the amount of time spent interacting with pupils at the expense of silent interactions such as monitoring pupils' progress and listening to pupils read. But in doing so they have not made radical changes to their existing practice. Instead, the present-day primary teacher has continued to engage in the same kinds of exchanges with their pupils as their predecessors did two decades ago.

Changes in silent and non-interaction

As discussed in the previous paragraph and displayed in Table 3.4, the use of the categories, *silent interaction* and *non-interaction*, where the teacher was mainly either monitoring, housekeeping or talking to a visiting pupil or another adult, has decreased over the two decades by nearly half. There have, however, been changes to the schedule in that in the 1996 version specific codings were made whenever the teacher was listening to pupils reporting back or was watching pupils read for an extended period. In the 1976 version of the teacher record, when the teacher was listening to an extended pupil response in this way it was generally coded as *non-interacting*. Only in cases where the teacher was hearing the pupil read would this have been encoded similarly under the silent interaction category *reading*. The other category where extended listening might have been coded in 1976 would be that of silent marking, where a pupil might make involuntary comments or offer explanations while the teacher was correcting work but received no verbal feedback in return. It is significant, therefore, that in Table 3.7 the two categories where the greatest change has taken place were *marking* (down from 10.1 per cent of all observations to 2.5 per cent) and in the *non-interaction* category (down from 17.5 per cent to 7.9 per cent). Although the listening and watching category has now been added to listening to children reading, the fact that the proportions have changed little would appear to indicate that overall there has been a decline in the amounts of time that teachers are able to give to various kinds of monitoring, such as questioning pupils about their work, listening to them reading a passage, or simply silently watching the children at work as, for example, when they were working in groups. Of the 7.9 per cent of observations in the 1996 non-interacting category, 5.8 per cent were *housekeeping* (a figure not available separately in the published data for 1976–77). Interestingly, the actual percentage of observations in which the teacher listened to children read did

Table 3.7 Types of silent and non-interaction[a]

	1976–77 % of all such interaction	% of all observations	1996 % of all such interaction	% of all observations
Gesture	4.4	1.9	5.5	1.4
Showing	6.0	2.6	11.9	3.0
Marking	23.4	10.1	9.9	2.5
Waiting	4.4	1.9	3.2	0.8
Story	2.1	0.9	4.7	1.2
Reading	7.9	3.4	15.8	4.0
Not observed	3.5	1.5	0.4	0.1
Not listed	0.0	0.0	0.0	0.0
Visiting adult	3.9	1.7	9.9	2.5
Visiting pupil	0.9	0.4	2.0	0.5
No interaction	40.5	17.5	31.2	7.9
Out of room	3.0	1.3	5.5	1.4
Total	100.0	43.2	100.0	25.3

Note
a This table is based upon the 6,708 observations.

not, as in the 1976 study, increase with age. In the 8+ group 1.2 per cent of all observations were given over to hearing children read. The figure for the 10+ and the 11+ was 1.1 per cent and 1.4 per cent respectively.

These changes appear to come about in two ways. First, the pressure of including all the National Curriculum subjects has reduced the amount of time spent hearing the children read. In one class, for example, we observed a teacher attempting to satisfy the headteacher's rule that every child should be heard reading every second day. The strategy adopted was that of hearing two children read at once. At his left ear was an excellent reader and at his right ear a poorer one. When the teacher heard pairs of children read in this way, he was observed to concentrate on the poorer readers for almost 90 per cent of the time.[2] Overall, therefore, this teacher reduced the amount of time spent hearing children read by around 50 per cent. Although this might have been an excellent strategy for meeting the statutory requirements of the National Curriculum (while at the same time satisfying the headteacher's quality assurance procedure of filling in the checklist showing that every pupil had been heard reading) it also, perhaps, conveyed an inappropriate message to the pupils about the importance the teacher placed on reading activities, particularly for more able readers.

A second reason for the reduction in the proportion of time devoted to reading between 1976 and 1996 follows from the increase in whole class subject teaching. In 1976, children would often work on their own research topic and the teacher would come and sit with the pupils while they read what they had written. Increased class teaching will have led to a reduction in such research activities, so that the opportunities to hear the children read aloud may have been considerably reduced.

The context of pupil–teacher interaction

In Table 3.8 we examine the pattern of interaction in different audience contexts. In other words we break down Table 3.4 to examine the variation in teacher interactions according to whether they involved the whole class, individuals or groups of pupils. The figures here are slightly different from those in Table 3.4 because some observers did not always record the nature of the teacher's audience for the silent interaction categories. Thus the overall proportions between the various main categories of questions and statements and silent interactions are different. What matter in this instance, however, are the relative proportions of individual, group and class as the teacher's audience, rather than the absolute values.

The largest variations in interaction patterns across different audiences were in the questioning and statement categories. Despite the continued perpetuation of the myth by the media over two decades that teachers in 'informal' or individualised settings 'are taking to extremes the belief that children must not be told anything',[3] in 1996 the use of statements was greatest during individual interactions and lowest in class settings. The reverse trend held for questioning. The same was true of the 1976 ORACLE data. Differences in the silent interaction and no interaction categories were less marked.

However, as Table 3.9 shows, these broad categories mask some important variations, particularly in the use of teacher statements. While most individual interactions involved talking '*at*' pupils, much of this talk also appeared to concern telling pupils what to do (task supervision) rather than, for example, providing them with task information. The figure of just below 51 per cent for individual task supervision interactions was double that for the class audience and, of course, also included some questioning. In contrast, it was in the whole class setting that both task statements and questions were highest. The figures for these two types of interactions are shown in the final two rows of Table 3.9. In general, task interactions were between two and two and a half times as frequent in whole class settings than when teachers were interacting with individual pupils, and the proportion of

Table 3.8 The context of pupil–teacher interaction in 1996

Activity	Individual	Group	Class	All
Questions	15.8	18.1	21.9	18.3
Statements	71.3	65.0	62.3	67.1
Silent Interaction	12.7	14.6	12.9	13.1
No interaction	1.7	3.8	4.5	2.9

Table 3.9 Percentages of interaction with different audience categories (1976–77 ORACLE data where available in brackets)

Activity	Individual		Group		Class	
Task	21.0	(22.4)[a]	35.9	(30.2)	48.8	(43.0)
Task supervision	50.9	(54.5)	39.0	(39.0)	24.7	(30.8)
Routine	28.1	(23.0)	24.8	(30.6)	26.5	(26.2)
Total	100.0		100.0		100.0	
Task statements	9.5		13.8		22.7	
Challenging questions (open and closed)	5.6		9.5		11.1	

Note
a ORACLE data given in brackets where available.

challenging questions, both open and closed, was also highest in class and lowest in individual settings. The picture of our typical teacher, then, is of someone who in class settings alternates between giving information or raising questions, whereas when involved with a single pupil he or she is more likely to be acting as a resource (defined in the sense that information or help from the teacher was essential for the pupil to complete the task) and offering help or feedback on the pupil's work. Routine statements, however, do not differentiate between the different audience categories in quite the same way as in 1976.

Comparisons with the original ORACLE data show that task activity has increased by around 5 per cent when the teacher interacted with either a group or the whole class. Routine interactions with individual pupils have also increased by around 5 per cent. In general, however, the figures, apart from these small differences, showed a degree of consistency over the two decades. In so far as changes in practice have occurred between 1976 and 1996, therefore, it has been largely due to the increase in the proportion of whole class teaching in the primary classroom. What does not appear to have changed significantly is the nature of the tactics (the individual moment-by-moment exchanges which take place between teachers and pupils) when teachers are involved with an individual pupil, or a group, or a class of children.

Variations in organisation across subjects

So far we have reported average values for the different observation categories that make up the Teacher Record. This has been done by aggregating observations across all teachers and all lessons to give a portrait of the typical teacher. However, as discussed in Chapters 1 and 2, since the advent of the National Curriculum there has been an emphasis on single-subject teaching, and it may be that patterns of classroom organisation differ considerably in,

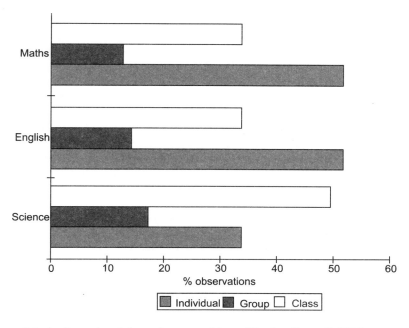

Figure 3.1 Audience breakdown by core subjects (Teacher Record) 1996

say, science as compared to art or history. Figure 3.1, therefore, looks at the use of individual, group, and class interactions in the core curriculum areas, English, mathematics and science. This kind of analysis was not carried out in the 1976–77 study so no comparison over time is possible.

Bearing in mind the strong links between certain kinds of teacher interactions and the use of individual, group and whole class organisation, there are some interesting findings when the 1996 ORACLE data on classroom organisation are broken down by subject. English and mathematics followed the typical pattern shown in Table 3.1, with around 34 per cent of activity taken up with whole class teaching. Science, however, was different, and some might argue disturbingly so, given that the pattern of the interaction within this setting follows that described in the previous paragraphs, with relatively limited opportunities for pupils to question or explore ideas. Here, approximately 50 per cent of the interactions during science took place in a whole class setting.

Such an emphasis on whole class teaching appears out of step with the constructivist theories of learing put forward by Driver (1983) or Harlen (1992). It conflicts also with the advice of Bennett (1992) in his monograph *Managing Learning in the Primary Classroom*, in which he summarises the constructivist view and quotes the dictum (Wells *et al.* 1990) that 'talk drives learning'. According to Bennett, this talk should involve activities

71

such as co-operative learning through peer tutoring and group work, and should include sustained questioning exchanges in which a proportion of questions stems from pupils as they attempt to interrogate their teacher, their peers or a text. Although this approach to developing pupils' conceptual understanding applies across the curriculum, it has obvious relevance to problem-solving activities in science involving hypothesising and other aspects of investigation.

Yet for science the level of group interaction was only marginally higher than for English or mathematics (16.9 per cent as against 13.4 per cent and 13.2 per cent respectively). The high proportion of whole class teaching relative to the average value was therefore accounted for by a fall in individual interaction between the teacher and pupils. For science the latter value is 33.5. per cent compared to 52.0 per cent for English and 52.7 per cent for mathematics. What is also of interest is the level of sustained interaction. This category was recorded if the teacher was engaged in conversation with the same group or the same individual pupil on the next time signal twenty-five seconds later. Sustained interactions are obviously more likely to occur when teachers are attempting to provoke thoughtful responses from pupils as in hypothesising, in contrast to more short-lived exchanges involved in giving out information or a task supervision instruction. In science, however, only 10 per cent of interactions were sustained, in contrast to mathematics and English, which were recorded at 20.3 per cent and 26.7 per cent respectively.

In foundation subjects there were also differences between art, history and geography, but this time it was art that did not follow the more typical pattern. The breakdown of the audience categories for these subjects is shown in Figure 3.2.

Whereas for both history and geography the percentage of whole class teaching was similar to that for mathematics and English (33.5 per cent and 34.3 per cent for the two subjects), in art it was only 13.4 per cent, the lowest of any subject. Although art is often thought of as a subject in which children work on their own individual tasks, the percentage of one-to-one teacher–pupil interaction was only marginally above that for subjects such as English at 59.5 per cent. It was group interactions which at 27.1 per cent (second only to physical education) compensated for the lower proportion of whole class teaching. Bearing in mind that many of the classrooms had art activity areas where groups of pupils could work, this finding does not necessarily mean that pupils were working on joint activities, but it would suggest that there was now more structure to art lessons with children working on the same theme or using a similar medium, so that when the teacher came to a particular table, or the art activity area, he or she could instruct the group rather than an individual child.

In the remaining subjects there were one or two interesting results. Music, which was not observed during the 1976–77 ORACLE study, but which in

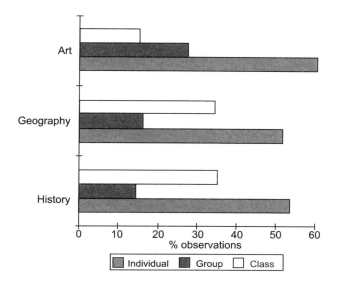

Figure 3.2 Audience breakdown by foundation subjects (Teacher Record) 1996

PRISMS (Galton and Patrick 1990) was typically a whole class activity, now has the highest number of individual interactions (80.6 per cent). Too much should not be read into this result since very few observations of music lessons were recorded. Apart from art and PE, only in technology and IT lessons did teachers conduct more than 20 per cent of interactions with groups. In history, where it might be surmised that a certain amount of discussion might best take place in groups, as for example when evaluating a piece of historical evidence, the figure for such interaction was only 13.4 per cent. This was comparable with the percentages for mathematics and English.

Teacher interaction in the core and foundation subjects

In this section we examine the teacher's use of questions, statements and silent interaction in each of the core and main foundation subjects. Table 3.10 expresses the various kinds of questions asked as a percentage of all questions within each subject, but also gives the percentage of questions as a proportion of all observations. Most questions were asked during geography (27.7 per cent) and mathematics (26.4 per cent) lessons, and fewest during art (8.5 per cent), a pattern which might, in general, be expected. Recall of facts was highest in geography and history and lowest in art. Closed questions were highest in mathematics and science. In every subject more closed than open questions were asked. In mathematics lessons the ratio of closed to open questions was just over ten, in science it was approximately two, while for art it was nearer one. English, history and geography were similar

Table 3.10 Teacher talk in the core and foundation subjects (as a percentage of questions, statements, etc.)

Activity		*English*	*Maths*	*Science*	*History*	*Geography*	*Art*
Question	fact	22.4	31.3	27.4	35.1	35.0	4.7
	closed	35.2	46.8	43.3	28.0	35.0	20.9
	open	12.8	4.5	20.0	11.9	10.7	16.3
	sup:	21.2	14.7	7.4	19.1	13.4	45.3
	rout:	6.4	2.7	1.9	7.1	4.7	12.8
	Total	100.0	100.0	100.0	100.0	100.0	100.0
% Observations		15.6	26.5	21.5	16.8	27.7	8.6
Statement	fact	17.6	19.9	21.8	12.1	17.0	7.8
	ideas	10.5	15.4	11.7	8.4	13.9	7.0
	tell	23.7	27.5	24.8	24.1	21.6	25.3
	praise	5.6	5.4	5.3	6.5	7.2	9.8
	s-feed	27.1	19.6	15.5	30.8	23.6	28.5
	Direct	7.6	6.6	11.0	10.3	7.3	13.1
	r-feed	3.7	2.3	6.5	5.0	5.7	5.3
	control	2.5	2.5	2.7	2.3	2.6	2.4
	s-talk	1.7	0.8	0.7	0.5	1.1	0.8
	Total	100.0	100.0	100.0	100.0	100.0	100.0
% Observations		59.0	64.8	60.0	63.4	64.8	86.3
Silent	show	9.1	19.5	23.6	29.8	17.3	55.0
	mark	22.4	31.0	14.8	9.1	40.0	0.0
Listen	read	24.4	2.2	0.0	0.0	0.0	0.0
	report	9.4	10.3	7.7	1.5	4.0	0.0
	Total	100.0	100.0	100.0	100.0	100.0	100.0
% Observations		25.4	8.7	18.2	19.8	7.5	5.1

with around three times as many closed questions as open ones. The highest levels of task supervision were found in art (45.3 per cent) and the lowest in science (7.4 per cent), again supporting the view that the latter subject, because of its content-dominated curriculum, affords pupils little opportunity to carry out investigations that might require teachers to give advice on the best procedure to adopt. Routine questions, probably to do with cleaning up and tidying away, occurred most frequently during art.

When, however, we turn to the section dealing with statements in Table 3.10, interesting differences between some subjects and similarities between others can be found. There was a degree of uniformity in the percentage of teacher statements across all subjects (art excepted, where they accounted for 86.3 per cent of all interaction). In the other main subject areas the figures hovered either slightly below or above 60 per cent. When this was added to teacher questions, then somewhere between 75 per cent and 90 per cent of class time consisted of teachers talking.

When detailed analysis of the different types of statements was carried out, the degree of uniformity across subjects was maintained. Statements of 'fact', which were highest in science (21.9 per cent), were observed around 18 per cent of the time in other subjects, with the exception of history (12.1 per cent) and art (7.8 per cent). There was slightly greater variation in the proportion of observations that were coded as a statement of 'ideas'; the lowest again occurring during history and art lessons and the highest, not unsurprisingly, occurring in mathematics followed by geography. In science, which might be expected to be similar to mathematics, nearly twice as many teacher statements dealt with facts rather than offering ideas or solutions to problems. There was a greater degree of consistency across all subjects in the case of task supervision where teachers were telling children 'what to do'. For every subject this category accounted for around a quarter of all statements. Praise or criticism were uniformly low, being highest in art (9.8 per cent) and around 5 per cent for all the three core curriculum areas. The next highest category was that of giving feedback about work, which somewhat surprisingly was relatively low for mathematics and for science (19.6 per cent and 15.5 per cent respectively).

Routine statements were also relatively infrequent. Particularly noticeable, given the media claims that children are now less well behaved, was the fairly uniform figure of 2.5 per cent for the combination of praise and criticism with respect to routine feedback. Even if the greater proportion of these observations involved critical feedback, this would still suggest that talk about increases in indiscipline in the modern primary classroom is somewhat exaggerated, unless most of the troublesome children are now excluded. The perception of the observers was that unacceptable pupil behaviour generally involved fidgeting and not paying attention. A teacher's instruction to 'sit up straight and listen' would then have been coded as giving *routine information*.

Finally, turning to the silent and non-interaction categories, these were around 20 per cent of all observations for history, science and English but only between 5 per cent and 9 per cent for mathematics, geography and art. 'Showing' (demonstrating) was highest in art (55 per cent), although this only represented just over 2.7 per cent of all observations in that subject. 'Showing' or demonstrating was next highest for history (nearly 30 per cent) followed by science (23.6 per cent). As might be expected, the only subject where there was a sizeable number of occasions during which teachers listened to children reading was English (24.4 per cent). For all other subjects the figures were either zero or very small. This finding confirms the explanation put forward earlier to account for the overall percentage decrease in the time that teachers spend hearing children read. It signifies a departure from the practice of twenty years ago, in which a feature of the primary classroom involved children reading aloud to teachers what they might have written about their research on a given topic during project work. Opportunities for children to report on their work are now relatively infrequent, and this again points to a concern in the way that subjects such as science and history are now being taught. It might be imagined that children would have been required to offer explanations to teachers about their ideas when called upon to investigate scientific or historical artefacts.

In summary, therefore, there are more similarities across the subjects than there are differences. Teaching in today's primary schools at KS2 is still very much a matter of teachers talking and children listening. Of this talk, by far the largest amount consists of teachers making statements. When questions are asked of children, these questions will require them either to recall facts or to solve a problem for which their teachers expect a correct answer. Open, speculative or challenging questioning, where children are required to offer more than one answer, is still very rare. Even in science, where the highest percentage is recorded, teachers are three times more likely to require a single correct answer than they are to invite speculation.

In the first chapter it was argued that the often quoted criticism that portrays teachers as never telling children anything, but leaving them to find out things for themselves, was untrue of the 1970s primary school. Those who perpetuate this myth in the 1990s appear to be guilty of a greater distortion of reality. The demands of the programmes of study in the various National Curriculum subjects, even after the Dearing (1993b) Review, still appear to place too heavy an imperative on teachers to cut down on the amount of pupil participation in order to 'get through' the curriculum content. This view emerges very clearly from the PACE analysis which has followed the curriculum over six years (Croll 1996a) and is also confirmed by the research on Discretionary Time carried out by Galton and Fogelman (1998). As one teacher commented in the latter study, 'There just isn't time now to listen to the children.' While it is true that there is now more task-related activity in the primary classroom than twenty years ago, the introduction of the National Curriculum appears to have resulted in an increase in the traditional secondary style of teaching, creating a one-way communication system where, for most of the time, teachers talk and pupils sit and listen.

Patterns of interaction across other subjects

Within the primary curriculum there were other curriculum activities besides those featured in the previous analysis. These subjects were also observed, although less frequently, and for this reason they have not been included in the main analysis. Nevertheless, it is of some interest to look at the patterns of interaction, particularly in a subject such as IT which was not part of the primary curriculum twenty years ago. In the 1976 ORACLE study neither PE nor music was observed. Because of the limited amount of observation, we report in Table 3.11 only those categories where more than 10 per cent of the interaction, expressed as a proportion of all observations was recorded, these being PE, music, IT and technology. For physical education, the highest percentages involved 'task supervision' (telling children what to do), followed by watching children, followed by giving feedback. In PE 44 per cent

Table 3.11 Audience and main interaction categories for music, PE, IT and technology

Audience	Music	PE	IT	Technology
Individual	80.6	24.1	54.5	82.9
Group		31.2	22.4	26.4
Class	19.4	44.7	23.1	20.7
	100.0	100.0	100.0	100.0
Activity				
Statements of fact	10.8		10.4	
Statements of ideas	10.8			
Telling	13.5	24.9	28.9	17.2
Feedback on task	21.6	11.0		17.2
Showing	10.8		20.0	10.0
Watching	11.9	20.8		
% of Observations	79.4	56.7	59.3	44.4

of all interactions were whole class, whereas for music nearly 80.6 per cent were with individual children. However, with only 100 observations in music, this finding may be atypical, since previous studies have generally reported that music was taught as a whole class activity (see, for example, Galton and Patrick 1990: 93). Of these music interactions, 21.6 per cent concerned feedback on work or effort, followed by 'telling children what to do' (13.5 per cent). Four other categories, 'watching', 'statements of facts', 'statements of ideas' and 'showing' ('demonstrating'), each accounted for approximately 10 per cent of observations in music. Technology and IT had shared audience profiles. In each case over half the interactions were with individual pupils, and around a quarter with groups, leaving the remaining quarter for whole class teaching. In information technology, 'statements of task supervision' were highest (28.9 per cent) followed by 'showing' (20 per cent). The only other category to exceed 10 per cent was 'making statements of fact'. In technology the two highest interactions again concerned 'telling children what to do' and providing feedback on work or effort. Here, the only other category to reach 10 per cent was 'showing'.

In all of these curriculum areas, therefore, there is a remarkable similarity in approach with almost a total lack of questioning of any kind or of statements of ideas. In every case, over half the observed interactions involved task supervision or demonstrations, or in the case of PE, watching children during an activity. The pattern was essentially one of coaching in which the teacher first demonstrates, then gives instructions, then watches the activity and then gives feedback in a continuous teaching–evaluation–re-teaching cycle. Technology seemed to provide children with very little opportunity to develop their ideas and this was in marked contrast to the situation investigated in the Rural Schools Curriculum Enhancement National Evaluation

(SCENE) Project (Galton *et al.* 1991) prior to the introduction of the National Curriculum. This project carried out an evaluation of educational provision in the fourteen local authorities which had received money under the Educational Support Grant (ESG) scheme for improving the curriculum in rural primary schools. Technology was one of the areas which received special attention, and it was found that, compared to the earlier study of small schools, the PRISMS project (Galton and Patrick 1990), there was a significant increase in the time devoted to subjects such as technology and science. In both these subjects it was noticeable that following the introduction of the ESG programmes, there were fewer activities, 'which consisted simply of the teacher giving information' (Galton *et al.* 1991: 67). This was compatible with an observed increase in the use of pupils' own work as a resource and a corresponding decrease in the use of workcards and of the teacher as major resource. The patterns seen in this present study, however, seem far closer to that observed in PRISMS. Since there was a close correspondence in patterns of teacher–pupil interaction across all curriculum activities where PRISMS could be directly compared to the 1976 ORACLE, there is no reason to think that practice in small rural schools is unrepresentative of primary practice in general. We may conclude, therefore, that these present results represent, in many respects, a return to a more teacher-dependent curriculum.

The typical teacher then and now

Commenting on the overall picture of the typical teacher of the 1970s, Galton *et al.* (1980: 97) remarked that a visitor to the primary classroom could not fail to be impressed 'with the high level of teacher activity' and 'the almost continuous interplay of talk and interaction generally between the teacher and pupils in the class'. When not interacting, the teacher was generally monitoring or checking pupils' work. However, the 1970s visitor may also have noted 'that few of the teacher's questions or statements make serious or challenging demands on the imaginative or reasoning powers of the child'. By far the greatest amount of time was devoted to English and mathematics, although some of this work tended 'to be repetitive and not very stimulating'. For the most part, the visitor would have seen little disruptive behaviour which 'speaks highly of the teacher's management skills and of the relative effectiveness of the system of teaching that has evolved in the junior school classroom' (Galton *et al.* 1980: 108).

Returning to the same classroom some twenty years later, the same visitor will now find our typical teacher working even harder and interacting more frequently with the class. More of these interactions will be with the whole class rather than as before with individual pupils. It will now be comparatively rare to see the teacher monitoring or checking work in progress. A broader range of subjects is now being taught. However, much of the morning session will still be devoted to English and mathematics. In most subjects, including science, the need to cover the specific content of the National Curriculum programmes of study would appear to have reinforced the tendency for many of the teacher's statements and questions to be insufficiently challenging or stimulating for pupils. Disruptive behaviour is infrequent, but the practice of bringing children away from their tables to sit on the floor during whole class exposition has required the teacher to spend more time on routine management matters. In most cases, pupils are moved elsewhere or gently cautioned before trouble develops. The fact that these routine interactions rarely involve strong negative feedback speaks volumes for the teacher's expertise in classroom management.

In the 1976 ORACLE study there were clear patterns in the ways that pupils reacted to the various strategies employed by their teacher. For example, the somewhat repetitive diet provided in mathematics lessons was dealt with by pacing the work carefully to make it last as long as possible. In this way pupils avoided the situation where completing one worksheet would be rewarded by being given another. In the next chapter, therefore, we examine primary practice largely from the typical pupil's point of view. In 1976 the life of a typical primary aged pupil could best be described as one of isolation within a very crowded, busy room. Given the emphasis on individual teaching, and the fact that there was one teacher to around 35 pupils, it was inevitable that for large parts of the day children would work on their own. What was not expected at the time was that they would also work with a very limited amount of contact with other pupils when the teacher was engaged elsewhere. Just how far the patterns of pupil behaviour have changed as a result of the changes in teaching described in this chapter will now be considered in the next one.

Notes

1 Most of the original primary school ORACLE observations were collected over two academic years, 1976–7 and 1977–8. For brevity in the text, however, we shall often refer to the 1976 ORACLE study when comparing the 1996 categories of observation with those of two decades ago.

2 One of us was an early years teacher in the 1970s and recalls that it was common practice for some colleagues to use this strategy. However, a survey of the teaching of reading by Southgate *et al.* (1981) concluded that the more usual method of hearing individual children read aloud was generally ineffective because the teacher's attention was often diverted to other pupils in the queue who needed help.

3 The claim that children must not be told anything but must find out for themselves was part of the open Letter to Members of Parliament which fronted the 1969 Black Paper, *Fight for Education*, edited by C.B. Cox and A.E. Dyson. It has been a charge repeated by the Chief Inspector (see, for example, his Royal Society of Arts lecture and the report in the *Daily Telegraph* by John Clare, Education Editor (27 Jan 1995) as examples).

4

PUPILS AND THEIR TEACHERS IN THE KS2 CLASSROOM

Introduction

The fourth chapter of *Inside the Primary Classroom* describes the general scene which might have greeted the passing visitor upon 'opening the door' onto a typical classroom of the late 1970s.[1] The general impression might well have been of an environment characterised by activity, interaction and co-operation, the kind of qualities which were characteristic of the 'informal' classroom. The original ORACLE studies were undertaken in the decade following the publication of the Plowden (1967) Report, which had argued that the class should be regarded as a 'body of children needing individual attention' (para. 75). The report recognised that, given classes of thirty or more, the 'essential principle' of individualisation could only be achieved by sometimes organising children into co-operative but flexible groups, which would enable the teacher to work closely with several children at a time, and facilitate both social and academic exchanges between the pupils.

While the fleeting impression may have been one of lively interaction and movement, more careful scrutiny would have revealed something quite different. By drawing on evidence collected from moment-by-moment observations, ORACLE 1976 revealed that beneath the apparent 'busyness' was a complex web of interrelationships, among and between the pupils and their teacher, as they worked their way through a typical school day. Observation of the pupil as well as the teacher provided detailed accounts of life in the typical primary classroom of 1976. In Chapter 3, we examined the data from the perspective of the typical teacher, comparing the findings of the 1976 research with those of the present study. In this chapter, we focus upon the experience of the child.

Visiting the primary classroom: then and now

One of the most striking features of the primary classroom which was to emerge from the ORACLE 1976 research was the essential asymmetry of classroom interaction when seen from the different perspectives of the teacher and the child. The typical teacher would spend more than three-quarters of a lesson interacting with pupils in some way, much of the time moving from base to base and talking to individual children. Occasionally, she or he[2] would stop to talk to a group as they worked co-operatively on an activity, or more often to address the whole class. For the rest of the lesson, the teacher would be moving around the class or sitting at the desk, quietly monitoring the children, preparing for the next lesson, organising materials, marking work or completing the register.

From the viewpoint of the teacher, then, a typical lesson consisted of giving pupils a lot of individual attention, informing, guiding, encouraging, enquiring and, very occasionally, remonstrating. Through the eyes (and ears) of the children, however, everyday classroom life was a very different experience. Despite the appearance of movement and action, careful observation revealed that the typical boy or girl rarely left their working base. Interaction with their teacher was infrequent, and experienced mostly as a member of the class, much less often as an individual, and very rarely as a member of a group. Communication with other pupils was also uncommon and when they did talk to one another (usually with those in their immediate group), it would mostly concern routine or non-task-related matters.

To illustrate this, let us assume that back in 1976, our classroom visitor was able to stay for a whole lesson. They would have seen that the typical teacher would have spent almost four fifths of the lesson involved with pupils in some way, and as we have already seen, the majority of this time – around twenty-eight minutes of an average lesson[3] – would have been spent interacting with individual pupils, a further few minutes would be spent in much the same way talking with children in groups or addressing the whole class. During the remaining ten or eleven minutes, the teacher might be quietly monitoring a particular pupil or group of pupils, or the class as a whole, organising materials for the next activity, marking or planning work, and so on.

Turning to observe the activities of our typical boy or girl, meanwhile, would reveal that the time that they spent 'on-task' – that is actively engaged in appropriate activity – would have amounted to around thirty-seven minutes of the average lesson. For twenty minutes of that time, they would be working entirely on their own, even though they would be mostly sitting in pairs or groups, and only for two or three minutes would they interact with their neighbours about the task in hand. In the remaining thirteen minutes or so they would have been distracted by other things going on in the class, such as what the teacher or another pupil was doing, or talking to their friends about last night's TV programme, their favourite pop star or some such thing. On average, each child would have had a minute and a half of the teacher's attention as an individual, and even less as a group member. For about six or seven minutes of the lesson they would mostly have listened to, or watched the teacher as she or he addressed the whole class.

81

That was the scene then, twenty years ago. If our visitor were to visit that classroom now, what would seem familiar, and what would have changed? The description in Chapter 3 might suggest that initial impressions would be that little has altered. The teacher still seems to spend most of the time with individual children, who still appear to be steadily engaged in the task in hand for much of the time, sometimes being distracted from their work just as pupils were all those years ago. More careful observation, however, would reveal that the teacher spends more time talking to the children than before, particularly to the whole class. Children sit together more than they did and seem to interact with one another more often than they used to. In particular, girls and boys talk to one another much more than they did before, particularly when they are together in pairs, and quite a lot of the conversation is about their work. While pupils still get relatively little of their teacher's time as individuals, they now spend over a fifth of the lesson, around 10 per cent more than before, interacting with their teacher in some way as part of the class.

Our visitor would probably conclude, on the basis of these observations, that the classroom of the 1990s is an even 'busier' place than it was back in the 1970s, and as we saw in Chapter 3, teachers are working much harder now than they were twenty years ago. But is this impression of activity something of an illusion, as much to do with 'a large number of children in a small space' as of 'general talk and movement' (Galton *et al.* 1980: 60), or has there been a genuine change? In order to answer that question, we will need now to examine the data in finer detail.

Interaction between teachers and their pupils

Table 4.1 clearly shows the pattern of pupil–teacher interactions already alluded to.[4] Although 80 per cent of observations in ORACLE 1976

Table 4.1 Forms of teacher–pupil interaction (Teacher and Pupil Records): % of total observations[a]

	ORACLE 1976		ORACLE 1996	
	Teacher Record	Pupil Record	Teacher Record	Pupil Record
teacher/individual	55.8	2.3	43.1	3.2
teacher/group	7.5	1.5	14.6	3.7
teacher/class	15.1	12.0	31.3	21.4
	(78.4)	(15.8)	(89.0)	(28.3)
no interaction	21.6	84.2	11.0	71.7
totals	100.0	100.0	100.0	100.0

Note
a All percentages throughout are rounded up or down, and do not, therefore, necessarily total 100.

recorded the teacher communicating with pupils in some way, the great majority, around 60 per cent, were interactions with individual children. The remainder were devoted to whole class teaching or, less often, interacting with children in groups. From the children's perspective (that is, from the pupil record), this pattern was reversed, so that 80 per cent or so of observations recorded pupils not interacting with the teacher at all. One-to-one communication occurred in brief episodes as the teacher moved from base to base, and on average pupil–teacher interactions of any kind occupied just eight minutes of a fifty-minute lesson, the bulk of which was experienced as a member of the whole class.

How much of this has changed since the 1970s? At one level, we can say that a great deal appears to have remained as it was. Individual children still have limited contact with their teacher, and when they do it is mainly when they are involved in some kind of whole class activity. Within this general pattern, however, there have been notable changes in the distribution of interactions, so that there is now a more complex pattern of classroom communication.

An examination of the teacher record shows that, while teachers are spending more time interacting with children in general, there is a considerable shift away from individual interactions, partly towards working with groups but mainly towards whole class teaching. In our average lesson, for example, this would represent almost seven minutes less time interacting with individuals, and around four minutes more with groups, and six minutes more with the whole class. The pupil record confirms this, showing an overall increase of almost thirteen per cent in the amount of time that the children and teachers communicate with one another. This translates as just over fourteen minutes of teacher's attention, approaching a third of an average lesson, instead of the eight minutes that the typical pupil formerly received.

When the ORACLE 1976 data were recalculated using the data for teacher–pupil interactions only, that is, excluding non-interaction observations, the 'perfect asymmetry' of classroom interaction became evident, showing that around three-quarters of all the teachers' interactions with pupils were with individuals, and only a quarter with groups or the class (Table 4.2). The experience of the typical pupil, meanwhile, was almost an

Table 4.2 Interaction and task activity (Teacher and Pupil Records): % of all teacher–pupil interaction

	ORACLE 1976		ORACLE 1996	
	Teacher Record	*Pupil Record*	*Teacher Record*	*Pupil Record*
teacher/individual	71.6	14.6	48.4	11.4
teacher/group	9.4	9.4	16.4	13.0
teacher/class	19.3	75.9	35.2	75.2
	100.0	100.0	100.0	100.0

exact mirror image of this, so that 75 per cent of all interactions with the teacher were as a class member. However, if we re-analyse the data from the present study in the same way, we find something quite striking. Comparing the teacher records of the two studies, the shift in teachers' attention away from individuals towards groups and the whole class is clearly apparent. What is remarkable, however, is that when we made the same comparison for the pupil record, the pattern, or distribution of those interactions has remained virtually identical. So, while levels of interaction overall may be higher now than before, we find that for the typical pupil, *75 per cent of all pupil–teacher exchanges are experienced as a member of the class,* exactly as they were twenty years ago.

The shift towards whole class teaching might seem to be a positive response to the recent calls for a return to this strategy documented in Chapter 1. However, a second – and, we would argue, more likely – explanation for this shift is a pragmatic response on the part of teachers to the increasing demands on their time, in particular the need to meet the requirements of the National Curriculum.

As Figure 4.1 shows, the cost, for the teacher, of greater interaction with the pupils is a reduction, by the same amount, in non-interaction time in the

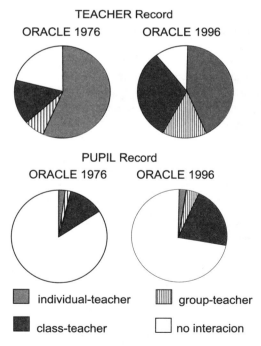

Figure 4.1 Interaction and task activity (Teacher and Pupil Records): % of all observations

classroom. This formerly provided the opportunity for silent monitoring of children's progress and behaviour, and for such activities as preparation of lesson materials, class layout and marking completed work, which are necessary 'to keep things moving in the longer run' (Galton *et al.* 1980: 107). It is from these activities, rather than from the time spent with individual pupils or groups, that teachers have found the 'extra' time to devote to whole class teaching. We must conclude, therefore, that many of these essential tasks, most of which would have been categorised as 'silent interactions' of one sort or another, are now undertaken outside of classroom time, that is, before the teaching day begins or after it is over. Since the National Curriculum has also increased the administrative load for individual teachers, and has introduced additional duties such as subject co-ordination, we can surmise that much of this additional work is also undertaken during non-contact time (Campbell and Neil 1994).

As Chapter 3 also demonstrated, teachers are now working much harder, in the sense that they are engaged in more interaction with the pupils, and are also spending longer periods working outside class time on other activities. The irony of this situation is that, as far as the children are concerned, little has changed. While the absolute level of classroom interactions has increased, the distribution of those interactions has remained almost identical, and the amount of attention the typical pupil receives, either as an individual or as a member of a group, still occupies no more than a minute or two of an average lesson. Furthermore, although class-based interaction has gone up from 12 per cent to 21.4 per cent, as we shall see later in this chapter, much of the content of this increase was concerned with routine instruction.

Group organisation: base and team

We have seen that the typical pupil rarely interacts with the teacher, at least on a one-to-one basis. Is this offset to any extent by interaction with other pupils? We have already described children in the ORACLE 1976 classroom as mainly seated in groups around flat-topped tables or desks, which would certainly facilitate the kind of collaborative activity and presumably, therefore, interaction, encouraged by Plowden. Furthermore, as Chapter 2 points out, a similar pattern of classroom organisation was found in the present study.

By recording whether children sat alone, in a pair or group, or as part of a whole class, it was possible to establish that children remained in their designated 'working base' for the vast majority of the time, a statistic which, for both the 1976 and present study, gives the lie to the notion that children in primary schools spend much of their time 'wandering about'.[5] As Table 4.3 shows, just as children in the ORACLE 1976 mainly sat together in groups or as a class, they also did so in the present study, indeed there has been a shift away from pairs and towards groups.

Table 4.3 Composition of base of pupil during observation sessions (% of all observations)

Base group	ORACLE 1976	ORACLE 1996
alone	5.1	5.0
pair	15.3	11.1
class	no category	13.3
group[a]	74.3	68.8
not coded	3.3	1.8
totals	100.0	100.0

Note
a There was no separate category for 'class' in the ORACLE 1976 study, so 'group' denoted any arrangement where more than two pupils sat together.

One of the anomalies of this situation in the ORACLE 1976 classroom was that, while children mostly sat with one another in groups, it became clear from the pupil–pupil interaction data (which we examine in detail shortly) that they rarely communicated with one another. Remembering that the interaction category included silent exchanges such as children passing materials to one another, as well as conversation, the logical conclusion was that pupils sat together, but worked alone. Thus the 'asymmetrical' nature of classroom interactions was mirrored by another imbalance – that is between how children were seated and how they actually worked.

Team

The ORACLE 1976 observation schedule was later modified to explore this issue by including a new category of *team*, or working arrangement, noting not only how children were seated, but also how they worked, that is, on their own, collaborating in a pair, a group, or as a member of the class (for example in a class discussion). Subsequent observational studies have confirmed this further example of asymmetry in the primary classroom, whereby most of the time children sit together, but work individually on tasks.

This is clearly demonstrated in Figure 4.2 which compares data from a study of classroom interaction (Hargreaves 1990),[6] which used this revised schedule as part of the Curriculum Provision in the Small Primary School (PRISMS) project. In the PRISMS study, pupils sat alone (*base* category) for around 7 per cent of the time, and in pairs or groups for over 70 per cent. In terms of working arrangements, however (*team* category), the pupils worked alone for over 80 per cent of the time.

Compared with children in PRISMS, those in the present study were more likely to be seated in groups, and more likely to collaborate with others, regardless of the actual seating arrangement. For example, while working together in either groups or pairs accounted for around 9 per cent of observations in PRISMS, the figure in the present study was more than double

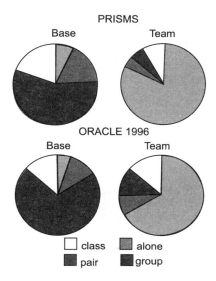

Figure 4.2 Differences between *base* (seating) and *team* (working) organisation (% of all observations). Comparison of PRISMS and ORACLE 1996 data (from the pupil record for Junior, now KS2, pupils)

that. This finding is perhaps surprising, given that PRISMS focused on small schools, where the majority of classes had fewer than twenty-five pupils and some as few as twelve. Nevertheless, the base/team dichotomy is clear in both studies, which suggests that, despite variations, such arrangements are a relatively stable feature of the primary classroom, regardless of class size. Only when, in the ORACLE 1996 study, children were brought together as a class, did the proportions of observations of 'base' and 'team' more or less coincide.

Interaction between pupils

We can see that, while the trend has been towards a general increase in communication between pupils and their teachers, the patterns of interaction have remained fairly constant. But what about interaction between pupils? How often, and in what circumstances, does communication between children take place, and has this changed over time? In Table 4.4 we see that as well as the 15.8 per cent of pupil–teacher interactions recorded in ORACLE 1976, a further 18.6 per cent involved interaction between pupils. Since in almost every case the two activities were mutually exclusive, communication of one sort or another was going on in about a third of all observations.

In the present study, an increase in pupil–pupil communication of just over 8 per cent, combined with the general increase in pupil–teacher interactions,

Table 4.4 Interaction and all recorded task activities 1976–96 (% of all observations)

	ORACLE 1976	ORACLE 1996
pupil–teacher interaction	15.8	28.4
pupil–pupil interaction	18.6	26.9
(total interaction)	(34.4)	(55.3)
no interaction	65.6	44.7
totals	100.0	100.0

has raised the level of classroom communication as a whole by some 21 per cent, so that interaction was recorded in more than half of all observations. The impression that the typical ORACLE 1996 primary classroom is much 'busier' place than the 1976 counterpart appears therefore to be generally supported.

Breaking down the content of these interactions further tells us that over 90 per cent of interactions were verbal. In half of all such interchanges, pupils either initiated interactions or responded to others, and in most of the remainder, about 45 per cent, pupils were engaged in sustained conversations – that is, having initiated or responded to an interaction, the target pupil remained in communication for at least twenty-five seconds – the length of time between observation signals – and often much longer. This is a higher proportion than in the earlier study, where sustained contact represented around a third of all pupil–pupil interactions.

A more active classroom is not, of course, necessarily a more productive one. What is of chief interest, therefore, is the extent to which the conversations between pupils were about their work. The fact that 83 per cent of pupil–pupil interactions occurred where the pupils were engaged in the same task – about 5 per cent more than in ORACLE 1976 – gives some indication. A truer test, however, is to examine the interaction data in relation to the different categories of activity.

We can classify the pupil observations as those which were *task-related*, where, as the observers' manual puts it, pupils were 'fully involved and co-operating on the task' and *non-task-related* (the sum of all other activities). In 1976, children were, on average, focused on the task for around three fifths of the time. The remaining two fifths of 'off-task' time was taken up with routine matters, waiting for the teacher's attention or being distracted. Much less frequently, children were distracted or disruptive.[7] If we now examine patterns of interaction within these two categories, we see that only a minority (5.2 per cent) of pupil–pupil interactions were directly related to the task. By comparison, we can see that the great majority (12.4 per cent) of pupil–teacher interactions were task-related (see Table 4.5).

There has been an overall increase in classroom interaction of 20.9 per cent, and of this, three-quarters was directly task related. The smaller rise

Table 4.5 Interaction and pupils' 'fully involved on-task' and 'non-task' activity 1976–96 (% of all observations)

Fully involved on-task	ORACLE 1976	ORACLE 1996	difference (1976–96)
pupil–pupil interaction	5.2	13.5	+ 8.3
pupil–teacher interaction	12.4	19.2	+ 6.8
	(17.6)	(32.7)	+ (15.1)
no interaction	40.5	28.9	−11.6
total	(58.1)	(61.6)	
totals	100.0	100.0	

Non-task related (all other recorded activities)	ORACLE 1976	ORACLE 1996	difference (1976–96)
pupil–pupil interaction	13.4	13.4	0.0
pupil–teacher interaction	3.4	9.2	+ 5.8
	(16.8)	(22.6)	+ (5.8)
no interaction	25.1	15.8	−9.3
total	(41.9)	(38.4)	
totals	100.0	100.0	

in non-task-related communication of 5.8 per cent consisted entirely of pupil–teacher interactions, meaning that all of the increase in conversations between pupils was task-related. So, not only were children talking to one another more, but the conversation was as likely to be about their work as not. They were also interacting with their teacher more often, and this increase was fairly evenly divided between off-task and on-task interaction. However, as we argue elsewhere, the general rise in the amount of whole class activity means that, for much of the time, what was coded as task-related interaction will have been passive – that is, the children listening to the teacher as part of a class – rather than active participation.

We have so far defined task-related activities as being 'fully involved', while non-task-related activities represent the remaining thirteen sub-categories of activity in the pupil record. This is something of a catch-all definition, however, since pupils may be engaged in teacher-approved activity which is not 'fully involved and co-operating on the task', but which is nevertheless task-related. This would include co-operating on routine tasks (getting out equipment, collecting materials and so on), and waiting for the teacher's attention, for example waiting for work to be checked over or for a question to be answered.

Table 4.6 shows that when these two categories are included, the proportion of time a typical pupil spends involved in the task in some way or other rises to around three-quarters of a pupil's activity. As *Inside the Primary Classroom* comments (p. 62), this helps to explain 'the general air of busyness'

Table 4.6 Actively engaged activity 1976–96 (% of all observations)

Category	ORACLE 1976	ORACLE 1996	difference (1976–96)
co-operating on-task	58.1	61.6	+2.5
co-operating on routine	11.9	11.9	0.0
waiting for the teacher	4.3	2.0	−2.3
total 'actively engaged'	74.3	75.5	+1.2

in the ORACLE 1976 classroom referred to at the beginning of this chapter. We will call this combined variable 'actively engaged' in the task.

The data show that the overall figure for 'active engagement' has remained remarkably constant across time, although there has been a slight increase in the time children spend directly on-task, with a corresponding decrease in the time spent waiting for the teacher. Clearly, the productive classroom will be one where our typical pupil is 'fully involved' far more than he or she is engaged in routine, if appropriate, activity, and this was indeed the case in both ORACLE 1976 and the present study. The amount of time being occupied with routine matters, meanwhile, has remained at exactly the same level.

Children are therefore just as much 'on-task' during their school day now as they were 20 years ago.[8] Since what might be called wilful disruption of the class (disruptive behaviour and horseplay) represents a fraction of observations in both studies, the remaining 25 per cent or so of 'off-task' activity can mainly be categorised as distraction of one sort or another. *Inside the Primary Classroom* argues that, in terms of describing the activities of a 'typical pupil', the most useful marker is the ratio of co-operation (active engagement) to distracted behaviour, given as 75:16. This figure ignores minor categories of distraction, however, such as taking an interest in what others are doing (other pupils, the teacher, very occasionally the observer) rather than focusing on the task, or daydreaming (coded as 'responding to internal stimuli'). Using the term 'diversion' to distinguish this group of behaviours from the single code 'distracted', we find that when we combine these variables, the total proportion of diverted behaviour rises to 24 per cent, giving a co-operation/diversion ratio for the ORACLE 1976 study of 75:24, virtually identical to that of 76:23 in the present study. Have we perhaps identified a ceiling effect, that is that around 75 per cent is the maximum level of 'active engagement' that we can expect from children? In order to test that hypothesis, we need to take the 'diversion' data apart again.

Examining the data for the individual sub-categories in Table 4.7, it can be seen that, while 'distraction' has gone down, 'co-operation/distraction' (partially co-operating and partially distracted) has increased, effectively cancelling one another out. Since this last category is one of the more difficult

Table 4.7 Diverted behaviour 1976–96 (% of all observations)

Category	ORACLE 1976	ORACLE 1996	difference (1976–96)
distracted	15.9	11.7	− 4.2
distracted by observer	0.3	0.3	0.0
co-operation/distraction	1.9	6.3	+ 4.4
interested in teacher	1.7	1.5	− 0.2
interested in other pupil	3.4	2.2	− 1.2
responding to internal stimuli	0.8	1.2	+ 0.4
total diverted behaviour	(24.0)	(23.2)	(− 0.8)

ones to code, it is possible that an increase in this sub-category is due, in part, to observer error. However, it is far more likely to reflect a genuine increase in the frequency with which observers were required to make this decision. As we argue above, it is during whole class teacher–pupil interactions, when children are often listening passively to the teacher, that it is most difficult to distinguish between attentive and distracted behaviour. Since we already know that whole class interactions have increased by around 12–13 per cent, we would expect a concomitant rise in the number of co-operation/distraction observations.

It could reasonably be argued that over the total number of pupil observations coded in this way, roughly half will be co-operating, and half will be genuinely distracted. If we add this in to the equation, we obtain total figures for active engagement of 76 per cent and 79 per cent for the ORACLE 1976 and 1996 studies respectively. This means that the level of on-task activity has indeed increased, and that the co-operation /diversion ratio in the ORACLE 1996 study is 79:20, compared with 76:22 for ORACLE 1976, suggesting that the active engagement 'ceiling', if it exists, may be nearer to 80 per cent than 75 per cent.

Attainment[9] and gender differences

So far we have described life in the primary classroom as it would be experienced by the 'typical child', based upon the mean or average of all pupil observations. This is a useful device, but classrooms are of course populated by individuals, not composites, and each child exhibits different behaviours, strategies and abilities. Although it is not possible here to examine the interactions of individual teachers with individual pupils, we can at least begin to look at interactions between teachers and different groups, or categories of children. As elsewhere in this chapter, we will take the lead from *Inside the Primary Classroom* which examined two areas of difference: attainment and gender.

Attainment

The need for the teacher to *differentiate* – that is identify, respond to and support the individual needs of children – is critical to their progress. How does the teacher accommodate the wide range of ability in a typical mixed-ability primary classroom, and how does that affect the patterns of interaction between teacher and pupil? Might there be a tendency for high attainers to be left to 'get on with it' for example, or alternatively, might their more rapid progress increase the demand on the teacher to ensure that they are being sufficiently challenged? Or perhaps the greater demands would come from the less able, who need more regular support and reassurance. What then, of the larger proportion of the class, the middle attainers? Might they lose out as the teacher attempts to meet the demands of the other two groups, or might they, through force of numbers, place the greatest demand on the teacher's attention.

By the time of the ORACLE 1976 studies, the process of 'unstreaming' in primary schools and the move towards the mixed-ability class, begun in the early 1960s, was almost complete (Thomas 1990). Faced with these arrangements, the teacher needed to organise classroom activities that allowed for differences in abilities and other characteristics but which also had 'a unity of purpose which transcend(ed) individual differences' (Richards 1988). One of the chief strategies to ensure this balance between individual difference and unity of purpose, the development of co-operative groups of children at 'roughly the same stage' for particular activities (Plowden 1967: para. 755), was little used by teachers in the ORACLE 1976 classroom, despite continuing to receive the official stamp of approval for some years (e.g. HMI 1980). The preferred approach, moving around the class engaging in a series of brief interactions with pupils, not only meant that, individually, children received relatively little attention, but also carried with it the possibility that the different demands and needs of a class of thirty or so meant that this attention was distributed unequally.

Examination of the ORACLE 1976 pupil–teacher interaction data for each of the three levels of attainment – high, intermediate and low – revealed that, although weaker pupils received significantly more individual attention than others, observations of this kind of interaction were relatively few, representing around 2 per cent in all. High attainers tended to receive slightly more attention as group members, while intermediate attainers interacted a little more frequently with the teacher as members of the whole class. In neither case were the differences statistically significant. Moreover, both task-related and non-task-related interactions were also evenly distributed among the three groups. These figures led to the conclusion that there was very little difference in the distribution of pupil–teacher interaction between the three attainment groups, regardless of interaction setting, and that 'no single group [was] either favoured or discriminated against' (Galton *et al.* 1980: 65).

Inside the Primary Classroom does not offer reasons for these findings, but simply points to their existence, and we venture here to explore the issue a little further. In the ORACLE 1976 era, the chief means of meeting the differential needs of the pupils was to set varying tasks which matched ability, or to allow children to select activities themselves from a range provided by the teacher. The role of the teacher was, therefore, to ensure that each child understood the task in hand and was making adequate progress. By and large this led, as we have seen, to high levels of individualised work, with pupils mainly working alone, and the teacher moving around the class for much of the time.

Since ORACLE 1976, schools have seen many changes, not least the introduction of a National Curriculum, the structure of which, with its clearly defined programmes of study, attainment targets and levels for each subject area, and end of Key Stage assessments, has resulted in much greater attention being given to the concept of differentiation, and the notion of what Croll and Moses (1990) call 'ordered progression'. In addition, it has provided teachers with the means of identifying the learning needs of individual pupils. Guidance for teachers on differentiation, in the form of published handbooks (e.g. Dickinson and Wright 1993) and in-service training courses have examined a variety of strategies for supporting pupils, including differentiation by content, resource, outcome and response as well as by task. Paradoxically, those currently arguing for a return to traditional front-of-class pedagogy propose an approach which, by definition, militates against differentiation.

How have teachers responded to these competing demands, on the one hand a renewed emphasis on the individual learning needs of children and on the other a concerted push to persuade teachers to 'lead from the front'? As we have already noted, whole class teaching has increased since ORACLE 1976, while individualised teacher–pupil interaction has decreased. We also know, however, that the general level of teacher–pupil communication was higher in the present study. But are those interactions still distributed in equal measure to children of differing attainment? Are we still able to claim that each attainment group was, by and large, 'neither favoured nor discriminated against'?

Certainly we can say that the general pattern has stayed pretty consistent. Table 4.8 shows that, as before, the lowest attainers received a significantly higher proportion of the teacher's attention than others in a one-to-one situation, and that group interactions favour the high attainers. However, what is of real note here is that these trends have become even more marked, so that there is now clear evidence of a relationship between attainment and interaction which has broken the equal pattern of distribution found in ORACLE 1976.

Only where pupils interact with their teacher in a class situation does the intermediate attaining group receive a greater proportion of the teacher's

Table 4.8 Attainment and pupil–teacher interaction (% of all interactions)[a]

	all observations	high attainment	intermediate attainment	low attainment
individual–teacher interaction	10.7	8.7	10.3	14.2[a]
group–teacher interaction	12.2	17.7	10.1	9.5[a]
class–teacher interaction	76.9	73.5	79.2	76.3
all pupil–teacher interaction	100.0	100.0	100.0	100.0
all task-related interaction	69.1	76.7	67.7	62.3
all non-task-related interaction	30.9	23.3	32.3	37.7

Note
a significant at $p < 0.01$.

[handwritten margin note: high attainers get greater teacher input on tasks.]

time than the other two groups. Of chief interest here are the bottom two rows of Table 4.8, which show the data broken down into task-related and non-task-related interactions. This demonstrates a clear association between attainment and on-task pupil–teacher interactions, whereby the proportion of task-related interactions is greatest for the high attainers and least for the low attainers. The reverse is the case for non-task-related, or routine interactions.

Attainment and attention to task

We have already seen that there have been changes in the way that teachers attend to children of differing levels of attainment. A related issue which was not addressed by the ORACLE 1976 researchers was the relationship between attainment and patterns of working. For example, might weaker pupils, finding that work is too difficult, be more susceptible to distraction? Or might more able pupils sometimes find work to be insufficiently challenging, and thus seek alternative off-task activities?

If we examine the composite variable that we have called 'active engagement', we find that the higher attaining pupils were more involved than the other two groups, with the intermediate group least so. Although these differences were not significant, high attainers were significantly more likely to be 'fully involved and co-operating on the task' than either of the other two groups, but less likely to engaged in routine activities. We can tentatively conclude, therefore, that while all pupils were actively engaged in approved work for the majority of the time, high attaining pupils were more productive (see Table 4.9).

Interestingly, the high attainment group were slightly more likely to have to wait for the teacher's attention, perhaps reflecting a tendency on the part of the teacher to assume that the less able children were in more urgent need. High attainers were also the most likely group to display deliberately disruptive behaviour, although the levels for all attainment groups were extremely

Table 4.9 Proportion of pupils (as a % of all observations) actively engaged on task (1996 data only)[a]

Category	All observations	High attainment	Intermediate attainment	Low attainment
co-operating on task	61.6	66.9	59.1	61.0[a]
co-operating on routine	11.9	9.9	11.7	11.7
waiting for the teacher	2.0	2.7	1.8	1.6
total actively engaged	75.5	79.5	72.6	74.3

Note
a significant at p < 0.05. (

Table 4.10 Proportion of pupil diverted behaviour by attainment level (% of all observations: 1996 data only)

Category	All observations	High attainment	Intermediate attainment	Low attainment
distracted	11.7	9.9	13.1	11.2
distracted by observer	0.3	0.2	0.2	0.6[a]
co-operative/distracted	6.3	5.1	7.1	6.4
interested in teacher	1.5	1.7	1.4	2.3
interested in other pupil	2.2	2.1	2.3	3.4
responding to internal stimuli	1.2	0.7	1.4	1.1[a]
total diverted	(23.2)	(19.7)	(25.5)	(25.0)
disruptive	0.0	0.2	0.0	0.0[ab]
horseplay	0.1	0.1	0.2	0.1
total disruptive	(0.1)	(0.3)	(0.2)	(0.1)

Notes a significant at p < 0.05 (anova)
         b significant at p < 0.05 (chisq)

small – 0.3 per cent, for example, represents just nine seconds of a fifty-minute lesson (see Table 4.10).

Higher levels of on-task behaviour naturally go hand in hand with lower levels of distraction, so that the high attainers were least susceptible to distraction, both overall and in individual categories of activity, with the lone exception of being interested in the teacher. In general, intermediate and low attainers were distracted to about the same degree, but the weaker pupils were more likely to be diverted by the activities of others, and significantly so by the observer and the teacher, although these represented relatively few observations.

These findings suggest that there is a relationship between attainment and attention to task. This is particularly true of the high attaining group, who were more fully involved in their work than the middle or lower ability pupils. Coupled with the results from the previous section which showed a relationship between attainment and teachers' attention to individual pupils, the most common form of pupil–teacher interaction, we might surmise that much of this extra time is spent in encouraging the less able pupils to focus on the task in hand. With the higher attaining groups, the teacher's attention is mainly gained when the pupil interacts as a member of a group. One explanation for this is that high attainment is likely to be associated with high confidence in the task, which might lead the child to assume the role of leader, and/or the teacher to regard that pupil as spokesperson for the group. The lower levels of interaction found with the middle attaining group – who represent around half of the pupils – also correspond with higher levels of distraction.

Gender

The first phase of the ORACLE 1976 research was undertaken at a time when gender was beginning to figure as a key issue in educational debates. A good deal of discussion and research at this time was from a feminist perspective, focusing upon what was seen as the greater power and influence of males in various educational domains. A major site of interest was to become the classroom itself, where, it was argued, boys dominated discussions and received disproportionate amounts of teachers' time and attention (Spender 1982; Clarricoates 1980).

The highly structured nature of the ORACLE 1976 observation schedule provided an ideal instrument to throw light on some of these issues, in particular the patterns of interaction between pupils and their teachers, and between pupils themselves, since it provided a detailed account of classroom processes. Furthermore, because the schedule was designed to be very low inference, its use ensured that findings were less susceptible to criticisms of ideological or other bias.

Teacher–pupil interaction

The ORACLE 1976 data revealed that, in general, teachers did not favour one sex more than the other in the distribution of their attention. Despite a slight trend for boys to receive more attention than girls, the differences were extremely small, regardless of the interaction setting, or whether interactions were task-related or not (Table 4.11). This was an important finding, and although little was made of it at the time, it throws doubt on some of the claims about male dominance of classroom interaction which were then emerging. Reviewing the contemporary literature on gender and classroom interaction, French and French (1984) reported on a number of studies which found that teachers favoured boys in classroom interactions, citing, as part of the supporting evidence, a comment from *Inside the Primary Classroom* that there was a slight tendency 'for boys to receive more contact than girls'. In fact, this was a proviso to the main conclusion of the section from which the quote was taken, which was that there was 'little difference

Table 4.11 Gender of pupil and patterns of interaction 1976–96 (% of all observations)

| | ORACLE 1976 | | | ORACLE 1996 | | |
	boys	*girls*	*difference (1976–96)*	*boys*	*girls*	*difference (1976–96)*
individual–teacher interaction	2.4	2.1	−0.3	3.4	3.1	−0.3
group–teacher interaction	1.6	1.4	−0.2	3.7	3.7	0.0
class–teacher interaction	12.0	11.7	−0.3	20.6	22.2	+2.4
other	0.5	0.1	−0.4	0.1	0.1	0.0
	(16.5)	(15.3)	(−1.2)	(27.8)	(29.1)	(+1.3)
all task-related interaction	13.6	12.8	−0.8	22.9	24.1	+1.2
all non-task-related interaction	2.9	2.5	−0.4	5.0	4.8	−0.2

in the distribution of teacher attention' according to the sex of the pupil (Galton *et al.* 1980: 66). The tendency was slight indeed (an average difference of less than 1 per cent), which, if anything, questioned rather than confirmed the findings of the other studies reported in the paper. In fact, the figures given by Galton *et al.* (1980) refer to interactions at the pupil level – that is, they derived from Pupil Record data – and described the average amount of the teacher's attention received by the *individual* boy or girl. A more accurate comparison would have been to use data derived from the Teacher Record, which would have given the average amount of attention the teacher gave to boys in general or to girls in general.

Twenty years later, and much of the debate about gender and equity has turned around, so that one of the greatest areas of current concern is the under-achievement of boys. In terms of performance, all pupils have made considerable progress in the intervening years, but it is girls who now out-perform boys in almost all areas of the curriculum, and at every phase of their education, spurring an Education Minister to announce a plan for 'co-ordinated action' to tackle the problem (DfEE 1988). Nevertheless, little appears to have changed in terms of the distribution of classroom interactions. As before, boys were slightly more likely than girls to interact with the teacher as individuals, or as members of a group, but again the differences in each instance were marginal. There has been a shift towards girls receiving greater proportion of the teacher's attention overall, as a result of an increase in whole class based interactions, but with this exception, the data show that, just as boys and girls received almost identical proportions of the teacher's time in the ORACLE 1976 primary classroom, so too did they in the ORACLE 1996 study.

We have the curious situation, then, that the pattern of interactions in both studies appears to show no gender effect at all, even though each was conducted during a time when claims were being made that girls (in the 1970s) or boys (in the 1990s) were losing out in, among other things, classroom interactions. Space does not permit a much more detailed examination of the issue here, and there are clearly a number of variables – ability, the curriculum setting, the content and style of pupil–teacher interaction and so on – which might reveal patterns of difference which are not evident at this level of analysis. As already mentioned, these data focus on the amount of attention receieved by the typical boy or girl, rather than, as is more common in studies of classroom interaction, that given by the typical teacher. Nevertheless, the findings as they stand would seem at least to begin to ask questions of long-held assumptions about classroom interaction and gender.

Sex of the teacher

The growing concern about boys' poor levels of achievement has given rise to renewed calls for a national drive to recruit more men into the primary sector (Byers 1998). Two of the underlying assumptions of the current campaign are the belief that men will represent positive role models for struggling boys in an otherwise female-dominated environment, and the notion that men and women interact differently with boys and girls. While we cannot test the first proposition here, our data can throw some light on the second.

We already know that the 'typical teacher' does not discriminate between boys and girls, but what patterns of interaction are to be found in the various permutations of male and female teachers, boys and girls, and various interaction settings?

An analysis of the ORACLE 1976 data showed that, in fact, the sex of the teacher appeared to make little difference to the pattern of classroom interaction. Similar analyses of ORACLE 1996 data did find a significant teacher effect, however. Furthermore, when we take into account the sex of the pupil as well as the teacher, an even more complex picture emerges.

First we examine the data according to whether the pupils interacted with their teacher as individuals, as members of a group, or as part of a class. In the case of class-based activities, the proportion of pupil–teacher interactions remained constant at around 75 per cent, regardless of whether pupils were taught by a man or a woman. However, pupils were much more likely to receive attention as individuals than as members of a group when taught by a man, while the reverse was true in a class taught by a woman (see Table 4.12).

Unlike the 1976 classroom, then, it does make a difference to the typical pupil if the class is taken by a man or a woman. But does it also make a

Table 4.12 Gender of teacher and patterns of interaction (% of pupil–teacher interactions: 1996 data only)

	Pupil interacts with…	
	male teacher	*female teacher*
individual	13.9	9.8
group	9.2	14.8
class	76.4	74.7
not coded	0.5	0.4
totals	100.0	100.0

difference if that pupil is a typical boy or a typical girl? In terms of class-based interactions, which account for the great majority of communications between pupil and teacher, the answer is 'not very much'. Both received around the same proportion of the teacher's attention in a whole class setting irrespective of the sex of the teacher, although there was a tendency for boys to get rather more attention from male teachers (77 per cent of all interactions) than females teachers (72 per cent) in this setting.

In one-to-one and group situations, however, these differences were more marked and, as Figure 4.3 shows, particularly in the case of boys in the classes of male teachers. The typical boy was twice as likely to interact

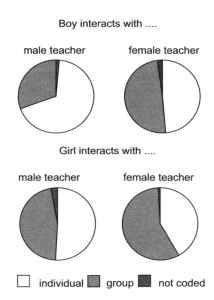

Figure 4.3 Gender of pupil and teacher; interaction patterns (% of individual and group interactions: 1996 data only)

with a male teacher on a one-to-one basis than when in a group, but in a woman's class interactions were more equally distributed between the two. The reverse pattern was found in the case of the typical girl, although the differences between the male and female teacher were much less sharp. In summary, the experiences of the typical boy and typical girl were much the same regardless of interaction setting or whether they were taught by a man or a woman, with one exception: the pupil most likely to receive the individual attention of the teacher was a boy in a class taught by a man.

Gender and pupil–pupil interaction

We earlier examined the seating (base) arrangements of children in the primary classroom (see p. 40), finding that the great majority of observations in both studies recorded children sitting together in groups. Here we further examine the gender-composition of the various base arrangements, and the patterns of interaction within them. In ORACLE 1976, almost half of the children were seated with others of the same sex, either in pairs or groups, while the same proportion sat with opposite-sex pupils. In fact, the category label for this arrangement, 'several opposite sex', is somewhat misleading, since it suggests a lone girl sitting with a group of boys, or a girl with boys. In fact the term denotes a *mixed* group of an indeterminate (that is to say, unrecorded) composition.[10] We can only be certain, therefore, that 2 per cent of targets were seated exclusively with opposite-sex peers, that is where they were in boy–girl pairs.

In the present study, 11 per cent of pupils were seated in pairs, while 82 per cent sat in groups or as members of the whole class, representing an overall shift of some 8 per cent away from pairs and towards group/class seating arrangements. Opposite-sex pairs have remained at a constant, if very low level at around 2 per cent, while single-sex pairings have decreased

Table 4.13 Composition of base of pupil during observation sessions: % of all observations

Base group	ORACLE 1976	ORACLE 1996	difference (1976–96)
alone	5.1	5.0	−0.01
same sex pair	15.3	9.6	−5.7
opposite sex pair	2.0	1.5	−0.5
(all pairs)	(17.3)	(11.1)	(−6.2)
same sex group	30.8	24.1	−6.7
mixed sex group	43.5	44.7	
class	no code	13.3	+14.5
(all groups and class)	(74.3)	(82.1)	(+7.8)
not coded	3.3	1.8	−1.5
totals	100.0	100.0	100.0

by some 6 per cent. Interestingly, same-sex groups have also declined by a similar amount, so that the increase in mixed groupings is almost 15 per cent. 'Mixed group' here includes 'class' of course, and, though we are not able to determine the level of such arrangements from the ORACLE 1976 data, we can say that 13 per cent of ORACLE 1996 observations recorded pupils sitting together as a class.

In general, therefore, children are much more likely to be seated in groups of some kind than they were twenty years ago. Within this change in classroom organisation, there is also a notable decline in the tendency for children of the same sex to sit together in exclusive pairs or groups. Is this change a result of choice or direction? Certainly some teachers in the present study deliberately encourage mixed-sex arrangements, but there is also the possibility that boys and girls feel more at ease working with one another than before.

Where teachers have encouraged boys and girls to sit next to each other, part of their rationale for doing so would be to encourage cross-sex interaction (see p. 47), and research also indicates that this is a successful strategy for reducing distracted behaviour (Wheldall and Olds 1987). The degree to which seating arrangements influenced communication between boys and girls was pursued in ORACLE 1976, revealing that overall around 80 per cent of all pupil–pupil interactions were between pupils of the same sex. Despite the shift in seating arrangements seen in the present study away from pairs towards mixed groups, most communication, 78 per cent, is still between same-sex pupils.

The ORACLE 1976 children were 'much more likely to interact with other pupils of the same sex than of the opposite sex' (pp. 74–5), and this was most likely to take place when children worked in same-sex groups or pairs. The lowest levels of communication occurred between pupils of opposite sex whether they were in a pair or a group. Belonging to a mixed pair or group appeared, therefore, to have a distinct 'dampening effect' on communication, and ORACLE 1976 pupils seemed therefore to make a considerable effort to avoid interacting with someone of the opposite sex.

The data in Table 4.14 represent gendered patterns of interaction *within* each type of base grouping, and are therefore 'percentages of percentages'. As in ORACLE 1976 (figures in brackets), the highest level of communication was between same-sex pupils in pairs or groups (rows (b) and (c)), while the lowest level (excluding pupils on their own) was to be found in between pupils of opposite sex based in mixed sex groups. Thus, while 'typical' pupils in the ORACLE 1996 study were more likely to be interacting with their peers than their ORACLE 1976 counterparts, boys still mostly talked to other boys, and girls to girls. There was, however, some increase in the opposite-sex communication, particularly where children were seated in pairs, which represents something of a culture shift.

Table 4.14 Pupil–pupil: base and interactions (% of all pupil–pupil interactions wihtin each base group: 1976 data in brackets)

Base Group	Same sex interaction		Opposite sex interaction		Total interaction	
(a) alone	7.6	(6.8)	3.3	(3.6)	10.9	(10.4)
(b) same sex pair	36.6	(16.1)	1.9	(2.0)	37.5	(18.1)
(c) same sex group	31.4	(19.4)	1.6	(0.7)	33.0	(20.1)
(d) opposite sex pair	3.9	(3.6)	24.8	(7.2)	28.7	(10.8)
mixed group	17.7	(10.9)	9.9	(5.7)	27.6	(16.6)
class	8.2		1.9		10.1	
(e) mixed grp + class[a]	25.9	(10.9)	11.8	(5.7)	37.7	(16.6)

Note
a equivalent to 'mixed group' in ORACLE 1976

The primary curriculum: the pupils' experience

In the 1970s, determining what comprised the primary curriculum was problematic. At a time when cross-curricular or 'topic work' was a staple of the primary curriculum, it was commonplace for many teachers to set a number of different tasks to different groups of pupils, some of which would require relatively little intervention by the teacher, while others (usually the 'basics', language and mathematics) were more teacher-intensive. This approach was particularly characteristic of the teacher styles described as *habitual changers* and *rotating changers*,[11] which together represented around 40 per cent of the 1976 sample. Furthermore, as we have discussed earlier in this chapter, in 1976 the 'asymmetrical' nature of pupil–teacher interaction meant that classroom life from the perspective of the teacher was very different from that of the typical pupil. It is not surprising, therefore, that there should be considerable disparity between what we might call the 'taught' curriculum, that is what the teacher delivered (to use the current idiom), and the 'received' curriculum, that is what the typical pupil actually experienced.

Growing concern about variability in the 'shape' and content of the primary curriculum led to various discussions about the development of a more structured approach. The 1980s saw the publication of numerous documents which focused on pupil entitlement and the need for a 'broad and balanced' curriculum, briefly discussed in Chapter 1, leading eventually to the introduction of a subject-framed National Curriculum. Since this required teachers to deliver a prescribed set of subjects, and to cover set programmes of study within each of those subjects,[12] the 'taught' and 'received' curriculum have moved much closer together. So what exactly does this 'new' curriculum look like now to the typical boy and girl in the classroom of the late 1990s, and how does it differ from that which children received in 1976?

102

Table 4.15 The observed curriculum: % of all observations of dominant subject

ORACLE 1976 curriculum	ORACLE 1996 equivalent	% of observations ORACLE 1976	% of observations ORACLE 1996	difference (1976–96)
language	English	36.1	30.1	−6.0
	mathematics	28.5	23.8	−4.7
		(64.6)	(53.9)	(−10.7)
	science		12.4	
	+ history		5.9	
	+ geography		7.4	
	+ RE		0.4	
	+ cross-curricular		3.2	
general studies		24.4	(29.3)	(+4.9)
art and craft	art	10.9	11.8	+0.9
no category	technology		4.0	+4.0
no category	IT		0.9	+0.9
no category	PSE		0.1	+0.1
			(5.0)	(+5.0)
totals		100.0	100.0	

For the reasons described above, there are some problems in making a direct comparison, since a range of curriculum areas – history, geography, music and, most notably, science – were subsumed in the ORACLE 1976 research under the heading 'general studies'. The data presented in Table 4.15 therefore compare the ORACLE 1976 curriculum categories with their nearest ORACLE 1996 equivalents.[13]

The two areas which, in ORACLE 1976 times, constituted the 'staple of the curriculum' – language and mathematics – together occupied almost two-thirds of the observed curriculum.[14] In ORACLE 1996, the two subject areas made up 53.9 per cent, something of a decrease since the 1976 study, but still representing a substantial proportion of a typical pupil's curriculum experience. With the gradual elevation of science to 'core' status, moreover, the three-subject core now occupies much the same 'curriculum space' as that of the old, two-subject version.

While there was no breakdown of the different areas that comprised the ORACLE 1976 category of general studies, and thus no possibility of directly comparing like with like, we can surmise that this new emphasis on science, coupled with the inclusion of new curriculum areas such as PSE, IT and technology, has meant that such subjects as history and geography account for a smaller proportion of the curriculum than twenty years ago. Activities categorised as art still occupy much the same proportion of the primary curriculum, and if we accept that at least some of what is now technology was part of the old art and craft curriculum, the amount of time devoted to these areas has probably increased by some 3 or 4 per cent. Also of note is the extremely low level of observations (eight in all) where

Table 4.16[a] Breakdown of mathematics and English 1976–96 (% of curricular area observations: dominant subject)

ORACLE 1976 category		ORACLE 1996 category	
MATHS		MATHS	
number work	14.0	handling data, number/algebra	12.0
practical	4.3	use/apply	4.0
abstract	10.2	shape/space/measure	6.2
	(28.5)		(22.2)
LANGUAGE		ENGLISH	
reading	4.4	reading	6.6
spoken Eng	2.0	speak/listen	8.4
general writing	21.2	writing	14.2
creative writing	8.5		
	(36.1)		(28.2)

Note
a Because of exclusion of data which do not fit comfortably in a given comparative category (for example, a few observations coded 'reading' in mathematics), cumulative figures for ORACLE 1996 data given in Table 4.16 do not exactly match those in Table 4.15.

IT was the dominant activity, which accords with the findings of Her Majesty's Inspectors (OFSTED 1997). Although IT might (indeed *should*) be used across the curriculum, only a further four observations of such use were recorded.

The ORACLE 1976 data were further subdivided into areas for mathematics (number work, practical mathematics abstract work) and for language (reading, writing, spoken, creative writing). These are again compared, in Table 4.16, with their nearest equivalents in the ORACLE 1996 study, and again these refer to the dominant subject recorded for each set of pupil observations.

Because of the inexact match between the ORACLE 1976 and ORACLE 1996 sub-classifications in the mathematics curriculum, precise conclusions are difficult to draw. Nevertheless, even given these relatively crude categories, there is some indication that there has been relatively little change in the balance of the mathematics curriculum.

The classifications used in language/English were fairly similar for both studies. Writing and reading are relatively straightforward categories, while 'spoken language' relates fairly closely to 'speaking and listening' (Attainment Target 1 in the 1996 English curriculum), and this level of correspondence allows us to make some further exploration of the data.

Although pupils now receive less English teaching overall compared with children in 1976 (Table 4.16), there has been quite a significant shift in the time spent on different areas within English, resulting in an increase in reading and oral English, while the amount of writing that the pupils engage in is at half its previous level. While it is not possible to determine from the ORACLE 1976 data the exact distribution of the three major divisions of English – reading, oral work and writing – a rough calculation gives us figures of around 13 per cent, 6 per cent and 82 per cent respectively. The comparable distribution for the present study was 23 per cent, 29 per cent and 49 per cent. Thus, writing still comprises the major part of English but no longer overwhelms the curriculum. This shift of emphasis, almost certainly as a result of the National Curriculum, has produced a much greater degree of balance within the English curriculum.

Summary

What then have we learned about the experience of the typical pupil in the modern primary classroom? The overriding impression is that much has remained the same as it was twenty years ago. In the light of the upheaval that primary education has experienced in the past decade or so, this is remarkable in itself. But there are important differences, some dramatic and some more subtle, and these changes too are of significance.

The thread which has run through this chapter has been 'communication' – who interacts with whom and under what circumstances; and the effects of various factors such as gender and level of attainment. We have already learned, in Chapter 3, that teachers spend a greater amount of their time interacting with the whole class, and this was confirmed by the pupils' experience. However, what is striking about the present study is that, while in *absolute* terms, pupils received more of their teacher's attention as a member of the class, in *relative* terms, things were almost exactly as they were in 1976 – that is, that three-quarters of all pupil–teacher interactions of any kind were still class-based.

When we turn to communication between the pupils themselves, we find the same rather curious mix of stability and change. Children still mostly sit grouped around tables, but still work mostly alone, for example. Most of their attention is still focused on the task in hand, and although they are distracted for around 16 per cent of the time, this is around the same proportion as before. Conversation among children, however, which in 1976 was relatively rare and mostly off-task, has increased substantially, and the talk is now as likely to be about their work as not.

Having looked at the children *en masse*, we next examined the effects of attainment on the patterns of work and interaction, and it is at this level that we begin to see real differences between the two studies. High attaining pupils were more likely than any other group to be actively engaged in the task in hand, and much more likely to be fully involved in their work rather than involved in routine activities such as sharpening pencils, organising materials and so on. Changes were found when it came to interactions with the teacher too. Whereas in 1976 teachers distributed their attention in very similar proportions to all pupils, regardless of attainment level, the very weak trends identified then have become much more marked. High attainers were much more likely to be engaged in task-related conversations with their teacher than any other group, particularly when they worked in a group situation. Lower attaining pupils, meanwhile, receive more attention as individuals, although much of this interaction is of a routine nature. Those that gained least overall were the average attainers, who comprised around 50 per cent of the whole sample.

An examination of gender differences also revealed subtle shifts since 1976. Analysis of the 1996 data for pupil–teacher interaction showed no evidence of favouring either boys or girls in terms of the attention they received. Neither were there any differences at the whole class level of inter-action between male and female teachers. However, at a one-to-one level, the typical pupil is now much more likely to get attention from a man. In a group, on the other hand he or she is more likely to get attention from a woman. Going a step further, and exploring the data from the different per-spectives of a boy and girl, we find that, while their general experience is pretty similar, individual attention from the teacher is most likely for boys who are in a class taught by a man.

Finally in this section on gender, we looked at patterns of communication between boys and girls themselves. The ORACLE 1976 study found that most interaction took place between pupils of the same sex. Although this general pattern has remained, that is that boys still mostly interact with boys, and girls with girls, a rise in mixed-sex pairings and groups, partly as a result of a deliberate seating strategies on the part of teachers, has con-tributed to an increase, since 1976, in opposite-sex communication.

We ended by examining how the curriculum has changed since the ori-ginal ORACLE studies. The introduction of a ten-subject National Curricu-lum, coupled with the inclusion of science in the core curriculum, together have had the effect of reducing the amount of English and mathematics that the pupils receive, so that the new three-subject core is equivalent, in terms of the amount of time devoted to it, to the old two-subject version. By further breaking down the mathematics curriculum, we are able to see that, inasmuch as it is possible to draw comparisons, the distribution of sub-areas within mathematics remains much the same. In English, however, the previous dominance of writing has given way to a much more balanced curriculum.

In this and the previous chapter, we have looked at life in the classroom from the standpoint of, first the teacher, and second the pupil, and have come to much the same conclusion in both instances. The classroom is, in many ways, a different place from that of the 1970s. That much might be expected given the passage of time, and in particular the dramatic shift in the attitudes of the policy makers, and the fundamental change in the struc-ture of primary education that has resulted. Yet what is perhaps more remarkable is how much has *not* changed. Teachers make statements and ask questions in the same proportion as they did twenty years ago, while the balance of attention that pupils receive as individuals, as group members, or as part of the class, is almost identical. These are striking findings, particularly in the light of the developments we have described, and say something about the essentially conservative nature of primary practice. Having said this, while the proportions may remain the same, teachers are working harder than ever before. Furthermore, as we argued in Chapter 2, this 'conservatism' may in fact be an attempt to maintain an element of stability in the primary classroom, a pragmatic response to a period of continual change.

In both Chapters 3 and 4, we have described the situation from the perspective of the *typical* teacher, the *typical* pupil, in much the same way that an opinion pollster might report what the 'average' person on the street may think about this or that issue. We have gone a little further in examining some simple group differences in the case of the pupils – gender and attainment – and we have already begun to see that there is a more complex and interesting story to tell beyond 'typicality'.

In the 1976 study, penetrating beneath this 'surface structure' uncovered a number of teacher styles or strategies to which we have already alluded. The analysis also exposed a number of pupil 'types' which described different behaviours, or ways of responding to particular situations. Examining the interaction between the two, teacher style and pupil type, revealed a symbiotic relationship in which strategy affected behaviour, and behaviour affected strategy, and it is to this that we now turn in Chapter 5.

Notes

1 Descriptions of the 'typical' pupil, teacher, lesson, etc. were based on the mean or average of all observations.
2 In *Inside the Primary Classroom* the convention was to talk of the teacher as 'she' (and the pupil as 'he'). In fact one third (35 per cent) of observed teachers in ORACLE 1976 were male, exactly the same proportion as in the present study.
3 References in this chapter to the 'average lesson' are based on fifty minutes. This does not represent an *actual* average, but is to make it simpler for the reader to convert tabled percentages (e.g. 34 per cent and 18 per cent translate as seventeen and nine minutes respectively) without constant reference to the text or a calculator. *Inside the Primary Classroom* used one hour as a standard period, and times that were cited in the original study have been recalculated.
4 Except where stated, all tables in this chapter are based on data from the Pupil Record.
5 This comment was noted by an ORACLE 1996 observer during a secondary school head's welcoming address to new pupils, in which he warned them that they would no longer be able to 'get up and wander about' in class as they had done in their primary schools.
6 The fieldwork for this part of the study was conducted in 1984–85.
7 A detailed examination of pupils' activity is presented later in this report.

8 Although the 'typical lesson' is a useful frame of reference, it should be remembered that these findings are based on minute-by-minute observations made throughout the school day.

9 As described in Chapter 1 (p. 32), pupils were assigned to one of three groups on the basis of their performance of standardised tests. Strictly speaking, this defines 'attainment' rather than the broader concept of 'achievement', the term used in *Inside the Primary Classroom*.

10 In the updated observers' manual an example of 'class' is given as when 'the children are grouped together, e.g. standing or sitting around the teacher's desk to listen to a story or watch a demonstration'. In ORACLE, there was no separate category for 'class'. A situation where target pupils worked for all or most of the observation period in a class setting would, therefore, have been coded as 'several opposite sex' (SOS). See Appendix 2 for a more detailed explanation.

11 See Chapter 5 for details of the various teacher styles identified in the 1976 study.

12 Even as we write, the requirement to follow the Programmes of Study for 'non-core' subjects is being 'relaxed' as part of the campaign to drive up standards in literacy and numeracy.

13 (a) The Pupil Record in the ORACLE 1996 study allowed for up to three curriculum areas per observation set to be noted (i.e. for each completed pupil record). In ORACLE 1976, only the main curriculum area was recorded for each observation set. In order to make valid comparisons, therefore, the ORACLE 1996 data in Table 4.15 are based on the *dominant* subject for each observation set.

(b) A number of new curriculum areas have appeared since ORACLE 1976. Since these take up classroom time which would, in ORACLE 1976, have been devoted to one of the four main categories, these have been retained in the analysis.

(c) PE and other extra-classroom activities (e.g. dancing, singing) were, however, not recorded in ORACLE 1976. In ORACLE 1996 a small amount of PE was observed, and this has been excluded from the analysis. Other categories which were not recorded in ORACLE 1976, (or possibly excluded from the analyses) were also excluded from the ORACLE 1996 data. These were the categories: 'cross-curricular', 'rapid change', 'routine' and 'other'. Appendix 1 presents the ORACLE 1996 data in its entirety.

14 As explained in note 13(c), some activities were not observed in the 1976 research. These figures therefore represent the observed 'classroom' curriculum, rather than the whole of the pupils' experience. By recalculating the 1976 data on the basis of a twenty-three and a half hour week, rather than the eighteen hours used for the data presented in Table 4.16 (see Galton *et al.* 1980; Appendix 4), Campbell (1994) arrives at a figure of 49 per cent for the two subjects combined. He points out that, despite a variety of methods for determining the make-up of the curriculum, numerous studies between 1977 and 1992 have found that English and maths account for around 50 per cent of the curriculum, what Campbell calls the 'basic instinct' of the primary curriculum.

5

ESTABLISHING A WORKING CONSENSUS
Teaching styles and pupil types

What do we mean by teaching style?

So far, our analysis of the data has been mainly based on the average inter-actions of the various categories on the two observation instruments, the Teacher and Pupil Records. This has provided detailed descriptions of typical practice from both the teacher's and pupil's point of view. However, within any sample of human behaviour there are likely to be variations, and in Chapter 4 we looked at the behaviour of pupils of differing attainment and gender. The purpose of this chapter is to examine other variations in the observed behaviour, first of teachers, then of pupils. We shall then go on to explore possible relationships between different patterns of teacher and pupil behaviour in the same way that it was done in the original ORACLE study. There we came to a view that for the most part, pupils reacted to what teachers did, but it was also evident that some pupils developed the ability to anticipate the likely teacher reaction to certain behaviours. These pupils became adept at manipulating events in the classroom so that the consequent actions of the teacher were to their (i.e. the pupils') liking. This was particularly true of some tasks requiring higher-order thinking. Often, if these pupils felt the work to be too challenging, they would behave in ways that forced the teacher to concentrate his or her attention upon them. The teacher might then decide that because he or she was unable to get around the class to provide help, the task should be abandoned or simplified. In this way, over time, an understanding developed whereby these pupils offered reasonable behaviour in return for relatively undemanding tasks. Pollard (1985), who has described such 'covert' bargaining in some detail, refers to this understanding as establishing a *working consensus*.

Before exploring this idea of the working consensus further, we first need to identify the various patterns of behaviour associated with different groups of teachers and pupils. We shall begin with the teachers. In the 1976 ORACLE study this was done by a statistical technique known as 'cluster analysis' which begins by bringing together the two teachers in the sample whose profiles across all observed categories are most similar. The values for these two teachers on each of the categories are then averaged to give a joint profile, so that, for example if 10 per cent of the first teacher's interaction involved *questions of fact* as compared to 11 per cent of the second teacher's, the joint profile would be 10.5 per cent. The exercise is then repeated but with the values in each observation category replaced by the joint profile. Two situations are now possible. First, the next highest association is between a third teacher and this average profile, in which case there are now three teachers who make similar use of the interaction categories. A new joint profile is therefore calculated. The alternative possibility is that the next highest association is between another two teachers, in which case a new group or cluster is constructed and their scores averaged to give a second joint profile, and so on. The exercise is completed when eventually all the different clusters have been merged into one. A point in this merging process is selected which yields a distinct number of groups, the basis of which is that the members of a particular cluster have more in common with each other than they do with members belonging to other groups. By examining the profile scores over the various categories for each cluster, it is then possible to see where the contrasts are greatest and so identify the particular characteristics of each cluster of teachers. The degree of association can be measured by a straight correlation or, more typically, by what is called a *distance* or *similarity* coefficient (Everitt 1994).

If we were to classify, say, the physical characteristics of a sample of people in this way, we might finish up with two groups – one consisting of tall people and the other consisting of short people. Lower down in the classification, however, there would be short people with fair hair who were female, and still further down, the classification might include a group of short, fair haired females with different coloured eyes. Applying this procedure to the interaction data from the Teacher Record, we have the possibility of distinguishing between groups of teachers who tend to ask questions and those who do not, and perhaps even differentiating between those who ask higher and lower order questions further down the clustering process.

When this procedure was carried out in the original 1976 ORACLE study, four main clusters of teaching styles were identified.[1] The first of these was called the *individual monitors*. Their name arose, as their title suggests, from their propensity to engage in monitoring and to interact mainly with individual pupils. The observers' descriptions of these teachers indicated that they were under considerable pressure so that most of the interactions with pupils were brief, such as telling a child how to spell a word. Their main concern was to keep waiting time, when pupils either formed a queue at the desk or put their hand up while sitting in their place, to a minimum (Galton *et al.* 1980: 122). In contrast, there was a group of *class enquirers*, who engaged in above-average levels of whole class teaching, during which there was an emphasis on challenge, either through task questions or by statements of ideas. These teachers frequently introduced new topics to the whole class through question and answer sessions, and when children worked on their own assignments they would continue these conversations with individual pupils as well as giving feedback on work. The third group, known as *group instructors*, favoured above-average levels of group work and were mainly concerned with task supervision. In whole class settings these teachers placed the main emphasis on informational aspects of teaching so that making statements of *facts* and to a lesser extent of *ideas* tended to dominate exchanges with pupils (Galton *et al.* 1980: 123).

Fifty per cent of teachers in the 1976–77 sample, however, were placed in a group which were labelled *style changers* because they tended to shift the pattern of teaching between the class, a group and individual pupils in various ways. A group known as the *infrequent changers* tended to alternate between the use of whole class teaching and individual instruction, but unlike the individual monitors, this individual instruction was more like that of the class enquirers, that is it involved above-average amounts of challenging questions. They might therefore have been subtitled *individual enquirers*, but gained their name because of the way in which they made deliberate changes in organisation either to deal with a specific problem or in accordance with a carefully thought-out strategy. Thus Galton *et al.* (1980: 124) describe how Miss S, who encouraged the children to 'think for themselves', increased the amount of whole class teaching because the presence of five disruptive boys in her class prevented her from giving sufficient individual attention to the other children. Mr H, however, began the year by using large amounts of class teaching until pupils had acquired 'correct learning habits' after which the formal arrangements were relaxed. The second arrangement, that of the *rotating changers*, alternated between individual and group work, characterised mainly by a particular curriculum strategy in which children either moved to or from different tables designated as subject areas, or else stayed at the same table but at frequent intervals ceased, as a group, to work on one curriculum activity and moved on to another in a different subject. With the final group, known as *habitual changers*, it was very difficult to identify any consistent pattern. They seemed to change the classroom organisation at whim largely as a means of trying to cope with classroom management problems. Thus, if the class were working in groups and the groups were too noisy, the teacher might tell pupils to get out their English books and work by themselves on a comprehension exercise. At other times they might call the class together and hold a mental arithmetic quiz. These constant shifts appeared to break the concentration of even the most able pupils in the class so that levels of 'time on-task' were the lowest among the six teaching styles.

Both Mortimore *et al.* (1988) and Bennett (1988) have argued that the notion of teaching style has outlived its usefulness. This is because for almost any analysis of this kind, the variations within a given cluster are as large as those between the clusters. Styles do not, therefore, differentiate sharply between the teachers, and, as a consequence, it becomes very difficult to attribute differences in attainment to a particular teaching style. For this reason, Mortimore *et al.* (1988) preferred instead to identify particular types of interaction, such as 'challenging questions', 'giving feedback' and 'demonstrating' which, independent of a teacher's style, could be shown to correlate highly with pupils' progress. As reported by Creemers (1994), these correlations are generally small, accounting for around 2 per cent in the total variation in pupils' 'gain' scores on tests. However, as we have demonstrated in Chapter 3, there is a remarkable consistency in the use of some of the main categories of teacher–pupil interaction independent of subject. In the original 1976 ORACLE study, this was certainly true of the two most contrasting groups, the *individual monitors* and the *class enquirers*, both of whom made a considerable number of 'statements of fact' and even more of 'task supervision'. Analyses of the kind carried out by Creemers (1994), in which the differences between student's pre- and post-achievement scores are partitioned across these teaching variables, can only demonstrate a statistically significant effect if the variation between the teaching variables is sufficiently large. In the case of primary teaching in English schools, research has repeatedly demonstrated that key variables, such as challenging questioning and giving feedback on work, are used relatively infrequently when compared to 'telling' and 'showing', whatever style of teaching is adopted. Furthermore, the evidence available would suggest that at no time has this preference among teachers for telling rather than enquiring not dominated their practice. This is true not only of teachers in the UK but in all parts of the world where a system of institutional schooling exists.[2]

In so far as the notion of a teaching style is a useful one, its purpose is not to enable tutors and mentors involved in the training of students to advise these novice teachers to 'use this style and you will be more effective'. Indeed, there are those in the School Effectiveness Movement who argue that, rather than changing the way teachers teach, we will do more to raise standards by concentrating on school variables such as professional leadership, shared vision and goals, and an academic ethos. This is because these school variables are correlated more strongly with attainment than are classroom process measures such as teaching style. Common sense, however, would suggest that what teachers do in classrooms has a significant effect on what pupils learn, and the statistical argument in favour of recognising the importance only of teaching variables which correlate strongly with attainment was refuted by Gage (1985).[3] Where, therefore, the concept of a teaching style can be helpful is by showing that certain patterns of classroom organisation tend to enhance or reduce the capacity to engage in certain kinds of teacher–pupil interactions and that further, certain interactions show small but positive correlations with pupils' test scores. By increasing the use of these specific interactions, therefore, it is potentially possible, as Gage (1985) argues, to improve pupil progress. What is not being claimed, however, is that teachers belong exclusively to one style or another, although one particular approach may tend to dominate a particular teacher's practice to a degree. Indeed, most teachers, when asked, claim that they use 'mixed styles' without necessarily being able to articulate what the term *mixed* involves. In this present research, it is therefore still of interest to look at the average profile for each of the four main clusters obtained in the original ORACLE study and to correlate these 1976 central values with the profiles of the twenty-nine teachers in the 1996 sample on the various interaction categories. We are then in a position to examine how far patterns of teaching have changed over the two decades.

When this was done, most of the twenty-nine teachers' profiles were associated with more than one of the 1976 ORACLE styles. Of these, only five, or 17.2 per cent, showed a significant correlation with the *individual monitor* style of teaching, which made up 22.4 per cent of the 1976 sample. Just one of these coefficients reached statistical significance at the 1 per cent ($p = < 0.01$) level. In contrast, only two teachers failed to achieve a significant correlation at the 5 per cent level with the 1976 profile of the *class enquirer* style. Of the twenty-seven teachers who did, only one did not reach significance at the 1 per cent level. The range of correlations at the 1 per cent level was from 0.96 to 0.66, with over half these values greater than 0.90. Twenty-four of the twenty-nine teachers also showed significant correlations with the 1976 *group instructor* style, but only fourteen were significant at 1 per cent, and only three values were above 0.75, with no values greater than 0.80. In terms of the relative strengths of the 1996 teachers' correlations with the various 1976 style profiles, we can conclude that the strongest association was with the class enquirers, the next with the group instructors, and the weakest was with the individual monitor style.

As a result of this strong relationship between the 1996 teachers and one or both of the 1976 clusters dominated by the use of whole class or group teaching, every one of the twenty-nine teachers could be expected to achieve significant correlations with the *style changers*' profile. This is because in the 1976 sample, style changers used a combination either of individual and class or of individual and group organisation. In the event, the profiles of twenty-seven of the 1996 sample of twenty-nine teachers showed significant correlations with the style changing profile at the 1 per cent level, and the profiles of the remaining two teachers reached the 5 per cent level of significance. To pursue the analysis further, therefore, we can look at several combinations in which a teacher is associated with the mixed style and with one or more of the other three styles. When we do this we find three distinct groups yielding four contrasting styles:

- Nine teachers whose profiles have a significant strong correlation with the *style changer* group and have only one significant correlation with another of the remaining 1976 teaching styles. Six of the nine

113

teachers have a significant correlation with the *class enquirer* style and three with the *group instructor* style. We may therefore treat them as two (distinct) contrasting styles.

- Fifteen teachers who have significant correlations with the *style changer*'s profile and with both the 1976 *class enquirer* and *group instructor* styles. This combination of class and group was not a feature of the 1976 ORACLE mixed clustering pattern, which was mainly dominated by combinations of individual interaction and either whole class or group activity.
- Five teachers who have correlations with the *style changer*'s profile and the *individual monitor* but also significant correlations with the remaining styles. The behaviour patterns of these teachers seemed to be a genuine example of a 'mixed' style, since their teaching profile was associated with all four of the clusters.

The next step in examining whether there have been changes in the patterns of teaching since 1976 is to compare the central profiles of the above four styles with those of the original ORACLE clusters. In the 1976 study, as in the present one, many of the differences between the observation categories making up the cluster profiles were not statistically significant. In the earlier analysis, to indicate the trends in the data, the values for a particular observation category within each cluster were placed in rank order and the range for that category was divided by four. By way of illustration, let us take a category of teacher behaviour where one cluster had the highest proportion of observations (14 per cent) and another the lowest (6 per cent) while the average value for all teachers was, say, 10 per cent. The range between the highest and lowest cluster would, therefore be 8 per cent so that a quarter of this range would equal 2 per cent. For this particular category of teacher behaviour, any cluster value greater than 12 per cent would be classified relatively 'high', while one which was less than 8 per cent would be classified relatively 'low'. This allowed the value of each category in every cluster profile to be described either as '*above average*' if located in the top quartile, '*below average*' if in the bottom quartile, or '*average*' if located in between these two extremes. What is gained is a simple pictorial representation of the trends across the clusters, but what is lost is any indication of the range or the relative use of a particular category compared to the others. In Figure 5.1, therefore, this representation is provided for both the 1976 and 1996 samples. The raw scores on which the figure is constructed for the 1996 sample can be found in Appendix 3 together with those for the 1976 sample which are taken from Tables 6.1 and 6.2 of *Inside the Primary Classroom* (Galton *et al.* 1980: 121 and 128). For the sake of completeness, the figures for all the 1976 ORACLE styles are given in Appendix 3A1, but in Figure 5.1 only the *individual monitor, class enquirer* and *group instructor* profiles are presented, since it is these three styles that the 1996 versions most closely resemble.

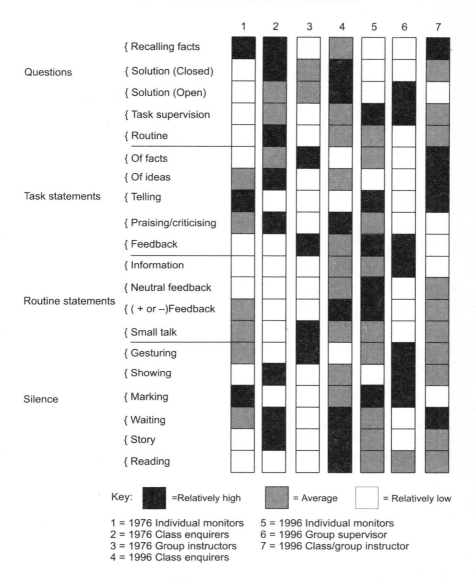

Figure 5.1 Comparison of 1976 and 1996 teaching styles (using 1976 and 1996 range and mean values)

Turning first to column 4 in Figure 5.1, this provides a profile for a teacher who emphasised challenging questions. Relatively high use was made of both *open* and *closed* questions, strong *task feedback* (in 1996 this category included instances of criticism as well as praise) and strong *routine feedback*.

As shown in Table 5.1, such teachers were interacting with pupils more frequently than teachers in the other clusters (93.5 per cent of all observations), and approximately half of these interactions were with the whole class (48.7 per cent). The style would therefore appear to represent a refined form of the 1976 *class enquirer* (column 2) since the 1996 version, unlike the original, made only average use of task statements involving *ideas* and of *showing* (*demonstrating*). One interesting characteristic was these teachers' use of above average amounts of routine statements, perhaps because of the increase in time children spent sitting in the carpeted area under fairly cramped conditions while the teacher read a story or heard a member of the class read out loud. This cluster profile strongly resembles one of the two identified by Alexander (1995: 246–8) in his CICADA project, in which some sixty transcripts of lessons from thirty teachers were analysed. Alexander's (1995: 246) cluster 2 involved high levels of explanation, questioning and eliciting. Compared to cluster 1 there was more whole class teaching. It would be reasonable, therefore, to claim that the profile in column 4 of Figure 5.1 represents the 1996 version of the *class enquirer.*

In the same way, the profile provided in column 5 exhibits some of the characteristics of the 1976 *individual monitor* displayed in the first column. In 1976, this style was distinguished by the relatively high use made of factual questions, telling pupils what to do and by what was termed *silent marking*, as when the teacher put a tick against a mathematics calculation without uttering a comment. The 1996 version (column 5) also made relatively high use of the marking and task supervision categories (both questions and statements). The picture is one where the teacher moves around the class checking pupils' work or offering advice on how to proceed with the task. At times feedback (both task or routine) will be offered, sometimes to individuals and sometimes to the class, since, whereas in 1976 only 6.9 per cent of teacher –pupil interaction involved the whole class, in 1996 this figure had risen to 25.2 per cent (Table 5.1). Individual interactions still, dominated, however,

Table 5.1 Cluster characteristics of 1976 and 1996 teacher styles by audience category (as % of total observations)

Audience	ORACLE 1976				ORACLE 1996			
	1	2	3		4	5	6	7
Individual	66.9	42.5	52.3		50.0	37.1	46.7	34.7
Group	5.5	5.8	17.7		8.6	7.7	31.0	16.8
Class	6.9	31.2	11.4		25.2	48.7	11.5	37.6
Total Interaction	79.3	79.5	81.4		83.8	93.5	89.2	89.2
N =	13.0	9.0	7.0	N =	5.0	6.0	3.0	15.0

Notes
1976: (1) Individual monitor; (2) Class enquirer; (3) Group instructor.
1996: (4) Individual monitor; (5) Class enquirer; (6) Group supervisor; (7) Class and group instructor.

accounting for exactly 50 per cent. Again, the 1996 version of the *individual monitor* appears similar to the profile of cluster type 1 in Alexander's (1995: 244) analysis with the emphasis on *task supervision* (directing and commanding in Alexander's terminology), and of *formative feedback*, which in Alexander's categorisation was coded when the feedback was a response to work or a pupil utterance, to distinguish it from the teacher's informative comments, 'which were given without reference to the work being undertaken'. Like the 1996 individual monitors, Alexander's type 1 teachers also engaged in more individual interactions with pupils than his type 2 teachers. By using transcripts collected during the PRINDEP evaluation (Alexander 1991) as well as those for CICADA, changes in the patterns of discourse were investigated over the period 1986–92. Alexander found that the clustering pattern was remarkably stable, despite the introduction of the National Curriculum. However, Alexander's CICADA study was completed before the pressure to increase the proportion of whole class teaching began to have a significant effect, as judged by the data presented in Table 3.1. The evidence presented here, however, suggests that a decade after the introduction of the National Curriculum, these two contrasting teaching styles, the *class enquirer* and the *individual monitor*, continue to survive, albeit in a modified form.

The pattern of interaction displayed in column 6 of Figure 5.1, however, which has the highest levels of group interaction of all the 1996 clusters (31 per cent of all observations), does not closely resemble the profile of the 1976 *group instructor* shown in column 3. The two clusters each made relatively high use of only two categories of the Teacher Record, task *feedback* and *gesture*. This latter category includes silent interactions, such as nodding approval, passing materials or, perhaps on occasions, frowning to convey a negative reaction to certain kinds of pupil behaviour. The 1996 version also made relatively high use of *open questions*, but was particularly identified by the emphasis on task supervision where there was relatively high use of both *task supervision* questions and statements, unlike *group instructors* in 1976. Among the silent interaction categories, *demonstrating* and *marking* were also emphasised. This suggests that in 1996 this style of teaching had less to do with instruction and more to do with helping pupils once they were engaged in follow-up work at their tables after the initial brief presentation to the class (only 11.5 per cent of teacher–pupil interaction was with the class). The relatively high use of marking was shared with the *individual monitor*, and this was not surprising given that this cluster nearly equals the monitors in the amount of individual interaction undertaken (46.7 per cent). As Table 5.1 shows, 89.2 per cent of all interactions consisted of talk, so that, overall, marking was still a small proportion of the teaching. The picture that emerges, therefore, is of someone who sets pupils problems by raising questions and then circulates among the tables offering advice, either to the whole group or to an individual pupil. This teacher tends to offer encouragement with a 'nod' or a 'wink' but at times may be willing to demonstrate a possible solution to a problem. This clear emphasis on supporting pupils in their work suggests that these teachers might be appropriately named *group supervisors*.

Just over 50 per cent of the 1996 sample of teachers were located in the remaining cluster (column 7). In Table 5.1 they have the second highest levels of group and class interaction (16.8 per cent and 37.6 per cent respectively). When teaching, the emphasis was clearly on instruction. These teachers made relatively high use of *factual* questions and statements of *facts*, *ideas* and also of task *supervision*. This pattern, in part, reflected a combination of the 1976 *class enquirers* (column 2), who also asked frequent factual questions, and the *group instructor* (column 3), who also made relatively high use of this questioning category. What appears to have happened, therefore, is a degree of realignment within these two 1976 teaching styles whereby the instructional aspects of teachers who tended to favour either a class or a group approach have been combined. The enquiring part of whole class activity has now separated to form a more sharply focused 1996 version of the *class enquirer* of the 1970s, while the supervision part of the 1976 *group instructor* (column 3) is now located in the 1996 *group supervisor* (column 6). The final cluster now encompasses the instructing element of the 1976 *class enquirer* and the *group instructor*. Hence its designation as a combined *class/group instructor* style. This teaching style would appear to be modelled upon the method known as direct instruction (Rosenshine 1979). Typically, at the start of the lesson, the teacher fires rapid questions at the class or a group to check they have remembered the content of the previous lesson. This is followed by further instruction in which both new facts and new ideas are introduced. Pupils are then set work in their groups or individually, during which time the teacher offers advice before bringing the class together once more to check that the new material has been correctly assimilated.

In summary, as can be seen from Table 5.1, almost 52 per cent (fifteen teachers) were in this *class and group instructor* category. Six, or 20.7 per cent, were a purer form of the 1976 ORACLE *class enquiring* style, compared to 15.5 per cent in 1976. Five teachers were a version of the *individual monitors*. This represented 17.2 per cent of the 1996 sample compared to 22.4 per cent in 1976. Three (or 10.4 per cent) were most closely associated with a *group supervisory* style, which was not present in the 1976 analysis. Given the limitations of a correlation analysis of this kind, these overall percentages suggest that there is now a sharper focus between the use of different forms of classroom organisation and the interaction profiles displayed in the clusters. The links between classroom organisation and the use of certain patterns of teacher–pupil interaction have been convincingly demonstrated by this present analysis, since in calculating the correlations between the 1996 teachers and the 1976 cluster profiles only the interaction categories and not the audience ones were included. The finding that the 1996 *individual monitors* were more likely to engage in individual interactions with the pupils, while the *class enquirers* recorded the highest levels of whole class interaction, only emerged after further analysis.

Partly as a result of a subject-based National Curriculum, the less effective styles of the 1970s such as the *rotating and habitual changers* have disappeared. But the emphasis now placed on whole class teaching has also eliminated the style known as the *infrequent changers*, who in the 1976 study were the most successful cluster of all and who were characterised by one-to-one challenging interactions which matched those of the *class enquirers*. What has now emerged, again partly as a result of the emphasis given to content in the National Curriculum, is the dominance of direct instruction with far less time being spent dealing with individual pupils' needs. How far what now appears to be the most frequently used pattern – a mixture of class and group work associated with low level cognitive questions and statements and increased levels of task supervision – presages a shift to a 'secondary' style of teaching at KS2 will be taken up in *Moving from the Primary Classroom: 20 Years On*, where the issue of transfer from the primary school will be considered.

In Figure 5.1, the mean values and the ranges on which the classification of the 1976 and 1996 sample of teachers has been calculated were, of course, different. For example, in 1976 *statements of facts* across the six clusters ranged from 11.9 per cent to 4.9 per cent of all observations and the overall average use of the category was 6.9 per cent. The corresponding overall mean in the 1996 study was 8.5 per cent, and the means for the four clusters ranged from 9.9 per cent to 6.6 per cent. The variation was, therefore, more restricted. Figure 5.2 thus provides an alternative version to Figure 5.1, where the values of the means and the range on which the profiles have been constructed for the 1996 clusters are those from the 1976 ORACLE analysis. This makes it possible to see shifts in the overall pattern of use of certain interaction categories over the two decades since 1976.

In Figure 5.2, therefore, because the percentage of observations occurring in the teacher–pupil interaction categories had increased between the two decades (see Table 5.1), all the 1996 clusters now tend to show 'above-average' levels of *closed* questions and statements of *ideas*, of *praise* and *criticism* and routine *information* coupled with *feedback*. For the same reason, among the silent interactions there were 'below-average' levels in categories such as *marking* and *waiting*. In other categories the pattern in Figure 5.2 tends to reinforce the previous analysis in Figure 5.1. For example, the 1996 *class enquirers* showed high levels of direct instruction when compared with their 1976 counterparts and therefore represent the original profile of this style of teaching more closely. With questions, the differences between the 1996 *class enquirers* and the *class and group instructors*, relative to the 1970s figures, were less marked, although in the latter cluster there was still

119

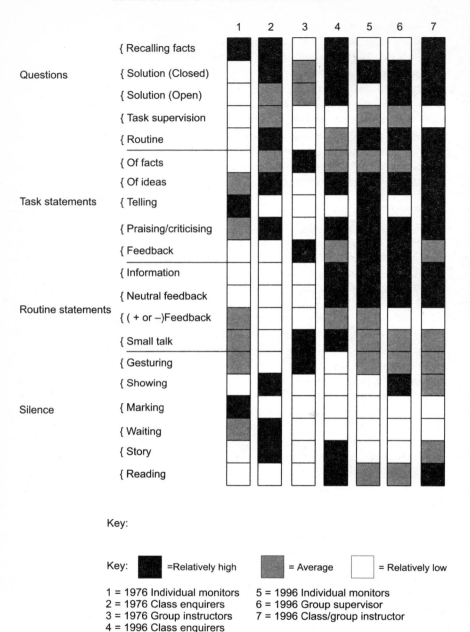

Figure 5.2 Comparison of 1976 and 1996 teaching styles (using 1976 range and mean values throughout)

greater emphasis on statements of facts. In contrast, the characteristics of the 1996 *individual monitors* were no longer as strongly represented as they were by the 1976 group of teachers. In the 1996 cluster there were 'below-average' levels of marking and more use of factual statements and other forms of telling. The cluster labelled *group supervisors*, although retaining this emphasis, also has become much more like the 1976 *group instructors*. In 1996 the problems of managing the classroom in order to meet the requirements of the National Curriculum appear to have increased. An interesting finding was the increased use of routine management interactions. Across most clusters there was an 'above-average' use of *routine* interactions. However, perhaps the most important conclusion, as Figure 5.2 demonstrates most convincingly, was that today's teachers engage in many more task related interactions than did their counterparts of two decades ago and this has resulted in higher levels of both questioning and telling. Nevertheless, relative to the different patterns of organisation, the differences between, say, *class enquirers* and *individual monitors* remained much as they were in 1976. Both styles asked more questions, but compared to colleagues in 1976, today's teachers now tend to challenge pupils more often in the whole class setting while also tending to engage in more direct instruction.

In the 1976 ORACLE study there were clear relationships between the different teaching styles and patterns of pupil behaviour, so that when a pupil moved from a class of, say, an *individual monitor* to that of a *class enquirer* then their behaviour changed to fit the pattern associated with that particular style of teaching. In the next section, therefore, we extend the analysis of primary practice, as seen largely from the pupils' point of view.

Patterns of pupil behaviour in the primary classroom

Just as there were differences between teaching styles in the 1976 ORACLE study, so pupils behaved in different ways when experiencing these styles. Using the data from the Pupil Record, four distinct types of pupil behaviour were identified. The first of these types was labelled the *intermittent worker*. These pupils tended to work when they were the focus of the teacher's attention, but at other times, when the teacher was fully involved elsewhere, these pupils sat at their tables engaging in conversation that rarely related to the work in hand. These *intermittent workers* were particularly noticeable in classes of *individual monitors*, because this was an ideal situation in which to practise their strategy of work avoidance. Pupils identified as intermittent workers, were always 'on-task' when the teacher was looking in their direction, but at other times, when the teacher was engaged elsewhere in the classroom, they would stop working and involve neighbouring pupils, usually those sitting at the same table, in conversations which were not about the work in hand. This behaviour has also been observed by other researchers, for example, Andrew Pollard (1985: 73) who called such pupils 'jokers' since they would do 'owt for a laugh'. In the 1976 ORACLE study, on average, such pupils were off-task for one day a week, but degree of intermittent working varied considerably, so that, in the more extreme cases a pupil might spend nearly half the week in off-task activity. Similar findings were reported from American studies, such as those of Berliner (1979). The categories on the Pupil Record which identified these pupils were the *distracted* (DSTR) and *partially distracted* (CODS) categories, which were linked to the observation that when such interactions were taking place, the teacher was occupied elsewhere in the classroom (T ELSE).

In contrast to these intermittent workers were the *solitary workers*, pupils who spent the greatest amount of time working on the tasks set them by teachers. They were always attentive during class discussion, but it was noticeable that they rarely actively participated, preferring instead to listen to the exchanges between the teacher and others in the class (PART). When they were working on their own assignments, although seated at the table with other children, they seldom engaged in conversations, unlike the intermittent workers. They therefore recorded the highest levels of on-task activity. The name *solitary worker* was given to this cluster of pupils because they were clearly similar to a group of older science students whom McClelland (1963) had identified in a study of American High School classrooms and had called 'undeflected' workers because, 'like human cannon-balls, they remained unaffected by the vagaries of the teaching'.

The third group of pupils were called *attention seekers*. This cluster consisted of two types of pupils who received above-average amounts of the teacher's individual attention. The first type were *attention getters* (STAR). Much of this attention usually had to do with routine or task supervision. These children were a source of frustration to teachers, because it was very difficult to be certain that they were, in fact, doing what they were supposed to. The teacher, for example, might set a practical task in which the pupils were required to make measurements of the perimeter of the classroom. These *attention seekers* would engage in conversations with other pupils near the area where they were carrying out their measurements. When asked by the teacher what they were doing they would reply, 'measuring Miss'. Teachers found it very hard to decide whether such pupils were indeed on task and would usually respond in a somewhat exasperated tone of voice by telling the pupil to 'get on with it then.'

However, the greater proportion of this type of pupil appeared deliberately to seek the teacher's help about relatively trivial matters (INIT). For the most part, they appeared to be less confident pupils who needed reassurance. They would stand in the queue at the teacher's desk either to show a few lines of writing to the teacher in order to have a tick placed on it or to enquire if, having done question number one, they should go on to number two.

Finally, there was a group of pupils who were labelled *quiet collaborators.* These pupils were given their name because, although they were often required to collaborate while working in groups, for the most part they appeared reluctant to engage in conversations about the work. When they did collaborate, it was usually to share materials so that such behaviour usually took place when the curriculum topic involved a practical activity. When not engaged in practical tasks, quiet collaborators in many respects behaved like solitary workers, that is, the former behaved in groups in a way similar to the way the latter type of pupil behaved during whole class activity. The cluster profiles, derived from the Pupil Record, are shown in Appendix 4. More detailed descriptions of each pupil types can be found in Galton *et al.* (1980: 143–6).

Identifying the 1996 pupil types

Using the same procedure we applied when identifying the 1996 teaching styles, the average profile of each pupil's behaviour, as recorded by the Pupil Record, was 'correlated with the average profile for each of the four 1976 pupil types'. The total sample consisted of 556 pupils of which 413 (74 per cent) could be identified from their correlation pattern (both positive and negative). Of these pupils:

- 133 pupils (23.9 per cent) showed significant positive correlations with *intermittent workers*. Some also to a lesser degree were associated with either *quiet collaborators* or the *solitary worker* type. These latter correlations are readily interpretable if we take into account the increase in whole class teaching reported in Chapter 3. As previously discussed, intermittent working in the 1976 ORACLE study was closely associated with the *individual monitoring* teaching style. In 1996, with the increase in whole class teaching, there is a decrease in the opportunities for pupils to engage in intermittent working. Hence these pupils will be more likely to co-operate on their tasks when involved in either teacher-supervised class or group activity but to revert to more typical behaviour when in their groups working on their individual assignments.
- The second group consisted of 109 pupils (19.6 per cent) whose highest correlations were with the 1976 *solitary workers*. Forty four pupils (7.7 per cent) in this group also had significant correlations with quiet collaborators. We saw in the analysis of the 1996 teaching styles that there was a separation of the enquiring part of class teaching from the part concerned mainly with direct instruction. These *class instructors* shared many of the characteristics of the 1976 *group instructors*, so that in the present analysis class and group instruction emerged as a single style. In responding to this pattern of teaching, this group of pupils (like the 1976 solitary workers) do not take an active part during class discussion, nor,

like collaborative workers, do they converse with their peers during group work, even when the talk is about the task. These pupils 'keep their heads down' and get on with their work. They appear to be an extreme version of the *solitary worker*, similar to a type of pupil identified in the 1978 ORACLE transfer secondary school who were called *hard grinders* (Galton and Willcocks 1983: 56).

The remaining 171 pupils (30.8 per cent) fell into two new groups not isolated in the original 1976 ORACLE analysis. They were distinguished by having strong negative correlations, either with the *intermittent workers* or the *attention seekers*.

The profiles of these two groups are shown in Table 5.2.[4] For the sake of brevity, only categories which accounted for over 1 per cent of the total observations are included in the table.

- The first group of these two groups consisted of twenty-two pupils (4 per cent) who had negative correlations with the 1976 *intermittent worker* profile but also showed positive correlations with either solitary workers or quiet collaborators. The reason for these latter correlations becomes apparent on inspecting the profile in Table 5.2. Like solitary workers these pupils were above-average on task behaviour (COOP TK and COOP R) and below-average on both the distraction (DSTR) and partial distraction (CODS) categories. They did, however, unlike the solitary workers, engage in above-average amounts of waiting for the teacher (WAITTCH) and also, interestingly, in daydreaming (RIS; responding to internal stimuli). Like quiet collaborators, they also shunned any form of interaction with other pupils. What distinguished them from other hard-working pupils was their relationship with the teacher. They were the centre of the teacher's attention (STAR) mostly as part of a class audience but also when involved in individual seat work. The picture which emerges is of pupils who are always the first to put their hands up to answer the teacher's questions during class discussion and who also sit patiently in their places with their hands up waiting for the teacher to come and help them with their work. Occasionally, while waiting, they may stare into space but this off-task behaviour rarely involves a neighbour. Pupils of this kind might be viewed somewhat cynically as 'teacher's pets' or as Americans say 'apple polishers'. They have been labelled *saints* by Bennett (1976) and *goodies* by Pollard (1985). Certainly, they are the kind of pupil every teacher would like to have during question-and-answer sessions because they help maintain the pace of the lesson. We shall therefore call them *eager participants* because of their contribution to whole class lessons and because, unlike the 1976 *attention seekers*, they waited for the teacher to come to them rather than pestering them for help.

Table 5.2 Pupil cluster characteristics of 'easy riders' and 'eager participants' as % of total observations – 1996[a]

Pupil Record 1996	All pupils N=556	A Easy riders N=149	B Eager participants N=22	sig.ev. between A&B
(ANOVA)				
PUPIL ACTIVITY				
TARGET ACTIVITY				
coop tk	61.4	64.7	60.7	
coop r	12.2	14.7[b]	15.0	
dstr	11.8	7.0[c]	7.0	
wait teacher	1.9	1.0[b]	5.0	1%
cods	6.1	4.1[c]	5.6	
intrst teacher	1.5	3.2[c]	0.2[c]	5%
intrst pup	2.3	3.3[c]	0.5[c]	
ris	1.2	1.1	3.6	1%
TARGET LOCATION				
P in	89.9	94.7[c]	85.4	1%
P out	6.0	3.0 [c]	10.3	1%
P mob	3.1	1.7[c]	2.7	
TEACHER ACTIVITY				
T pres	34.6	37.0	92.5[c]	1%
Telse	56.4	49.2[c]	4.6[c]	1%
Tmntr	2.4	3.8[c]	1.0	
T hskp	4.4	8.4[c]	0.9[c]	5%
PUPIL–ADULT INTERACTION				
TARGET'S ROLE				
init	1.8	1.3	2.5	
star	1.9	1.5	6.7	1%
part	21.5	20.3	60.6[c]	1%
lswt	4.4	5.7	16.2[c]	1%
INTERACTING ADULT				
teacher	27.9	27.8	83.0[c]	1%
ADULT'S CONTENT				
tk wk	24.5	23.4	71.2[c]	1%
rout	4.5	4.4	13.9[c]	1%
ADULT'S COMMUNICATION SETTING				
target individual attention	3.1	2.3[b]	7.1	1%
group	3.5	5.1	6.3	
class	23.1	21.2	72.4	
PUPIL–PUPIL INTERACTION				
TARGET'S ROLE				
bgns	6.9	6.4	1.9[c]	1%
rspnds(coop)	6.2	2.9[c]	0.2[c]	1%
sust	11.4	9.3	0.2[c]	1%

Table 5.2 Contd

Pupil Record 1996 (ANOVA)	All pupils N=556	A Easy riders N=149	B Eager participants N=22	sig.lev. between A&B
MODE of INTER'N				
mtl	1.8	2.2	0.5[c]	
vrbl	23.5	17.8[c]	2.0[c]	1%
OTH PUP TASK				
s tk	21.8	18.2[b]	2.7[c]	1%
d tk	4.3	1.8[c]	0.0	
OTH PUP NO.& SEX				
SS	16.6	14.4	1.3[c]	1%
OS	3.7	1.5[c]	1.4[c]	
SevSS	3.4	3.1	0.0	
SevOS	2.4	0.9[c]	0.0	
OTH PUP BASE				
own base	22.2	17.9[c]	2.2[c]	1%
oth base	3.5	2.0[c]	0.5[c]	

Note
a Individual coding categories which constitute less than 1% of total observations are excluded.
b = 5% significant difference *below* rest of sample (t-test)
c = 1% significant difference *above* rest of sample (t-test)

- Finally, there remained some 149 pupils (26.8 per cent) who might be thought of as friendly *ghosts* because they were seen but rarely heard. These were pupils whose profile correlated negatively with attention seekers, but who had even higher levels of on task behaviour than the eager participants. Like *hard grinders*, they appeared to shun contact with other pupils and preferred to be inactive when part of a class audience. Table 5.2 shows that these pupils got most of the teacher's attention as part of a group. When working on their tasks they rarely needed to wait for the teacher's help. Where they did engage in above average levels of activity was in watching the teacher talk to other pupils (INT TCHR and INT PUP). The picture of these pupils which perhaps begins to emerge is of a group similar to one labelled *easy riders* in the 1976 ORACLE transfer schools (Galton and Willcocks 1983: 56). This name came about because such pupils were able to give the appearance of being on-task, so as not to attract the teacher's attention while going about their work as slowly as possible.

Galton (1989: 66), describes one such boy pupil who was observed carrying out the teacher's instruction to draw a margin of 2.5cm with a 'sharp

126

pencil'. This easy rider made this activity last considerably longer than his classmates. First he withdrew the various articles required, pencil, ruler, rubber, one by one from his bag. Then he accurately measured 2.5cm from the top, the middle and the bottom of the left-hand side of the page. He then repeated this procedure, at the same time glancing up to see that the teacher was not showing a particular interest in what he was doing. When, at last, he began to draw the margin, he kept one eye upon the teacher, and when she was engaged elsewhere, deliberately broke the pencil point. This then required him to retrieve his pencil sharpener from his bag and resharpen the point. He continued sharpening the pencil until it appeared to the observer that if the activity had gone on a second longer it might have elicited an adverse comment from the teacher.

In the secondary transfer schools such pupils were on task for 71.5 per cent of the time they were under observation, of which 11.4 per cent involved routine activities such as pencil sharpening. Our 1996 *easy rider* was on task for 79.4 per cent of the time of which 14.7 per cent involved routine (COOP R). The pupils in 1996 engage in proportionally more routine activity, and this perhaps explains the below average levels of distraction and also partial distraction compared to the 1976 easy riders. During legitimate routine activity it is much more difficult for the observer (and it would appear also from these results for the teacher) to determine how much of it is purposeful and how much is a device to avoid getting on with the task. Drawing margins with care, underlining the heading on a page or an answer to a sum, rubbing out errors can contribute either to the production of a neat piece of work or to getting through a few minutes of the lesson without too much intellectual effort. In many circumstances teachers tend to give such pupils the benefit of the doubt.

In summary, therefore, the present pattern of pupil behaviour, in part, reflects practice as it existed twenty years ago in the primary school and, in part, practice in the secondary transfer schools which were also part of the ORACLE project. In these 1976 transfer schools a more 'formal' approach operated irrespective of whether, as in most of the feeder schools, children continued to sit in groups around tables or else sat in single-sex pairs with the desks set out in rows. Irrespective of seating arrangements, whole class teaching was the norm, so that a typical pupil received 93 per cent of attention as part of a class audience (Galton and Willcocks 1983: 43). Although from Table 5.2 the corresponding figure, as a proportion of interactions, is not as high (78 per cent) as we saw in both Chapters 3 and 4, this still reflects the fact that <u>one of the main changes in primary schools</u> <u>over the two decades has been not only the increase in whole class teaching</u> <u>but also the largely didactic way the curriculum is delivered.</u> In Chapter 3 we saw that the proportion of 'fact giving' had increased considerably. What is perhaps depressing about the pupil types identified in Table 5.2 is that, faced with such teaching, KS2 pupils cope by adopting strategies which studies of secondary classrooms have shown are widely used by their older peers to pass each day enjoyably without being 'picked upon' by teachers for perceived lack of effort.

This situation is exacerbated because of the uniformity in practice across the core and foundation subjects. In Chapter 3, for example, we noted that science teaching was rarely investigative in nature, but like the other subjects was largely dominated by teachers giving information, and to a more limited extent, ideas. This is similar to the science teaching provided in secondary schools in the pre-National Curriculum period as described by Delamont and Galton (1986).[5] Hargreaves (1982) in his book *The Challenge for the Comprehensive School*, also argues that teaching is dominated by lessons which, irrespective of subject, tend to be extremely repetitive. It would seem, from the evidence presented here, that within these 1996 pupil types, many pupils have responded to the teaching they receive by adopting almost identical strategies to those they will need to survive in the bigger secondary school. In this sense, at least, an element of continuity within the transfer process that was not present in 1976 has now been established.

Creating a 'working consensus': the distribution of pupil types across teaching styles

One of the key findings in the 1976 ORACLE study was the existence of a set of relationships between the different teaching styles and the various pupil types (Galton *et al.* 1980: 148). These relationships appeared to be remarkably stable from year to year, such that when pupils moved to a new teacher who made greatest use of a different style, they tended to adopt the characteristics of the pupil types associated with that style. As described in the first part of this chapter, such relationships are a manifestation of what Pollard (1985) described the 'working consensus', a state of equilibrium in which certain teacher behaviours produce certain pupil reactions, while at the same time other pupil behaviours appear to condition the teacher's actions. For example, attention seeking was almost non-existent in classes of the group instructors, which perhaps explains why, in the present study, it has largely disappeared, because of the extent to which direct instruction now accounts for a large part of the primary diet. On the other hand, nearly half the 1976 children (46 per cent) in the classes of individual monitors were intermittent workers. Nearly two-thirds (64.5 per cent) of children who were taught by the *class enquirers* were solitary workers. The highest number of attention seekers were found among teachers who were *style changers*. Table 5.3 shows the distribution of pupil types by teaching style for the 1996 sample. Where there is a direct comparison with the ORACLE figures, as in the case of the intermittent workers, the 1976 percentages are given in brackets. The same data is also presented in a pie chart (Figure 5.3).

Table 5.3 Distribution of pupil types across teaching styles

Pupil types	Individual monitors	Class enquirer	Group supervisor	Class or group Instructor	All
1 Intermittent workers	40.8 (47.6)	25.3 (9.2)	43.5	29.8 (32.1)	32.2
2 Hard grinders	25.4	30.7	10.9	28.3	26.4
3 Eager participants	4.2	4.4	6.5	5.8	5.3
4 Easy riders (ghosts)	29.6	39.6	39.1	36.1	36.1
	100.0	100.0	100.0	100.0	100.0
N	71	91	46	205	413

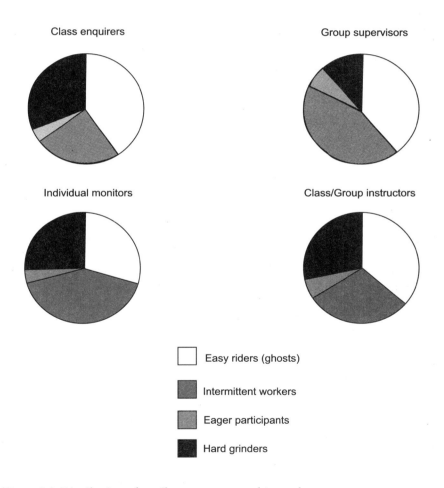

Figure 5.3 Distribution of pupil types across teaching styles

The first point to strike one is that, across all four teaching styles, there was a sizeable proportion of easy riders. This is best seen pictorially in Figure 5.3. The smallest proportion can be found when the individual monitoring style was being used (29.6 per cent). With this style, however, the number of pupils involved in some form of task avoidance was reinforced by the presence of others engaged in intermittent working (40.8 per cent). This latter figure is very close to that recorded under the same style twenty years ago. However, the highest proportion of easy riders were in classes taken by class enquirers (39.6 per cent) and the group supervisors (39.1), some 3 per cent greater than during the use of the *direct instruction* approach by the class and group instructors. Furthermore, the number of intermittent workers also increased dramatically when the class enquiry style was used (25.3 per cent compared to 9.2 per cent twenty years ago). The group supervisor style also appeared to afford plenty of opportunities for intermittent working as the teacher moved from table to table making suggestions about how pupils could proceed with their tasks. Group supervisors also had the lowest number of hard grinders (10.9 per cent).

These patterns make sense, if it is remembered that the teaching styles of the 1990s are not as distinct as those of the 1970s. Now, all of the teaching styles, except that of the group supervisor, involve sizeable proportions of whole class teaching. This is particularly applicable to the case of the 1976 individual monitors, who recorded just below 7 per cent of whole class interaction compared to their 1996 counterparts' figure of around 25 per cent. Inevitably, therefore, the pupil characteristics in the 1996 sample will be more evenly distributed across the different teaching styles, because there are now higher levels of whole class teacher–pupil interaction with correspondingly less individual attention. In the 1976 study most of the variation in pupil behaviours was attributable to differences between the relative use of group and individual interaction by the teacher. Since we also know that most of the increase in whole class interaction recorded in 1996 consisted of direct instruction of a kind offered in the secondary school, it is not surprising to see the large numbers of easy riders across all the categories. The same argument applies to the hard grinders, a sizeable presence in all cases except for that of the group supervisor teaching style.

What is not so easily explained by this line of reasoning, however, is the proportion of intermittent working when the class enquiring style is being used. Intermittent working accounts for 25.3 per cent of pupil behaviour compared to only 9.2 per cent two decades earlier. However, here again it should be remembered that intermittent working in 1996 is not the same as intermittent working in 1976. In general, intermittent workers, although they still take opportunities to be off-task when the teacher is engaged elsewhere, nevertheless exhibit higher levels of on-task behaviour (COOP TK, COOP R and CODS) than did their counterparts in the 1970s. This is because intermittent working is not a very practical strategy for task *change opps.for work avoidance*

avoidance when one is sitting on the classroom floor, grouped closely around the teacher. It is much easier and safer to operate when the teacher is talking either to a group or to an individual pupil at another table elsewhere in the room. One possible explanation for the present situation lies in the finding that much of this increase in whole class teaching has been accompanied by a decline in the use of the silent and non-interacting categories. In 1976 around 20 per cent of the class enquirer's time was spent on activities such as demonstrating to the class or glancing around the room to monitor pupil activity.

During such times there would be few opportunities for pupils to work intermittently. Now in 1996, however, class enquirers interact with pupils for 93.5 per cent of the time (Table 5.1), because of this decrease in the use of the silent and non-interaction categories. Consequently, although, in direct proportion to the amount of class teaching, the number of individual interactions has declined, because of the overall increase in teacher–pupil interaction, the actual time class enquirers spend in conversation with either individuals or groups (44.8 per cent) was not so different from the 48.3 per cent recorded by the 1976 class enquirers. What appears to be happening, therefore, is that some pupils in these classes (given that they spend nearly half of their day on whole class activities, many of which involve sitting in a confined space, listening to the teacher) regard an instruction to work on one's own, or with a group of pupils, as welcome relief. At such times, more opportunities to relax and enjoy a joke are being taken than was the case in 1976. At the same time, despite the proportionate increase in off-task behaviour, more work was done by pupils, because the overall levels of engagement in the 1990s are now much higher that was the case in the 1970s.

The findings presented here tell a story that reinforces the conclusions arrived at in the earlier chapters. The decision deliberately taken a decade ago, to leave the design of the primary phase of a National Curriculum to subject panels dominated by experts whose teaching experience was mostly gained in secondary schools has produced a curriculum dominated by subject content. As a result, much of the teaching at KS2 appears to be similar to that which operates in the bottom half of the secondary school. As Hargreaves (1982) and others have argued, a feature of this secondary approach is that it regularly produces a sizeable number of disaffected pupils, particularly in the year immediately after transfer from primary school. In its extreme form, this can result not only in an increase in the number of serious incidents of misbehaviour but also in a hiatus in pupil progress, so that some children do less well on tests of attainment at the end of the first year after transfer than they did at the end of their last year in the primary school. Our present data might suggest that the first signs of this disaffection, easy riding and intermittent working, are now being practised by a sizeable number of primary pupils. The recent SATs results would demonstrate that pupils still perform reasonably well in examinations despite these manifestations of disaffection in much the same way that secondary school pupils would appear to overcome the first year hiatus in progress, since GCSE examination standards have continually risen. Nevertheless, the present findings suggest that there is a degree of truth in the observations which teachers made to the PACE researchers Croll (1996a), and to Galton and Fogelman (1998) in their study of 'The Use of Discretionary Time in the Primary School', that for many KS2 pupils, in particular, school is no longer as enjoyable as it was before the National Curriculum.

The main focus of the 1976 ORACLE study was upon the effectiveness of different teaching styles. In each year of the primary school, the pupils were tested in September and then again in June. Thus it was possible to explore the effectiveness of different styles by looking at the yearly gains made on the tests by pupils in classes of, say, the individual monitors as against those made in classes of, say, group instructors. Such an analysis is not possible with the 1996 sample, because the focus of interest in the present study was on transfer and whether the introduction of the National Curriculum had helped to reduce the hiatus in progress, consequent on the lack of continuity between the primary feeder and the secondary transfer schools. This present sample of pupils was, therefore, only tested at the end of the year in primary school, so there is no means of judging yearly changes in pupil progress across the different teaching styles identified in this chapter.

Nevertheless, the fact that some attainment data were collected during the primary year does allow certain comparisons to be made. As we observed in Chapter 1, there have been continual complaints over the last two decades, not only about primary teaching methods but also about the (alleged) decline in standards of numeracy and literacy. In this study we have used the same tests that we used twenty years ago. It is, therefore, possible to say something about changes in standards over the two decades. This is what we do in the next chapter.

Notes

1 Full description of these teaching styles can be found in *Inside the Primary Classroom*, pp. 120–30.
2 The essentially conservative nature of teaching has been noted, for example, by Cuban (1984) in his review of teaching practice in American schools during the period between 1890 and 1980.
3 Gage (1985: 11–14) discusses the conditions under which certain weak relationships may still be important when formulating policy. Taking a hypothetical case, he points out that an experiment in which a new treatment reduced the percentage of bad outcomes from 60 per cent to 40 per cent would only give a correlation of 0.2 and account for around 4 per cent of the variation in the outcome measure. Applying this to a medical trial using beta-blockers to reduce death due to heart attacks, where, in a sample of 3,800 men, only a 2.5 per cent increase in survival resulted from administering the drugs, Gage calculates that their use saves 21,000 lives a year in the United States alone. Yet the correlation coefficient was a

mere 0.2 (*Journal of American Medical Association* 1982 (247): 1707–13). In the same way Gage argues that, in teaching, correlations do not have to be large to be important. What matters is the relative cost of even small gains when spread over large numbers of pupils. In the case of classroom practice, cost is measured in terms of teachers' and pupils' time and effort as well as academic results.

4 The percentages of pupil–teacher interaction within individual, group and class settings for all pupils in the Table 5.2 differ slightly from those given in Table 4.1. This is because in this analysis only pupils with complete records, including attainment profiles, have been included. This sub-sample was then used to chart changes in pupil behaviour and performance after transfer to secondary school.

5 The next volume, *Moving from the Primary Classroom: 20 Years On*, will describe science lessons which are remarkably similar to the ones observed by Sara Delamont and her team of participant observers during the ORACLE transfer study.

6

PUPIL PERFORMANCE IN BASIC SKILLS

1976 and 1996

Three issues have been prominent in the education press during the 1990s. These concern questions of whether standards are falling, whether, given the rising costs of schooling, money is being wisely spent, and finally, the relatively novel issue of whether boys are 'under-achieving' in comparison with girls. A selection of headlines from the *Times Educational Supplement* (*TES*) for two weeks in January 1998 illustrates the point. For example, on 16 January we find:

> 'Weakness in numeracy runs across the board'
> '£1bn' inspection regime fails to raise standards'
> 'More spent on tests than textbooks'

while in the previous week (9 January 1998) the paper's headlines read:

> 'Tory competition fails to raise standards'
> 'Minister promises to act on boys' failure'
> 'Whatever happened to the likely lads?'

Two of these questions, those concerning standards and boys' achievement, are central to both this and the next chapter.

We begin by looking at recent developments in relation to these two key issues, before outlining the major changes which have taken place in assessment at primary level in the twenty years since the original ORACLE study. Following that, we describe the tests used in this present replication of ORACLE, and present the results of giving, as far as possible, the same tests, to children of the same ages, in the same schools, in 1996 as we gave in 1976. In the course of this and the next chapter, therefore, we will attempt to answer the following questions:

- What has happened to standards of performance in these tests in the twenty years since the first ORACLE study?
- If standards have changed, can this finding be related to any differences in the relative performance of girls and boys in the tests?

134

- What has been the impact of the National Curriculum on performance in these tests and how might this, in part, explain our findings?

We begin with the issue of standards in education.

Falling standards or a sea of confusion?

News of falling standards is somehow familiar. In 1975, The Bullock Report, for example, opened with statements of concern dating from the 1920s about worsening standards; in 1997 the issue was still causing such concern that the new government created 'Ministers for School Standards'. Yet, within two weeks of the *TES* headlines at the opening of this chapter, the Chief Inspector of Schools acknowledged improvements in teaching *and standards* in his Annual Report for 1997, but went on to identify a dip in progress in the early years of KS2. The recently created Schools Standards Minister, Stephen Byers, announcing the report, welcomed the good news, but said that there was no room for complacency, and re-emphasised 'the Government's drive to raise standards' (DfEE 1998a).

The annual publication of primary school 'league tables', unthinkable in 1976, shows the percentage of children in each of England's 13,500 primary schools that achieved the 'standards expected of eleven-year-olds' (i.e. Level 4 or above) in national assessments of mathematics, English and science. The average proportion of eleven-year-olds that achieved Level 4 or beyond in these three subjects was 54 per cent in 1995, 58 per cent in 1996, and 65 per cent in 1997. Although these figures do not reflect the 'value-added' by a school in relation to the children's entry standards, which will be incorporated into the 1998 results (but see Chapter 8, note 1), they do suggest a gradually rising standard of performance. If we look more closely at English, for example, there appears to be a gradual improvement in the standard between 1995 and 1997 (48, 57 and 63 per cent of eleven-year-olds achieving at least Level 4 in 1995, 1996 and 1997 respectively), provided that the measures of achievement used are reliable and valid (e.g. Galton 1995; Sainsbury 1996).

International comparative studies, however, suggest that England's performance has been falling relative to that of other countries, particularly those situated around the Pacific Rim, such as Singapore, Japan and Korea. This conclusion is based on successive surveys of International Education Achievement (IEA). In mathematics, for example, among thirteen-year-olds, the English ranking fell from 6th to 11th to 16th in the First, Second and Third International Mathematics Studies (Reynolds and Farrell 1996; Keys *et al.* 1996). In an attempt to put these results into perspective, Brooks *et al.* (1995) have pointed out that among all ten 'educational systems' in the first two surveys, there was a general decline with respect to number, geometry, measurement and statistics. Unfortunately, this trend did not hold for algebra, where the results deteriorated for England and Wales only. This has led to expressions of serious concern about standards in the UK, leading to an extensive review, which was funded by OFSTED and carried out by Reynolds and Farrell (1996). This review recommended the adoption of teaching methods from the above-mentioned Pacific Rim countries whose rankings were much higher than those of the UK. We engage in a fuller discussion of these international comparative studies in Chapter 8.

Given the widespread respect once accorded to the English education system (Richards 1998), the current position represents a dramatic turn-around from the time when 'English primary education was the envy of the world.' The present situation also represents something of a paradox, since the conclusion that, on international comparisons, standards are continuing to fall has been reached at a time when it is also claimed, from evidence provided by the SATs and GCSE results, that national standards have been steadily rising.

The debate about national standards at primary level was set alight in 1990 by Martin Turner's 'blistering' attack on 'the many-headed hydra' of approaches such as 'real books', emergent literacy and apprenticeship reading, which he claimed were being used to teach reading and writing in most primary schools. Basing his case on reading tests carried out in ten south-eastern Local Education Authorities, Turner argued that the results provided evidence of a 'downturn in reading standards...unprecedented in peace-time educational history'. He predicted a 'far greater haemorrhage in literacy standards moving up the system' which would appear at ages eleven or sixteen (Turner 1990: 6). This 'sharply downward trend' was being 'sponsored' by parents as taxpayers because of 'local government in which such havoc [could] be perpetrated without accountability', and the timidity of politicians in the face of 'experts' (Turner 1990: 7–8). Strong counter-arguments to Turner's views were put forward by 'literacy experts', such as Hazel Francis, David Barton, and Peter Pumfrey and Colin Elliott and can be found in the 'Open Dialogue' following Turner's 1992 paper. However, we should perhaps note that one of Turner's concerns, which was largely uncontested, had to do with the widespread adoption of these new methods and techniques in schools without any rigorous trials or comprehensive evaluation.

While Turner provides an alarming picture, Brooks *et al.* (1995) who reviewed standards in literacy and numeracy between 1948 and 1994 for the National Commission on Education, concluded that:

> The major feature of the results throughout the UK is their great stability over time; most comparisons reveal no change, a few show a rise, even fewer show a fall... and there is certainly no warrant for doom-laden pronouncements of inexorable decline.
>
> (Brooks *et al.* 1995: 3)

On the other hand, OFSTED (1996b), following a one-day reading 'raid' in forty-five inner London primary schools, reported that reading perform-ance was 'well below the national average, judged against test norms' and was 'lagging 12 months and 15 months behind children's chronological ages, in Years 2 and 6 respectively'. This report became the basis of major policy initiatives, including the setting up of the Literacy Task Force by New Labour while still in opposition. This, despite what was regarded by many as a 'damning' critique of OFSTED's methodology by Mortimore and Goldstein (1996) who concluded that 'a series of methodological errors and limitations made these conclusions largely invalid.'

Further support for the argument that standards have fallen comes from Davies and Brember (1997). These researchers report gradually declining standards in their analysis of the scores of seven successive cohorts of Year 6 children taking the Primary Reading Test (France 1981). They attribute this decline to a shift in the distribution of individual scores around the mean, the result of an *increase* in the numbers of very low achieving children coupled with a *decrease* in the proportion of high achievers. When the low achievers were excluded from the analysis, however, the decline in standards no longer occurred.

Thus, the evidence for a general decline in standards of literacy, which has probably been the most consistently tested area of basic skill in primary schools, is somewhat equivocal. Nevertheless, not only has the new Labour government set national targets for literacy and numeracy; namely that, by 2002:

- 80 per cent of eleven-year-olds will be reaching the standards expected for their age in English; and,
- 75 per cent of eleven-year-olds will be reaching the standards expected for their age in maths

(DfEE 1997a: 19)

it has also set individual LEA targets (DfEE 1998b). In two programmes, which will cost billions of pounds, primary schools must devote two hours a day to teaching literacy and numeracy using highly prescribed teaching programmes. In English, the programme embodies OFSTED's conclusions (1996b) that more 'whole class teaching and group work and a greater use of phonics' are needed in the teaching of reading, despite Mortimore and Goldstein's critique (1996), and despite the localised nature of OFSTED's 'one-day raid'. The programme being implemented for National Literacy remains, as yet, without a complete UK evaluation.

Even supposing that the literacy target is met, and 80 per cent of eleven-year-olds *do* achieve the standard expected for their age, unless a large pro-portion of those pupils fails to make any further progress, which seems un-likely, 'the standard expected for their age' will inevitably become higher than it is now. This is because when targets are defined in these terms, 'standards', even those referenced by observable performance criteria, are destined to rise as soon as they begin to be achieved. Once there are indications that these targets are being achieved, we might then attribute the actual rise in pass rates to teachers' growing expertise in enabling children to acquire the knowledge, understanding and skills that they need. The danger here is that the teachers may then be accused of 'teaching to the test'. In 1995, only 19 per cent of KS2 teachers who took part in a survey said they were teaching to the test more than they thought 'was reasonable'. However, these teachers expressed great concern about the narrowing effect of the tests on the curriculum (ATL 1996a). In 1996, when the league tables of SATs results were to be published for the first time, the figure had nearly doubled to 36 per cent (ATL 1996b), but, given the continuing emphasis on driving up standards, this may now be a conservative figure. When test results have important consequences, such as the publication of the results in league tables, which ultimately affect school recruitment, funds and resources, the assessment is referred to as 'high stakes' (see Nuttall 1989). In the United States, 'teaching to the test' or 'measurement-driven instruction' (MDI) is acknowledged as a means to promote the teaching of particular curricula or to drive up standards (Popham 1987; Gipps 1994). In England and Wales, (but not Scotland or Northern Ireland) this type of high stakes assessment now holds sway in primary schools, a situation which could not have been imagined at the time of the original ORACLE project.

Gender differences in achievement: why are boys doing badly?

Evidence of gender differences in achievement in various subject areas has been growing since 1988, with the publication of GCSE results which showed, for example, a 4 per cent difference in favour of girls, even in a stereotypically 'masculine' subject such as physics, a lead which has been maintained in subsequent years (Stobart *et al.* 1992a). Since then, there have been numerous reports of girls' increasing academic success, while boys have continued, in the euphemistic terminology of the day, to 'underachieve' (Nuttall 1980), not only at GCSE but also in some subjects at GCE 'Advanced' level, in the Standard Assessment Tasks (SATs) and Teacher Assessment (TA) (SCAA 1996, 1997; OFSTED 1996c; Elwood and Comber 1996). Most recently, the publication of DfEE figures for the 1997 SATs and Teacher Assessment have shown boys lagging behind girls in 'reaching the standards expected for their age' in SATs by 5 per cent in English (but not in mathematics) at KS1 and 2 (DfEE 1998c), while the 1997 Teacher Assessments of pupils at KS3 showed that 'girls appear(ed) to be performing better than boys, particularly in design and technology, history, music and modern foreign languages'. Concern about boys' under-achievement has reached such a pitch that the Government has announced a co-ordinated campaign involving LEAs, OFSTED and the Qualifications and Curriculum Authority (formerly SCAA) to tackle the problem (DfEE 1998d).

There are several plausible hypotheses as to why this gender gap has arisen in recent years. Some researchers attribute it to factors residing within the tests themselves, some argue the explanation can be found within the culture of schools, while others look to the process of young people's socialisation by way of explanation (Stobart *et al.* 1992a; Gipps and Murphy 1994). Hypotheses associated with the tests themselves concern the effects of the content, context and format of the items. The widening gender gap in tested performance may be explained in terms of the removal of biases which favoured boys' performance, such as items about traditionally masculine interests or a predominance of items which featured or were about men or boys. Nuttall (1989) identified three factors in the 'context and circumstances' of testing which can facilitate or inhibit performance. These include motivation to do the task, the relationship between the assessor and individual being tested, and the way the task is presented. Any or all of these may lead boys and girls to view the same tests and tasks differently. In terms of item types, boys tend to do better on multiple-choice items (see Stobart *et al.* 1992a), and are more successful at abstracting the essence of a problem from its context than are girls. Open-ended tasks may also be interpreted very differently by boys and girls (Murphy 1989). Increasing care to eliminate gender bias in tests, which was generally unfavourable to girls may, therefore, explain some of their recent 'success', or the boys' apparently declining performance.

Among the socio-cultural hypotheses are those which concern the teachers' treatment of boys and girls in school, teachers' different expectations of boys and girls, and pupils' own relative levels of self-confidence and expectation. Differential 'treatment' of boys and girls can involve a number of processes, from grouping arrangements to classroom display to teacher–pupil interaction. In the case of the latter, the distinction is between *quality* and *quantity*. Writers such as Spender (1982) and Clarricoates (1980) claim that boys have benefited in both domains. However, as we pointed out in Chapter 4, while further detailed analysis of the observation data might yet reveal differences in the nature of such interactions, there was no evidence, either in 1976 or in the present study, of systematic differences in the distribution of teachers' attention to boys or girls.

The effects of teachers' expectations of girls' and boys' self-confidence were examined by Stobart *et al.* (1992b). They found that, while the majority of candidates for GCSE mathematics were girls, boys were more likely to be entered for the Higher tier, reflecting a tendency for teachers to see them as more confident than girls, and by association more capable of success. Substantially more girls than boys were entered for the Foundation and Intermediate tiers, on the other hand, the latter in particular representing a 'safety first' approach on the part of teachers, who were given to underestimate girls' ability to achieve at the highest level. Other recent explanations of boys' low levels of performance include the notion that 'school is uncool' for boys, who do not wish to be perceived by their peers to conform to what might be expected of them in terms of behaviour or academic endeavour (Connell 1989). This may be further borne out by the revelation that 83 per cent of permanently excluded students are boys (DfEE 1998d). The Government's co-ordinated plan, referred to above, requires LEAs to address the issue of disaffected boys and to challenge the 'laddish anti-learning culture which has been allowed to develop'. Such a culture may in part be a reaction to the success of schemes designed to increase girls' academic aspirations.

We shall return to these issues in Chapter 7 when we consider possible explanations for the results presented in the following sections. First, however, we outline the considerable developments in primary educational assessment in the last twenty years. The most prominent have been the work of the Assessment of Performance Unit (APU) and the imposition of a compulsory national assessment system, following the crucial if somewhat problematic report by the Task Group on Assessment and Testing (TGAT 1988).

Changes in assessment at primary level since ORACLE 1976

The 1976 ORACLE study took place at a time when testing in schools was at an all-time low (see Gipps *et al.* 1983)[1] following the ending of eleven-plus, and in response to concern about the narrowing effect of testing, both for selection on the curriculum and on children's self-esteem (Bullock Report 1975; Barker Lunn 1970). Ten years earlier, the Plowden Report (1967) had urged teachers to reclaim the role of assessor, and devise their own curriculum related tests, while advising test developers to

> be diverted from the design of tests for the purpose of selection to the development of tests suitable to the changing primary curriculum, and helpful to teachers who need to diagnose children's difficulties in learning.
>
> (para. 421)

Thus a move away from norm-referenced tests to formative assessment was encouraged. Teacher-made tests were not widely used however, and in Bassey's survey of 900 primary teachers (1978), less than a third of the teachers reported using them. In 1975, the Bullock Committee emphasised the long-standing concern about falling standards of literacy, and recommended the setting up of a new system of monitoring which would include light sampling and the development of a pool of items, to be screened initially by teachers to ensure face validity. The Committee said that, '*as a general rule, a school would be selected only once in several decades.*' Indeed, '*many children would complete their school days without ever encountering the monitoring process*' (para. 3.19). These words have a very hollow ring nowadays, when a school, a child or a teacher who can escape the monitoring process is a rarity.

Bullock's recommendations, however, slipped neatly into the brief of the newly formed Assessment of Performance Unit (APU). This was set up in 1974, and found its niche after Jim Callaghan's Ruskin College speech (1976), when concern about falling standards was linked to calls for greater accountability in education (Gipps and Goldstein 1983). The APU's initial purpose was to identify and define standards and subsequently measure and assess pupils' achievements against them. Before it became defunct in 1991, it commissioned national surveys of the performance of seven-, eleven- and fifteen-year-olds in English, mathematics and science, among other things, but it failed in its intentions either to define or to measure standards. By 1989, as Galton (1995) points out, the APU had abandoned its concern with 'standards' and was merely 'monitoring' levels of pupil performance (APU 1989). It did, on the other hand, pilot new types of assessment, and, while failing to pave the way for the introduction of national assessment, for better or worse, it reintroduced the idea of external assessment into the primary professional vocabulary.

In retrospect, the APU bridged the gap in primary education between an under-assessed past and an over-assessed present; a time during which other major theoretical changes were taking place. Concurrently with the APU's work, serious challenges were being made to the implicit bases of education and traditional ideas about ability and assessment. Social cognitivists, such as Donaldson (1978), and Tizard and Hughes (1984), emphasised the effectiveness of children's learning in real-life contexts. There were also challenges to our understanding of intelligence, from notions of how the intellect develops which ranged from Vygotsky's 'zone of proximal development' (1978), to ideas about 'practical intelligence' (Sternberg and Wagner 1986) and multiple intelligences (Gardner 1983). Parallel with these moves in psychology, was a gradual shift towards a process-oriented and skills-based curriculum, in which children in some classes were encouraged to think like scientists (Harlen 1985), be composers (Paynter 1982), and to use metacognitive thinking strategies (Nisbet and Shucksmith 1984). All of these moves represented constructivist views of learning, and the appeal of 'emergent literacy' (Hall 1987) and 'whole books' (Waterland 1985) approaches to writing and reading were symptomatic of the *Zeitgeist*. Thus, although Galton (1989) concluded that, as far as classroom *practice* was concerned, little had changed in primary education since Plowden, the *ideas and attitudes* of some primary educators were undergoing a renaissance. These renaissant educators and teachers, unfortunately, represented the visible tip of an iceberg, which had an unseen, and much greater mass beneath it, waiting to shipwreck, or at least seriously damage, the recommendations of the imminent TGAT report (1988) on National Curriculum assessment.

Assessment in the National Curriculum: the TGAT report

The new ideas led to a shift to a process-oriented curriculum enshrined in what became the 'Attainment Target 1s' (AT1s) or process skills components of National Curriculum areas, such as mathematics, science and geography, although not without a struggle against those on the National Curriculum Council who wished to emphasise content and knowledge. In its attempt to facilitate inter-school comparisons, the Task Group on Assessment and Testing (TGAT) had the difficult task of marrying formative and summative assessment, and of seeking to strike a balance between assessing process skills and testing knowledge, within the context of the inherently social constructivist and anti-testing mind-set of the primary teaching profession. To do this it proposed the development of Standard Assessment Tasks, possibly reminiscent of tasks developed by the APU, as the more formal means of assessment which would be used alongside teacher assessment (TA). The intention was that the administration of the SATs would be so like children's normal activities that they would not be aware of being assessed. Thus a brave attempt at implementing a form of 'authentic' assessment was put in place.

The assessment, whether by SAT or TA, was to be criterion-referenced, in that it specified behavioural competencies or 'statements of attainment'. After moderation by groups of teachers,[2] the aggregated statements of attainment had then to correspond to one of ten levels of achievement which were to span the eleven years of compulsory schooling (for example, it was expected that children at the end of KS1 would have achieved Level 2). The model was fraught with difficulties in its application. Nuttall (1989; 1993) and Wiliam (1992), for example, discuss its inherent difficulties, and, as Nuttall said of the attempt,

> In an imaginative and trail-blazing set of proposals, TGAT almost managed to find a way to combine assessment for formative, summative and evaluative purposes into a single system that gave equal status to each of the purposes.
>
> (Nuttall 1991, reprinted in Murphy and Broadfoot 1995: 208)

but, as he continued,

> Subsequent developments have squashed this notion irrevocably (if indeed it was ever achievable) – the system that is being developed is incontrovertibly 'high stakes'.

The teachers' difficulties in implementing this system,[3] coupled with considerable protests in 1993 when it was confirmed that SATs were to be administered at eleven and fourteen, began to cause concern about the use of these new procedures. The practical difficulties for teachers who were unused both to working with collaborative groups (a high proportion of teachers at that time: see Chapter 4), and to observing certain children while the rest of the class worked independently, were not foreseen – the hidden part of the aforementioned iceberg. There still remained considerable concern about the workload associated with the 1995 national assessment, particularly at KS1, while at KS2, 80 per cent of the teachers surveyed thought the process stressful for the *pupils*, and over 90 per cent found it stressful (38 per cent very stressful) for *themselves* (ATL 1996b). Sainsbury (1996) provides an interesting 'dramatisation' of these issues in the development of the SATs (with Accountability, Manageability, Authenticity, Reliability and Agency as the cast), while both Abbot *et al.* (1994) and Gipps *et al.* (1995) describe in detail the reality of the teachers' experience when attempting to assess children's performance in this way. Further, given the difficulties inherent in administering them reliably enough to justify their use for 'high stakes' purposes, it was inevitable that these innovative, 'authentic', context-based forms of assessment would be largely replaced by exactly what teachers had feared most, namely, externally marked pencil and paper tests; tests which were just what some right-wing Conservatives had envisaged back in 1979 would be the mechanism by which to raise standards (Gipps and Goldstein 1983).

The tests used in the 1996 ORACLE study

The present study tested children's performance in basic mathematics, reading and language skills in June 1996, four to six weeks before they left the primary phase schools. The tests used were the same as those used in the 1976 ORACLE study, apart from the minor changes to correct anachronisms, such as those discussed in the earlier section on gender bias.[4] The cyclostyled sheets of the 1970s were replaced by three booklets, one for each test, and each with a separate answer sheet designed for optical mark reading, in common with many contemporary published test materials. The tests were administered in standard test conditions, a procedure which, incidentally, highlighted the Year 5 and Year 6 children's familiarity with doing tests in some classes. For example, the transformation of a typical 'groups around tables' classroom, to seating arrangements such that children could not see each other's work, was a well-rehearsed routine, triggered in one classroom by a mere 'Get into your assessment places' from the teacher. In some classes cardboard screens were issued which were erected between children to prevent copying. Three months earlier, however, one observer's fieldnotes recorded the teacher's dilemma, when administering a formal test on behalf of the local secondary school to which the pupils transferred:

> She did not want to raise their levels of apprehension by emphasising that this was a test but by not doing so she caused puzzlement in that they [the pupils] did not totally understand the reason for being made to sit by themselves, not able to consult one another.
>
> (Observer's fieldnotes)

By June 1996, however, familiarity with testing was the norm in the Year 5 and 6 classes.

The ORACLE tests themselves are 'abbreviated' versions of the Richmond Tests of Basic Skills (RTBS, France and Fraser 1975). Each consisted of thirty items for the two older age groups, and up to twenty items for the youngest age group, and required between twenty and thirty minutes' administration time. Galton and Simon (1980) reported high correlations, ranging from 0.86 to 0.89, between children's scores on the ORACLE tests and on the full RTBS. In 1976 the RTBS were new tests, in the forefront of those described as 'criterion referenced' in that they consisted of a series of sub-tests in which items demanding the same type of cognitive operation (e.g. 'mathematical problem solving' or 'the use of capital letters'), were grouped together and arranged in ascending order of difficulty. Galton and Simon (1980) suggest that they are better described as 'domain referenced' however, since even within the sub-tests there are a range of different task demands.

A child's performance can be reported as a profile of scores within each main domain, enabling the teachers to identify any area of relative weakness in the child's profile and teach accordingly. The Language Skills Test components are: Punctuation, Use of Capital Letters, Language Usage, and Spelling. The reading test is divided into sub-tests of Vocabulary and Comprehension; and the Mathematical Skills test is subdivided into two parts, Mathematical Concepts and Problem Solving. The test manual provides a detailed item-by-item classification of the specific skills tested and offers strategies for improving performance in specific areas. (In Appendix 6, Tables 6A1a, 6A1b and 6A1c provide item-by-item details linked with National Curriculum content for the three tests.) All of the test items are in standard multiple-choice format,[5] but in the test of mathematics problem solving, the fourth option is always 'Not given', and in Language Skills it is 'No mistakes', to reduce the likelihood of a child's reliance on recognition or guesswork, as opposed to working out the right answer.

Validity and reliability of the ORACLE tests

Galton and Croll (see Galton and Simon 1980) discuss the validity of the tests at some length. In the absence of a prescribed curriculum, they refer to teachers' aims (Ashton *et al.* 1975) and the curriculum observed in the ORACLE classrooms. The highest ranked aim among the primary teachers of the 1970s was for children to be 'happy, cheerful and well-balanced', and the second was for them to 'read with understanding'. Knowing how to use mathematical techniques in everyday life was ranked joint fifteenth along with 'having a wide vocabulary', while knowledge of the four rules of arithmetic was ranked twentieth. 'Basic grammar' was regarded as merely 'important'. Although spelling was ranked the lowest among aims 'of major importance', nevertheless, it was tested weekly in nearly three-quarters of the classrooms.

In the present study, however, we need not resort to teachers' aims as we have a National Curriculum (NC) against which to test the content and construct validity of the tests, as well as observation-based information concerning the extent to which children had sufficient 'opportunities to learn' the skills we are testing. We will refer again to these when interpreting the test results.

Although the correspondences between NC Programmes of Study and the test items are listed in full in Appendix 6.1, we will summarise the main points of correspondence to illustrate that the tests, although devised over twenty years ago, continue to have a considerable degree of content validity.

The items in the tests of Language Skills are congruent with the NC orders for English at KS2, and relevant extracts from the NC Orders are shown in Appendix 6. For example, the Orders clearly state, that at KS2, under the Key Skills of the Writing Programme of Study (point 2c) pupils should be taught, in punctuation, to:

> use punctuation marks correctly in their writing including full stops, question and exclamation marks, commas, inverted commas, and apostrophes to mark possession.
>
> (DfEE 1995: 15)

The Reading Vocabulary test fits neatly into the NC Writing Programme of Study requirement that pupils should be taught 'to distinguish between words of similar meaning'. The Reading Comprehension test includes three passages, one narrative, one informational and a poem, all three of which are required forms of text for KS2 Reading. According to the Richmond Test manual (Hieronymous *et al.* 1988), the comprehension skills which are tested are: finding the main point of a passage, recognising and understanding important facts and details, implied facts and relationships, understanding how a passage is organised, and being able to evaluate the aspects of the passage.[6] The Key Skills for Reading at KS2 include (point 2b):

> Pupils should be taught to consider in detail the quality and depth of what they read. They should be encouraged to respond imaginatively to the plot, characters, ideas, vocabulary and organisation of language in literature. They should be taught to use inference and

deduction. Pupils should be taught to evaluate the texts they read, and to refer to relevant passages or episodes to support their opinions.

(DfEE 1995: 13)

This covers the relatively narrow content of the ORACLE reading comprehension and vocabulary tests and shows that the implementation of the National Curriculum has by no means invalidated the content of the tests.

Lastly, the task demands in the mathematics tests all fall within the NC Programmes of Study for 'Number', 'Shape, Space and Measures' and requirements of 'Using and Applying Mathematics'.[7] The last, for example, specifies, in point 3a, that pupils should be taught,

to understand and use the language of:
- numbers,
- the properties and movements of shapes,
- measures,
- simple probability,
- relationships, including 'multiple of', 'factor of' and 'symmetrical to'.

(DfEE 1995: 26)

Test reliabilities

Table 6.1 shows the reliability coefficients (Cronbach's alpha) that were obtained based on the internal consistency of the 1996 tests. All of the reliabilities were 0.8 or above, except the short form of the Language Skills tests which was 0.76. These are all acceptable values for the purpose of drawing inferences from the test scores.[8]

Table 6A3 in Appendix 6.3 shows the sub-test reliabilities, in which in the language skills of Punctuation and Use of Capital Letters are too low to support any inferences based solely on these sub-tests. However, the overall Language test reliability can be accepted, since it is not usual practice to quote internal consistency values for sub-tests with relatively few items. For example, in the new NFER Mathematics 7 Test manual only an overall reliability figure is provided, although the twenty-eight items are said to cover five different mathematical processes (Hagues and Courtenay 1994).

Table 6.1 Reliabilities obtained in the ORACLE 1996 tests (Cronbach's alpha)

Test	1996 long N = 389	1996 short N = 623
Mathematics skills	0.83	0.80
Language skills	0.80	0.76
Vocabulary and Reading Comprehension	0.81	0.80

Changes in standards: can we compare like with like?

The test of basic skills, 1976 and 1996

As we have seen earlier, it is always difficult to determine how, or indeed whether, standards have changed, because direct comparability between two sets of scores is difficult to establish. Reynolds and Farrell (1996), for example, list the problems inherent in making international comparisons, which require the assessment of performance on the same skills, understanding or knowledge, with the effects of the many educational and non-educational variables isolated, controlled or accounted for. However, even when making what appears to be a straightforward comparison of children's performance on the same tests across a twenty-year divide, we encounter problems.

This is mainly because the purposes of the 1976 ORACLE study and the 1996 ORACLE studies were not exactly the same. The 1976 study aimed to identify the effects of teaching style on pupil progress. The 1996 study was principally concerned with the effects of transfer across educational phases on children's performance. In the ORACLE 1976 study, therefore tests were carried out in September, at the beginning of school year 1976/7 and again at the end of the school year, in June 1977, so that progress during the year could be related to the styles of teaching to which the children were exposed.[9] In the 1996 study, however, test data were collected at the end of the children's final primary year, and again at the end of their first secondary phase year. The most *direct* comparison therefore is between the children's scores on tests taken sometime in the summer of 1977 with those taken by the present cohort in the summer of 1996. This comparison is shown in Table 6.2.

There are, however, difficulties with the above analysis because we may not be comparing like with like. The 1976 ORACLE analyses of the effects of teaching style were based on the summer 1977 test scores pooled across age group and gender for all the children. This was necessary to optimise the size of the samples of teachers who tended to use each style. We do not know, therefore, whether in the *direct* comparison the samples were matched by age and by gender. If, for example, there were more younger pupils or more boys in the 1996 sample, it might explain a decline in the mean test scores. In order, therefore, to examine whether age and gender have had differential effects on performance and to look at children's performance within the three basic skills areas, we need to refer to the 1976 ORACLE September data, which are broken down according to these categories in Table 3.3 of Galton and Simon (1980: 50).

One way of achieving comparability is to work backwards, that is to ask what a pupil in September 1976 would have scored if the test had been taken in June 1976. Research shows that pupils' scores regress over the summer

147

holidays (Cooper *et al.* 1996), so we would need to make an adjustment for this effect. Beggs and Hieronymous (1968) carried out a study of this regression effect using the Iowa Tests of Basic Skills (ITBS), from which the Richmond Tests were derived, and found varying degrees of regression for different groups of children in the different skills areas. Since we have not used the full ITBS, nor the complete version of the Richmond Tests of Basic Skills, this estimate would be difficult to make.

We therefore decided to work forward and to calculate what a pupil who took the test in September 1976 would have been likely to score in June 1977. To do this we have estimated 'year progress factors' which have been calculated and added to the September 1976 scores to render them '*as if*' the children had taken the tests at the end of the school years in question (i.e. in June 1977 instead of September 1976). The method of calculation is explained in Appendix 6.6.

In summary, therefore, we have used two types of comparison in comparing standards between 1976 and 1996:

1   The *direct comparison* of the end-of year raw score results achieved by children in the summers of 1977 and 1996, regardless of age group or gender.
2   The '*as if*' *comparisons* which enable us to take account of the children's:
    • age groups;
    • performance on the sub-tests within each skill area;
    • gender.

The comparability of the 1976 and 1996 samples

When making the direct comparisons there is a further adjustment to be made. We need to take into account the age composition of the ORACLE 1976 sample which contained almost twice as many eight-year-olds (580) as it did nine- and ten-year-olds (306 and 315 respectively). The effect of this will have been to deflate the overall 'pooled' test results for the 1976 cohort because: (a) younger children get fewer items right; and (b) the eight-year-olds did a shorter test consisting of only twenty items. In the absence of a 'ceiling' effect, the eight-year-olds' scores were converted into percentages on the basis of the total number of items (30) in the tests taken by the nine- and ten-year-old children. Thus, even if an eight-year-old child did get every item correct he/she could only achieve a maximum score of 67 per cent. In order to compare the results of the 1996 cohort with those of the 1976 cohort as fairly as possible, therefore, we constructed a 1996 sample which was drawn at random from the three age groups to reflect the same age group proportions as those in the 1976 ORACLE September sample. The larger proportion of Year 4 children relative to the Year 5 and 6 children should now exert an equivalent deflationary effect on the 1996 results.

The purpose of this rather lengthy foregoing explanation has been to demonstrate our attempt to take the 'worst case' situation in order not to suggest 'no change' or a rise in standards where this does not exist. However, as the next section of the chapter will show, even without the weighted sample in the direct comparison, and in some cases without the substitution of 'as if' scores, the results of the 1996 tests tell the same story: namely that standards of achievement on all three tests appear to have fallen.

Having explained the various adjustments and assumptions that we have made, we now present the results, starting with the simple direct comparison.

ORACLE 1996 tests of basic skills: have standards fallen?

The direct comparison

Figure 6.1 and Table 6.2 show the overall ORACLE 1996 test results, using raw scores pooled from all year groups, and compare these with the equivalent scores for the 1976 children. (Tables 6A4a and 6A4b in Appendix 6.4 show the same comparison based on the raw scores.) The figures reveal a highly significant drop in performance in these tests of Mathematics, Language Skills and Reading between 1976 and 1996. This despite the greater test-taking sophistication of the 1996 children, which would be expected, if anything, to have enhanced their results. Although, as discussed earlier, the content of the tests fell well within the National Curriculum in mathematics

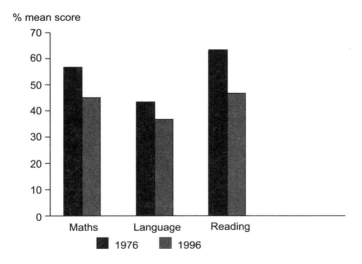

Figure 6.1 Mean percentage scores for the 1976 and 1996 cohorts in the three basic skills

Table 6.2 Comparison of basic skills performance for children in Years 4, 5 and 6 at the end of the school year: 1976 and 1996

| | ORACLE 1976a | | | ORACLE 1996b | | |
	%	s.d.	N	%	s.d.	N
Mathematics	56.0	17.7	409	45.4[c]	20.4	476
Language skills	43.3	17.7	410	36.2[c]	17.3	476
Reading/vocabulary	62.7	19.9	410	47.7[c]	18.6	476

Notes

a ORACLE 1976 figures derived from Tables 4.1, 4.2 and 4.3 of Galton and Simon (1980).

b ORACLE 1996 sample is a weighted random sample derived to reflect the same relative age composition as the 1976 study. Table 6A4a in Appendix 6.4 shows the raw means and unweighted total sample for the 1996 cohort.

c $p < 0.01$ (anova)

and English, the observational evidence of children's 'opportunities to learn' (see Table 4.14) showed a clear reduction in the proportion of observations which included English and mathematics activities. Ironically, the achievement of a broader and better balanced National Curriculum may explain the drop in tested basic skills over twenty years. English has fallen by 6 per cent, from 36 to 30 per cent of the observations, while mathematics observations have fallen by nearly 5 per cent.

This coincided with a drop of over 10 per cent in the time available for teaching basic skills – time which now appears to be devoted to science, technology and other foundation subjects (excluding music and PE which were not observed during the 1976 study). The decrease in the time devoted to teaching basic skills must contribute to the explanation of this fall in performance levels. In 1976, reading was the children's strongest area and language skills their poorest area of performance. In 1996, the decline in reading performance has reduced its mean value to the same level as that for mathematics skills. Language skills, however, still remained the weakest area, although these general comparisons in Table 6.2 may mask differences in performance across the three age groups and within the sub-tests. We examine the effects of these variables in the next section, using the estimated 'as if' scores for the ORACLE 1976 pupils.

The 'as if' comparisons of basic skills performance across three age groups: 1976–96

In Table 6.3 we show the comparative results across the three age groups. As explained earlier, these scores are based on the September 1976 tests and have been adjusted so that it is *as if* we had results for the same children at the end of the 1976–77 school year. These 'as if' scores were then compared with the scores of equivalent groups of pupils tested in the 1996 summer term.

The differences in percentage scores in Table 6.3 showed a deterioration in performance on each of the tests in all three year groups. The overall

Table 6.3 Comparison of 1976 and 1996 overall test results for each age group

	ORACLE 1976[a]			ORACLE 1996		
	8/9[b]	9/10	10/11	Y4[b]	Y 5	Y6
	(mean percentage 'as if' scores)			*(mean percentage scores)*		
Mathematics skills	42[c]	62	75	31[d]	55[d]	62[d]
Language skills	31	49	55	28[d]	41[d]	47[d]
Vocabulary and						
reading comprehension	50	74	86	36[d]	53[d]	61[d]
N children	*580*	*306*	*315*	*235*[e]	*193*	*196*

a Extrapolated from beginning of year 1976 figures in Table 3.3 (Galton *et al.* 1980).
b Scores are taken as a percentage of the total items (30) on longer test.
c Percentages rounded to nearest whole number.
d $p < 0.01$.
e Ns shown are for mathematics; Ns for language skills: 238, 194, 200; Ns for reading: 242, 189, 198.
NB: This Table is shown in full with standard deviations in Appendix 6.4.

differences between the 1976 and the 1996 results were largest in reading and appeared to increase as the children got older. It is important to remember, however, that this study was not a longitudinal one. Consequently, any conclusions which are drawn about year by year progress must be treated with caution.

Comparison of basic skills performance on sub-tests across three age groups

In this section, we examine differences within the sub-tests for each of the three 'basic skill' areas, beginning with mathematics. At this level of comparison, there is considerable uncertainty in applying the 'as if' correction factor to the sub-tests, so their values are not given in the Tables 6.4a–6.4c. In terms of confidence limits, the 'as if' score for a particular sub-test could possibly represent somewhere between a 20 and 50 per cent improvement on the score obtained in September 1976. Thus although no absolute comparisons can be made, it is possible to look at trends across the two decades.

Mathematics sub-tests

In Table 6.4 we compare the 1976 and 1996 cohorts in mathematics skills and also examine overall progress from year to year. The pupils in 1996 recorded higher scores in mathematics concepts than in problem solving, which is a reversal of the position in ORACLE 1976, when the children were more successful at problem solving. This is made particularly clear by looking at the columns headed Y5 June 1996 and 10/11 September 1976. Here we see the results of same age children in the two cohorts

Table 6.4 a: Comparison of 1976 and 1996 children's scores by year group on the test of mathematics skills

	8/9[a] Sept[b] 1976	8/9[a] 'June[c] 1977'	Y4[a] June 1996	9/10 Sept 1976	9/10 'June 1977'	Y5 June 1996	10/11 Sept 1976	10/11 'June 1977'	Y6 June 1996
Maths concepts	28		32	41		58	51		64
Problem solving	30		29	46		50	53		59
All mathematics	29	42	31[d]	43	62	55[d]	52	75	62[d]
N	580	580	235	306	306	193	315	315	196

a All totals as a percentage of 30 items although the 8/9 and Y4 children did a 20-item maths test.

b ORACLE 1976 figures from Table 3.3, Galton *et al.* 1980: 50.

c 'as if' scores: see Appendix 6.6.

d $p < 0.01$ for the difference between 'June 1977' 'as if' score and 1996 score.

separated only by the summer holiday, after which Year 5 pupils moved to Year 6. Even allowing for a reduction in the 1976 scores for summer holiday regression (Cooper *et al.* 1996), the 1996 performance appears relatively stronger in mathematics concepts, but weaker than the 1976 in problem solving. This reversal could have arisen as a result of the general drop in reading skills, since most of the questions on the latter mathematics sub-test were 'word problems' which required the pupil first to comprehend the question before he/she could exercise the appropriate mathematical skills. An alternative, and more likely explanation, however, is the decrease in the time set aside for the mathematics curriculum and problem solving activity in particular. Our observations show that, compared to the 10 per cent of time given to what in 1976 was classified as 'abstract' mathematics (which included problem solving), there has been a reduction in 1996 by 6 per cent (see Table 4.15).

Language skills sub-tests

The figures in Table 6.5 indicate that there have also been changes in performance within the various language sub-tests since 1976. Performance in the spelling test appears to have deteriorated considerably, with the 1996 children in Years 4 and 6 being no better spellers than the previous generation had been at the start of a school year. Year 5 pupils appear to have done considerably worse. On the Capitals and Punctuation sub-tests, however, the 1996 children did better than their 1976 counterparts who took the test at the beginning of the same school year. This superiority was maintained, even if allowance was made for the 1976 children's progress over a school year. Furthermore by comparing the 1996 Year 5 scores with the September 1976 ten/eleven-year-olds' scores, we can see that the 1996 children's scores were higher than those of the oldest 1976 children at the start of their next school year. However, given the low base from which the 1976 cohort operated, and also the lack of internal consistency recorded for this sub-test, the above result should perhaps be treated with a degree of caution.

Nevertheless, the skills of punctuating correctly and using capital letters are an important part of the English National Curriculum, and we tentatively suggest that this may explain the improvement in this case.

The decline in spelling performance is more difficult to explain, particularly as it is one of the English SATs at KS2. Spelling tests were a regular feature of classroom life even in 1976, as Galton and Croll (see Galton and Simon 1980) pointed out. Several hypotheses can be put forward to account for the deterioration in performance over the two decades. The first has to do with recent approaches to teaching literacy and the possible subsequent reduction in the emphasis on the teaching of phonics. Although neither of the two ORACLE studies collected information about how the children were first introduced to reading and writing, we suspect that while the use

Table 6.5 Comparison of the 1976 and 1996 children's scores by year group on the test of Language Skills

Language skills	8–9[a] Sept 1976	'June 1977'	Y4 'June 1996'	9–10 Sept 1976	'June 1977'	Y5 'June 1996'	10–11 Sept 1976	'June 1977'	Y6 'June 1996'
Spelling	26		28	43		34	48		49
Use of capitals	12		22	25		45	32		47
Punctuation	18		30	26		40	25		42
Usage	27		31	38		45	40		52
Total Language	21	31[b]	28[b]	33	49[b]	41[b]	37	55[b]	47[b]
N	580	500	238	306	306	194	315	315	200

Notes
a Totals based on 30-item version of the test.
b p < 0.01 for difference between 'as if' total scores and Sept. 1996 total scores.

of 'phonics' has not been abandoned, the frequency with which the approach is used has declined over the last decade. This is because there has been an increased emphasis on working with books chosen for their literary appeal, as against working through reading schemes which mainly consist of words chosen for their phonic structure, or visual profile. The result may have been to reduce children's exposure to exemplars of phonic rules or distinctive outlines and this could have had a negative effect on spelling ability.

The second hypothesis relates to the overall reduction in 'opportunities to learn' in the 1996 primary classroom. Compared to 1976, observations of curriculum activities show that the proportion of time given to English has fallen from 36 to 28 per cent (Table 4.16). Within this overall figure, the proportion of observations involving writing tasks associated with English has more than halved; down from 30 per cent to 14 per cent (Table 4.16). Since the data presented in Chapter 3 also pointed to a decline in the amount of time teachers spent correcting work during lessons, it appears that children are getting less support in this key area, even though spelling drills and quizzes continue to be a regular feature of life in the primary classroom in much the same way as they were two decades ago

In summary, therefore, the findings indicate an overall decline in scores on tests of language skills over the two decades. This has arisen mainly because of a deterioration in spelling performance across all three age groups, mitigated, in part, by evidence of a slight improvement in the use of correct punctuation and capital letters.

Reading sub-tests

As shown earlier, reading sustained the largest drop in performance between 1976 and 1996. Table 6.6 shows that this decline extended across all age cohorts, such that the scores of the 1996 children at the end of each school year were about the same as those of the 1976 children starting that school year. The consistency in the magnitude of these differences in scores across the age groups allows us to say with a degree of confidence that today's children are lagging behind those of 1976 by at least a school year.

The table also shows that, whereas the 1976 children did better on the comprehension items than on vocabulary, the reverse is true for 1996. The recent emphasis on books and reading for understanding suggests that there should be gains in both areas. It can be argued, however, that the real test of the 'whole books' approach to learning to read must wait until these pupils mature as adults. Only then will it be evident whether these young people read books more frequently than their parents who learned to read through a more traditional approach.

To sum up, the 1996 primary children appear to lag behind the 1976 children's performance on all three tests of basic skills. Additionally, the main

Table 6.6 Comparison of the 1976 and 1996 children's scores by year group on the test of Vocabulary and Reading Comprehension

	8/9[a]		Y4[a]	9/10		Y5	10/11		Y6
	Sept 1976	'June 1977'	June 1996	Sept 1976	'June 1977'	June 1996	Sept 1976	'June 1977'	June 1996
Vocabulary	33		36	47		56	51		63
Comprehension	35		37	52		51	62		59
Total Reading	34	50[b]	37[b]	50	74[b]	53[b]	58	86[b]	61[b]
N	580		242	306		189	315		198

Notes
a Totals based on 30-item version of the test.
b $p < 0.01$

conclusions to be drawn from the tables are that the children in our 1996 study found mathematics problem solving, reading comprehension and spelling relatively more difficult than did their 1976 counterparts. Given that the issue of declining standards has become a central feature of the contemporary debate, it is surely important, in the light of the above findings, that we make a careful appraisal of all the evidence before apportioning blame for this situation. This includes the evidence presented in the earlier chapters based upon careful observation of classroom practice. It is all too easy to lay the blame for this drop in children's performance at the feet of their primary teachers. But if we wish to improve matters as quickly as possible, then it may be advisable to take a more dispassionate view and consider a number of other alternative explanations for the fall in the test scores. This is what we shall now attempt to do.

Notes

1 Gipps *et al.* (1983) reported a major reduction in the number of LEAs using English and mathematics attainment tests between 1960 and 1972, although intelligence testing remained a common practice.
2 The teachers, however, were without previous experience of the process of moderation (unlike their secondary counterparts), and were from schools which, through the simultaneous introduction of Local Financial Management, were acutely aware of local competition for pupils. They were expected to disregard, in some saintly fashion, the potential effects of the outcomes of the assessment on their schools' recruitment and subsequent resources, and moderate completely equitably.
3 Nuttall (1991) reported, for example, that the 1991 pilot SATs which were supposed to take thirty hours, actually took nearly fifty hours' administration time and the same amount in out-of-hours preparation and reporting.
4 Given today's levels of sophistication and sensitivity in these matters, the ORACLE tests might be expected to have eliminated gender bias. Nevertheless, some items, and in particular two of the passages chosen for the comprehension test, might appeal more to boys than girls: one is about a father and son having an accident in their car; the other, a poem extolling the power and ferocity of a male eagle. A third piece not only implied stereotypical gender roles but also placed a moral value on these. A few words were changed for the 1996 tests to neutralise the more obvious of these biases, and it is acknowledged that this might have depressed boys' scores on these tests compared to the previous version, where if unaltered, the words might have artificially inflated them.
5 Although multiple-choice tests are said to favour boys, Stobart *et al.* (1992a) report conflicting evidence from Murphy (1982), who suggested that this effect had decreased, and cite Schmitt *et al.* (1991), whose review concluded that the effect remains strong. If this is so, then the boys' test results should be considered to be enhanced on tests such as those used here.
6 In terms of the observed curriculum, work on passages occurred in 10 per cent of the observation sets, but work involving poems was very rarely observed (0.8 per cent).
7 ORACLE 1976 included assessment of study skills, which included activities which would appear in the Mathematics attainment target: Data Handling. In

the RTBS similar tasks are covered in the work study tests. In ORACLE 1996 no attempt was made to measure study skills. We acknowledge, however, that the present tests represent only a narrow range of the mathematical skills listed in the NC Orders. For example, our tests do not examine pupils' use of calculators, and in the present study we have not assessed pupils' skills in data handling or use of co-ordinates, which were assessed as study skills in ORACLE 1976.

8 The full list of sub-test reliabilities appears in Appendix 6, Table 3 and shows very low internal reliability in the Punctuation and Use of Capitals sub-tests. These sub-tests contain very small numbers of items, however, and even in the full RTBS these sections have the lowest, though acceptable, reliabilities of all the sub-tests (Hieronymous *et al.* 1988).

9 Galton and Simon (1980) refer to these results as the 'pre-tests' and 'post-tests' respectively in 'Progress and Performance in the Primary Classroom': Tables 3.3, 4.1, 4.2 and 4.3; Appendix C.

7

WHY HAVE STANDARDS FALLEN?

Given the detailed analysis in the previous chapter, we arrive at a conclusion that some aspects of mathematics and language performance have stood still but that, in general, the scores on the tests of mathematics, language and reading have all declined over two decades, with the biggest drop in reading. There seem to be at least three possible explanations:

- That these findings are the result of the 'disastrous mistakes [that have been] made in modern education, the result of progressive ideas which are now in the ascendant... so that students do not know as much as they should' (Cox and Dyson 1969: 6). As we saw in Chapter 1, this theme has been often repeated throughout the last two decades.
- That the decline in the performance of boys has contributed substantially to these differences, in that a separate analysis of the results by gender might indicate that the fall in standards is partially a social and cultural phenomenon, and not attributable to a general all-round educational decline.
- That the decline is a consequence of the introduction of the National Curriculum, which does not test the same things in the same way as the ORACLE measures and that, further, the broad and balanced curriculum now in operation restricts the amount of time available for teachers to teach basic skills of the kind assessed here.

We will deal with each of these possibilities in turn, beginning with the argument that the decline in standards is the result of poor teaching, which has largely come about because of the continued adherence by a substantial part of the profession to aspects of progressive ideology. A little thought, however, indicates that such an explanation does not hold water. Even if we accept, in the face of all the evidence, that there was a primary revolution based upon progressive ideas following the Plowden (1967) Report, it is generally accepted that this revolution was in decline following the intervention by the then Prime Minister, James Callaghan, in his 1976 Ruskin speech, and the accession of Margaret Thatcher to the premiership

159

in 1979. Whole class teaching, as we saw in Table 3.1, had increased by the time that studies such as that by Mortimore *et al.* (1988) had taken place in the mid-1980s and, furthermore, Mortimore could find little evidence of any integrated classroom activity, a supposed feature of progressivism. Even more conclusive, however, are the results from the PRISMS study (Galton and Patrick 1990) which took place over a three-year period beginning in 1983. This study involved sixty-eight schools from nine local authorities, with no school having more than one hundred pupils on roll. In the middle year of the project, eight-, nine- and ten-year-olds were tested using a shorter, but representative, form of the 1976 ORACLE tests. PRISMS pupils did better overall than their ORACLE counterparts on punctuation, language use and spelling. On vocabulary, mathematical concepts and problems the younger eight-year-old PRISMs children out-performed their ORACLE counterparts, but for the two older groups of children the results were more even.[1]

At the time, we interpreted this result cautiously: first, because eight years had elapsed since the ORACLE study, and we argued that the increased emphasis on testing arising out of the development of the APU could have meant there had been a general all-round rise in scores since 1976. Second, we were aware that, because of the social class composition of small schools – the result of a movement of population among the mobile, prosperous, well-educated and articulate middle class from city suburbs to rural villages – it was only to be expected that small schools should out-perform larger ones. We, therefore, reached a conservative conclusion that, in terms of their performance on these tests, pupils in small schools did no worse than their peers in larger suburban and urban settings.

However, in terms of the present discussion, whether the pupils tested in 1984 in these small schools actually performed equally as well as, or even better than, the pupils tested in 1976 is irrelevant. The important point is that they did not do *worse*. This means that the decline in standards described in the previous section must have begun or accelerated over the period from 1984 until 1996. Unless, therefore, we wish to claim that the drift to progressivism and the resultant poor teaching has also been on the increase since 1984, we must conclude that this present decline in pupil performance over the two decades has largely come about because of other factors.

Gender differences in basic skills' performance

The second possible explanation is that differences between pupils' scores in 1976 and 1996 are the result of social and cultural changes associated with the under-achievement of boys. We have already examined in the previous chapter the possible gender bias within the test items. Now we will look at the scores of boys and girls separately and compare them over the two decades.

Table 7.1 Test results in basic skills for boys and girls in 1976 and 1996[a]

	Mean percentage scores for end of school year[b]			
	1976/7 boys[b]	*1976/7 girls*[b]	*1996 boys*[c]	*1996 girls*[c]
Mathematics skills	57	56	47	44
Language skills	40	43	34	38
Vocabulary and reading comprehension	65	65	47	49
N	205[d]	205[d]	242	234

Notes
a All differences between the 1976 and 1996 scores are significant at $p < 0.01$ for boys and girls.
b September 1976 scores from Table 3.3 (Galton *et al.* 1980) converted into 'as if' scores for June 1977 (see Appendix 6).
c Estimated, since ORACLE 1976 figures are not available (see Appendix 6).
d Sample made to reflect age proportions of the 1976 sample.

Girls and boys achieved almost identical overall test scores in 1976, as shown by the first two columns in Table 7.1. The reading scores were identical, but boys did 'slightly better' in mathematics and girls did 'slightly better' in language skills. The biggest difference found was of 4 per cent in the use of capital letters (Galton and Simon 1980). In contrast, gender differences in performance have emerged at several points in our analyses of the 1996 test results. In this summary, we will look first at the overall results, compared with those of 1976, and then look in more detail at gender differences in performance within the 1996 tests.

Table 7.1 which uses two sets of adjusted scores (as explained in Appendix 6.5) so that comparisons can be made more easily, shows a significant drop in performance in all three tests since 1976. The drop in mathematics skills performance was very slightly greater (12 per cent) for girls than for boys (10 per cent). In language skills, the scores for both sexes have deteriorated by about the same amount. In reading, the drop in the boys' result was very slightly greater (18 per cent) than the girls' (16 per cent).

In Table 7.2 we look at overall gender differences within the basic skill areas of each test by comparing pooled data for the year groups. The results for the 1976 children are included, but this time based on their actual beginning-of-school-year scores. Table 7.2 shows no gender difference in performance in mathematics skills. As in 1976, the boys did 'slightly better' than the girls, with a slightly bigger gap in favour of boys in problem solving, but the differences between the test scores were not significant. In language skills, however, there were more striking differences within the 1996 sample. In particular, the 1996 results showed girls' superior performance in each language skill except the use of capital letters. This result adds to the evidence that shows that girls are increasing their lead in language skills at primary level, and matches the findings of the 1996 SATs:

Table 7.2 Overall girl/boy differences in tested basic skills for ORACLE 1976 and ORACLE 1996

Test	Boys Sept. 1976 (mean % score)	Girls Sept. 1976 (mean % score)	Boys June 1996 (mean % score)	Girls June 1996 (mean % score)
Maths concepts	38	36	51	49
Maths problems	41	39	47	43
Maths total	*40*	*38*	*49*	*47*
N	*586*	*615*	*318*	*306*
Spelling	35	37	33[a]	40[a]
Capitals	19	23	36	39
Punctuation	22	22	35[b]	38[b]
Usage	33	33	39[b]	46[b]
Language total	*27*	*29*	*35[b]*	*40[b]*
N	*586*	*615*	*321*	*311*
Vocabulary	41	41	49[b]	53[b]
Comprehension	46	46	47	49
Reading total	*44*	*44*	*48[b]*	*51[b]*
N	*586*	*615*	*316*	*313*

Notes
a $p < 0.01$
b $p < 0.05$

> As with most other assessments of children's achievement in English, girls continue to achieve significantly better than boys in both the tests and Teacher Assessment.
>
> (SCAA 1997: 3)

In reading, again the girls out-performed the boys significantly in the 1996 cohort in vocabulary, but, perhaps surprisingly, there was no significant difference in comprehension skills. We will look for further clarification of this in the later section which examines the item difficulty levels, but first we will investigate the 1996 data further to see whether gender differences in performance are in greater evidence in any particular age group.

Table 7.3 is derived from a full Table in Appendix 6A5, which shows boys' and girls' scores for each sub-test and each year group in the 1996 study. It shows the results of subtracting the girls' mean percentage score from that of the boys in each category, revealing an age-related pattern. The youngest boys vastly out-perform the youngest girls in mathematics, but there is, at this stage, no significant difference between them in literacy skills. Among the older groups of children, however, gender differences in mathematics skills were no longer evident, but there were now differences in literacy, such that girls performed significantly better than the boys in both language and reading skills.

It is worth pointing out that in the language and reading tests, although ten of the differences did not reach statistical significance, seventeen out of

Table 7.3 Differences between boys' and girls' scores by year group

	1996 Year 4 boys–girls % difference	1996 Year 5 boys–girls % difference	1996 Year 6 boys–girls % difference
Spelling	−8	−7	−9[a]
Capitals	−4	−6[b]	−3
Punctuation	+3	−6[b]	−6[b]
Usage	−5	−8[b]	−11[a]
Language total	−4	−6[b]	−8[a]
Vocabulary	−5	−6[b]	−5[b]
Comprehension	−1	−5	−1
Reading total	−3	−5[b]	−2
Maths concepts	+7[a]	+1	−2
Problem solving	+10[a]	+2	+1
Maths total	+9[a]	+2	−1

Notes
a $p < 0.01$
b $p < 0.05$

the possible eighteen differences favoured girls. Too much should not be read into this pattern, however, partly because it might be an artefact of the reading demand (which would favour the girls), or the gender bias of the items within the tests themselves (which would favour the boys). We must remember too that this was a cross-sectional, and not a longitudinal study. While, therefore, we can attempt to link these effects to differences between age groups, we cannot talk about progressive changes from Year 4 to Year 5 of primary school.

To sum up this section on gender differences in tested performance, the equivalence between boys and girls found in 1976 has remained intact in mathematics, but has broken down in the tests of language skills and reading. Girls, overall, have achieved higher scores in spelling, punctuation, usage and reading vocabulary. The gender differences vary according to age, however, with boys achieving significantly higher scores in Year 4 in mathematics, and girls doing better in Years 5 and 6 in language and vocabulary skills. In searching for explanations for the overall decline in standards, our conclusion must be that these are not principally the result of either gender bias in the tests or superior performance of girls, since the latter's superiority was often not large nor was it consistent across all tests and across all age groups. Clearly, however, it has been a factor.

We therefore turn to the third of our possible explanations, the effect of changes brought about by the introduction of the National Curriculum. In the previous chapter, when discussing the validity of the ORACLE tests, we observed that some items were more closely associated with specific attainment targets than were others. By charting changes in performance over the two decades on specific items (where this information is available), we can examine the extent to which teaching to the National Curriculum has required some aspects of mathematics, language and reading to receive less attention, with consequent deterioration in pupil performance on corresponding items from the Richmond Tests.

Item facilities: how difficult were the test items?

To engage in this analysis we need to compare the item facility indices, typically expressed as proportions or as percentages of the children who answered a question correctly. A facility index of 0.76, for example, would inform us that 76 per cent of the testees responded to the item correctly. The facility index is, therefore, an indication of the ease or difficulty of a particular item on the test. Easy items have high facilities, and in timed tests, items are usually arranged in ascending order of difficulty based on these indices (i.e. pupils begin with items with high facilities before moving to items with gradually reducing values). A full list of item facilities for boys and girls in each year group appears in Appendix 6.2. This shows that, overall, the order of the 1996 ORACLE test items matched this desired pattern.

Mathematics skills[2]

The mathematics test had two components, namely 'mathematics concepts' and 'problem solving'. The mathematics concept items are set out either as simple problems, such as 'Al's mother bought 1 dozen oranges...', or as straightforward arithmetic equations. In the 1996 cohort, the facilities followed a smooth descending progression, from over 85 per cent of the children who answered the first few items correctly, to under 20 per cent who were unable to answer the last few items correctly. More than 70 per cent of the Year 5 and Year 6 children could do items involving addition, subtraction and shape; 60 to 70 per cent could answer items involving measures, particularly time and money correctly; but less than 45 per cent could answer items involving division, or number operations involving fractions, and decimals. The most difficult items, with facilities of under 20 per cent involved recognition of fractional and decimal fraction equivalence and a division item involving the expression 'n'. Year by year progression was as expected, with mean facility levels over 60 per cent for the first four items at Year 4, the first seven items at Year 5 and the first eleven items at Year 6.

These findings parallel almost exactly the information provided by Galton and Simon (1980) for the 1976 children, and show that little has changed in arithmetic in twenty years, since they also match closely the results of the SATs at age eleven in 1996, as the following extracts show:

Children's performance on the tests generally shows:

- As in 1995 there is a more secure understanding of addition and subtraction than of multiplication and division.
- Questions on fractions and percentages were not well answered even by the children achieving the highest level.
- Children showed a good understanding of basic shapes and their properties...

and

- In both tests and Teacher Assessment, proportionally more boys than girls achieved level 5.

(SCAA 1997: 11, 12)

To return to the gender difference issue, in the present study, more boys than girls could answer items correctly in all year groups, although the differences were significant only in Year 4. It is worth mentioning again, however, that a high proportion of the items in the mathematics test, particularly in the test of problem solving, included boys' names or were about topics such as cars, ships, trains and sport. This might have had a demotivating effect on the girls.

English

In Table 7.4 we can compare the scores of children of about the same age by looking at the 1976/7 ten to eleven-year-olds and the 1996 children who were ending Year 5.

The 1996 results are shown separately for boys and girls because the differences between their facility levels were so distinct. Starting with punctuation, 22 per cent *more* of the 1996 Year 5 girls recognised the omission of a question mark, but in spelling, 26 per cent *fewer* 1996 girls recognised 'radeo' as a mis-spelling, although in 1976, 86 per cent of the children had spotted this. 'Feild' is less likely to be spelled correctly by today's children; only 45 per cent of the girls and 36 per cent of the boys recognised the incorrect 'e' before 'i' compared with 57 per cent in 1976, although more children spotted 'gloomey' as a mis-spelling in 1996. According to Galton *et al.* (1980), spelling was the strongest area of the 1976 children's language skills, but their 'use of capital letters' was 'rather poorer'. As shown when the mean test scores were presented in the previous chapter, the 1996 children showed an inversion of that situation. The remaining striking feature of the language skills item facilities is that the girls found the items easier than did the boys in most cases, and this gender difference was more marked in Year 6 in the tests of usage and punctuation. The greatest difficulties were in the use of apostrophes, speech marks and commas, but the 1996 children were able to recognise the omission of a question mark and a full stop.

As in the case of mathematics, these results are also reflected in the 1996 English SAT scores for eleven-year-olds. In the SAT Writing test, for example,

Table 7.4 Item facilities in language skills for ten-year-olds in 1976 and 1996

Language skills	1976 10/11 year olds Item facilities (%)	1996 Year 5 children Item facilities (%)	
	boys and girls Sept 1976	boys June 1996	girls June 1996
Punctuation			
question mark	31	36	53[a]
Usage			
me and him	67	63	71
Us boys	40	30	31
delightfulest	24	26	31
Spelling			
radeo	86	50	60
feild	57	36	45
gloomey	18	19	26
Reading: Vocabulary			
even	> 80	81	88
healed	> 80	74	82
suburb	< 25	34	25
leisure	< 25	37	58[a]

Note
a $p < 0.01$ Significance of gender difference.

it was reported that children had most difficulties with speech marks, commas and apostrophes, while in spelling:

> many of the errors suggest that children are not properly analysing the sounds in the words and then relating these to different spelling patterns. Other errors ... appear because the children fail to apply their knowledge of common transformations or spelling patterns, and as a result resort to their knowledge of phonological relationships to spell relatively common words.
>
> (SCAA 1997: 7)

In the SATs, it seems that the children 'are *not* analysing the sounds in words and applying them to spelling patterns', but that they *are* using phonological relationships to spell common words – that is, they are using 'phonics' but for the wrong words – such are the irregularities of English spelling.

Vocabulary and reading comprehension

In 1976, reading, and specifically 'reading comprehension' was the children's most successful basic skill. The recent emphasis on understanding and love of literature should have sustained, if not increased, this strength, and yet, as shown in the previous chapter, the 1996 children found reading comprehension much more difficult than did the 1976 children, although they found the vocabulary test relatively easier. Few of the 1996 children had difficulties with the first passage on the test, however, which is narrative text. Over 67 per cent of the Year 4 and well over 80 per cent of the Year 6 children were able to answer the first four items correctly, showing that they could identify and understand implied facts and relationships, and generalise correctly from the meaning of the passage. The girls' item facilities were higher than the boys' in most of the items, particularly in Years 5 and 6. In the second passage, which is informational text, 40 per cent of Year 4, about 50 per cent of Year 5, and over 60 per cent of Year 6 could identify important and implied facts and details, but only about 35 per cent of each year group could select a title which expressed the main purpose of the passage. Girls, in Years 5 and 6, however, were significantly better at this than the boys. Significantly more boys than girls in Years 4 and 6 were able to answer a comprehension question dealing with the various uses of nutmeg, but there were no other differences between boys and girls in this section. This would be slightly surprising, if the culinary theme interested girls more than boys, except for the fact that the passage was really about the dishonest sale of sawdust in place of nutmeg.

The final piece, a poem about the power and isolation of a male eagle, represented a considerable leap in item difficulty, as Gray (1980) pointed out, and was not part of the Year 4 test. Less than 60 per cent of the children could answer any of the items. Of those that could, items testing ability to deduce the meaning of words were easiest, while less than 20 per cent could abstract the main idea of the poem. Interestingly, boys were more likely than girls to get these difficult items right.

In the vocabulary test, all age groups in 1996 performed well in the shorter form of the vocabulary test. The best-known words, with facilities of well over 80 per cent at all ages, were 'final' and 'destroy', while the most difficult words, understood by under 25 per cent of the Year 4 and under 40 per cent of the Year 6, were 'fairly' and 'explain'. There were considerable gender differences in the vocabulary test in Years 5 and 6, but not in Year 4. The older girls were significantly more likely to know the meanings of 'final', 'healed', 'weed' and 'knit' than boys, and the last three might arguably align with feminine interests. 'Destroy' was the only word where there was no apparent gender bias across all year groups.

Comparing the 1996 facilities with those of the 1976 children, Table 7.4 shows little difference on the easier words, but slightly more of the 1996 children knew the meaning of the difficult words 'suburb' and 'leisure', perhaps, as a result of work done in National Curriculum geography.

To conclude this section, the item facilities reflect the general drop in performance on the tests in 1996, although a small number of items that proved difficult in 1976 were relatively easy for the 1996 cohort. The pattern of the item facilities of the vocabulary test, the more difficult spellings and the comprehension tests suggest that today's children may have slightly wider vocabularies, and we might speculate that this is a positive result of learning to read with 'real books' and a broader curriculum. But again, these results are not consistent enough or large enough to explain the major part of the decline in standards in terms of the changes in task demand since the introduction of the National Curriculum.

Detecting the effect of the National Curriculum

To sum up, in a search for an explanation for the decline in standards we have rejected the explanation that is due to progressive teaching methods. Part of the decline can be attributed to gender differences, particularly on the language tests, but these differences are neither large enough nor consistent enough to 'provide the total picture'. Increasingly, therefore, our attention is focused upon the extent to which the National Curriculum may have influenced these results. As we have seen, the direct positive effects appear to be the slight improvement in performance in basic technical aspects of writing, such as punctuation. In mathematics, children are proficient at correctly answering items involving basic arithmetic concepts and straightforward questions about shape and measures, all topics emphasised in the National Curriculum. The cost of these improvements, however, may have been in the areas of comprehension and spelling, in English, and problem solving skills in mathematics.

Turning to the possible indirect effects of the National Curriculum, the general fall in performance in mathematics and English may be an unintended consequence of the expansion of subjects such as science, history and geography into the time once occupied by practice in these basic skills. As Galton and Fogelman (1998) and the PACE studies (Pollard and Broadfoot 1997) show, the process of implementing a broad and balanced National Curriculum has existed uncomfortably alongside continued concern about falling standards in 'the basics'. The National Curriculum Council and its successors, SCAA, now the QCA, appear to have succeeded in broadening the curriculum experienced by primary children, and in so doing must be regarded as having improved educational standards, at least qualitatively. The recent results of SATs and Teacher Assessment (SCAA 1997) show that primary children can now demonstrate scientific processes, such as carrying out fair tests, and have acquired concepts of forces, for example, which were probably not part of the repertoire of most children in 1976. This expansion in children's skills, knowledge and understanding clearly represents an improvement in educational standards of one kind.

We also saw in Chapters 3 and 4 that the National Curriculum appeared to have encouraged teachers to place greater emphasis on whole class teaching, which mainly consisted of direct instruction. Teachers have been mainly concerned to deliver curriculum content and not to engage in curriculum processes. A consequence of this shift in practice has been the decline in both task supervision interactions and what we termed *silent* or *non-interactions*. The latter included monitoring, listening to pupils report on their work, and marking work while sitting alongside the pupil. It is just on such occasions that a mis-spelt word tends to be pointed out. There is now, clearly, less time for such immediate feedback of this kind, which is known to be very important in reinforcing whole class practice drills.

In addition to this reduction in teacher activity of the above kind, this broadening of the curriculum has perhaps also been at the expense of the time available for the more cognitively challenging aspects of numeracy and literacy, namely problem solving and literary comprehension. The only area of modest improvement has been in the most basic para-literary skills of being able to 'speak proper', use capital letters and punctuate sentences correctly. These are all aspects of the curriculum that have been given prominence over the last few years. Our conclusion concerning the fall in standards is that it mostly reflects this change in emphasis between the curriculum of the 1970s which was narrower across subject areas but may have offered more breadth within the basic skills, and the broader, more balanced 1990s curriculum with its shift to the technical or mechanical aspects of basic skills.

Conclusion

Before leaving the question of national standards, we need to address the nature of the somewhat problematic relationship between teaching and assessment. We began to open up this issue in the discussion at the beginning of Chapter 6 when discussing developments such as the APU and TGAT. After the considerable investment in the development of techniques of assessment suitable for use in a broad and challenging primary curriculum, the gains (such as they are) are precisely those which are most easily measured by means of tests. These competencies are most susceptible to what Askew *et al.* (1997) have called 'transmission teaching'. In their study of effective teachers of numeracy, however, they found that the most effective practitioners were those characterised by what they termed a 'connectionist' approach, and, interestingly, not those who had the highest qualifications in mathematics. Askew *et al.* express the concern that reports of low standards of numeracy may lead increasingly to the adoption of transmission modes of teaching. The Numeracy Task Force consultation paper, (DfEE 1998e) appears to offer hope, however, in that it stresses 'genuine communication about mathematics' in which teachers give pupils the opportunity 'not only to show what they know, but to explain the reasons behind it and suggest creative ways of tackling new problems' (para. 42). The report goes on to say that teachers must ask open questions and provide cognitively challenging problems in interactive whole class settings (para. 43). Yet, at the top of the list of 'desired outcomes' are:

- All children have the opportunity to take part regularly in oral and mental work that develops their calculation strategies and recall skills;
- Teachers know how to illustrate, demonstrate and explain mathematical concepts, offering models and contexts from which key ideas can be extracted;

(DfEE 1998 d: 51)

and these points are coupled with high praise for education systems that emphasise oral and mental practice in working with numbers no greater than 99 until the age of nine (para. 28). While the current numeracy and literacy hour proposals appear to offer opportunities for a balance of organisational strategies and teaching which should cover a range of levels of challenge, the emphasis on a large number of very narrowly specified objectives, at least in literacy, places a strong emphasis on the less challenging aspects of this curriculum: i.e. those areas that are easier to assess.

As Plowden (1967) pointed out long ago, we have considerable experience of the development of sophisticated methods of assessment, as shown subsequently by the endeavours of the APU and TGAT. The more subtle the learning to be assessed, the more sensitive the form of assessment must be, and so the more difficult the development of a means to make valid and reliable judgements of achievement, as Terwilliger (1997) has shown. In the effort to drive up standards in England, it is surely important to continue in the attempt to develop reliable procedures for implementing systems of authentic assessment in order to tap these more subtle aspects of learning. As Daugherty (1997) suggests, this may be achieved through the use of frameworks for teacher assessment, as well as through standard tasks and tests. As it is, the proposed literacy and numeracy programmes may simply hone children's abilities to perform simple operations which can now be accomplished with increasing speed and accuracy by machines, provided that *their users know how to exploit them*. Instead, we need to ensure that all children know how to exploit the technology to solve their problems. In other words, as children's horizons expand, so does the need for a broad curriculum consisting of cognitively challenging tasks and appropriately sophisticated and valid forms of assessment, whose reliability would increase as teachers gained more experience, confidence and faith in its value. This will not be achieved, however, as long as we have such 'high stakes' assessment – as long as teachers feel that the aim of assessment is to move their schools up the league table, rather than to support children's learning.

These last paragraphs have begun to touch once more on matters first raised in Chapter 1 where we considered the nature of present society and the appropriate education for a child such as Hayley. We shall now, there-fore, take up the issue of primary education in the next millennium, having first summarised the main findings to emerge from this present study.

Notes

1 Details of these results can be found in the full report (Galton *et al.* 1987). Reading was not included on this occasion in an effort to shorten the time taken up by the testing. One of the reasons for this decision, interestingly enough in view of the dis-cussion in Chapter 6, was that many of the schools were already carrying out their own programmes of standardised testing.
2 In *Progress and Performance in the Primary Classroom* (Galton *et al.* 1980: 50–52) fewer details of the facility indices for mathematics were given in the text, in contrast to English. For this reason, no table of comparisons is available for mathe-matics, unlike Table 7.4 for English in this chapter.

8

PRIMARY EDUCATION FOR THE MILLENNIUM

We began this book by speculating on the differences between the 1970s classroom experience of our semi-fictional parent, Donna, and her own eldest child, Hayley, some twenty years later. We concluded that on the surface little had changed, a view supported by the evidence collected in Chapter 2. In that chapter, we saw that the physical layout of primary classrooms has remained largely the same, despite research evidence collected over the twenty years that sitting children around tables in mixed-sex groups and requiring them to work on individual activities, the most common arrangement, generally led to the highest levels of off-task behaviour. A number of studies have suggested that seating arrangements should be more flexible so that a better fit is obtained between the context and the purpose of the task (Hastings *et al.* 1996).

The above conclusion is based on a summary of five studies over the period of 1979 to 1995. When children were seated in groups the average time on-task was around 60 per cent, whereas when children were placed in rows the percentage time on-task increased to an average of around 78 per cent. However, in summarising these results, these researchers note that such flexible arrangements are only possible if there is a good deal of space available (Hastings *et al.* 1996: 42). They suggest, for example, setting aside one room as a quiet study area where children can choose to work and where all talk is forbidden, or placing study booths along a wall of a corridor or the classroom. Where space of this kind is not available, some flexibility can be created by arranging the classroom in different ways for different parts of the day, so that group seating may be used for collaborative tasks, but 'L' and 'U' shapes as well as rows are available for individual seat work. In response to claims that it takes time to set up these arrangements, it is argued that this time loss is compensated for by the quality of learning and the amount of work that results. In particular, according to Wheldall and Congreve (1981), it is the most disruptive pupils who when seated alone progress most.

In the twenty-eight 1996 ORACLE classrooms there was one teacher who adopted this flexible arrangement, but in the rest of the classrooms the pattern remained much the same as it had done twenty years ago. Particularly noteworthy, given the observed increase in whole class teaching, much of which involved direct instruction, is that such activity often took place away from the children's tables, while they were seated around the teacher either in the quiet corner or in close proximity to the teacher's desk. Twenty years ago this class activity typically involved ten minutes at the beginning and end of the morning and a quarter of an hour at the end of the day when the teacher read a story. Now the time that children can spend sitting close to one another in the quiet corner may run up to half an hour in any one session. It is not surprising that under such conditions children tend to become distracted, as evidenced by the increase in teacher–pupil routine feedback interactions.

Another issue concerned the use of space within open-plan classrooms. Many of these open-plan schools were built in the late 1960s and early 1970s and were not designed either for whole class teaching, nor for a content-dominated, subject-based National Curriculum. Open-plan class-rooms tend to be crowded and relatively noisy compared to more traditional arrangements, so that careful planning is required in order to keep the dis-ruption of one teacher's lesson by another to a minimum. Nevertheless, the habit of working together in an open-plan base has led some teachers to adopt very flexible but imaginative approaches to their planning and deliv-ery of the National Curriculum.

There have also been changes in the way that different subject specialisms are presented. In Donna's day it was usual to combine two or more subjects into a topic, typically in the humanities (history, geography and social stu-dies). Pupils normally spent the morning on mathematics and English, and then did their topic or their art and music in the afternoon. Topic webs were created around themes so that, in English, the *potato* might generate poems about potatoes while in mathematics there would be calculations about the cost of potatoes or the yield of potatoes and subsequent profit made by farmer, wholesaler and shopkeeper. Pupils could grow potatoes in science; in history, hear the story of Sir Walter Raleigh and the discovery of the potato; and study the location of potato growing in geography. They might undertake crisp-making in home economics and potato printing in art. Note, however, that apart from studying the discovery of the potato and its current locations, much of the work would be done as discrete sub-jects, although pupils might be set a programme of work and allowed to choose the order in which they worked on the various tasks. Some of this work might be collaborative, so that a group of children would produce a folder in which there would be poems, facts and pictures. These folders tended to contain a lot of material that was directly copied from other sources.

During the 1980s, therefore, those who advocated the continued use of topic work attempted to shift the emphasis towards projects that were more investigative. It was argued that in the pursuit of a broad and balanced curriculum, such topics should not be mainly confined to humanities but should also involve mathematics and science. To give a specific example, a survey by children might present in various graphical forms (pie charts, graphs, etc.) their fellow pupils' preferences for chips, boiled or mashed potatoes. This might be based on careful observation of school dinners over the course of a week.

All these attempts at experimentation, however, changed with the introduction of the National Curriculum (Webb 1993b). It appears that teachers find it easier to demonstrate to bodies such as OFSTED that they are providing the statutory amounts of time for each curriculum subject by setting it within a distinct timetable in a similar manner to that of secondary schools (Galton and Fogelman 1998). Many schools now convert the percentage of time required for each subject at KS1 and KS2 into hours and allocate these as lessons in the timetable. In practice, therefore, Donna would notice very little difference between her own and Hayley's morning activity, in that the majority of time is still, as it was then, given to English and mathematics. The main difference would be that in Donna's time there was a certain amount of choice as to how pupils organised the afternoon.

Writing and listening to the teacher still dominates most lessons, particularly in the core and foundation subjects. In the 1996 study of English, these two activities accounted for exactly 65 per cent of the lessons. In science the figure was nearly 50 per cent, in geography around 56 per cent, and in history 53 per cent. Few higher order intellectual demands were made upon pupils. Only in art was a significant degree of creativity displayed. Work cards, published schemes, books and the teacher were still the major resources, the use of the teacher as a source of information being highest in science and geography. In science, no equipment was in use during nearly two-thirds of the observations. In these respects, therefore, the curriculum of the 1990s, when compared to that of the 1970s, has changed little in terms of the cognitive demands placed upon pupils.

This similarity in primary practice over the two decades is reflected in the patterns of teacher–pupil interaction which were described in Chapter 3. Class teaching has increased so that it now involves nearly 35 per cent of all the teachers' interactions with pupils, compared to 19 per cent twenty years ago. This increase has largely been at the expense of the time that was previously spent monitoring children's activity or marking their work. However, within the different observation categories on the Teacher Record, the pattern of teacher–pupil interaction has remained remarkably stable. For example, the ratio of teacher questions to teacher statements has remained unchanged. What has increased, however, is the proportion of statements concerning task and routine matters in comparison to those concerning task supervision, indicating, as suggested earlier, that there is now less emphasis on active learning, and that more time is spent on direct instruction as in the typical secondary class. These patterns are remarkably stable across subjects, so that in areas such as science, for example, where one might have expected a greater emphasis on experimentation, there appears a tendency for pupils to be told what to do rather than being asked to find out. One consequence of this emphasis on instruction is that there are now fewer situations where children are engaged in activities designed to provide a broad range of language acquisition other than in English. In the 1970s, Donna would on occasions have been told to go and research a topic which would have required her to collect information, summarise it, and then go to the teacher and read out what she had written. In Hayley's classroom, however, the only significant number of occasions where the teacher was observed hearing the children read was in English and, to a lesser extent, geography. Looking at the classroom from the pupil's point of view, as we did in Chapter 4, the stability of these teaching patterns was confirmed. In 1976 a key finding concerned the asymmetry of interactions from the perspective of the teacher and the pupil. Then, 72 per cent of the teacher's interactions were with individuals, whereas from the pupil's perspective, 76 per cent of their interactions with the teacher were experienced as a class member. This was because with over thirty pupils in a class, each pupil received approximately six minutes of the teacher's personal attention each day. Now, however, because of the increased use of whole class teaching at the expense of silent and non-interactions, the proportion of individual attention that teachers give pupils is reduced to 48 per cent, while class interaction has increased to around 35 per cent. From the point of view of the typical pupil, however, these changes have not affected the way in which he or she interacts with the teacher, since proportionally speaking, three-quarters of all pupil–teacher interactions on the Pupil Record are still experienced as a class member, exactly as they were twenty years ago. There have been slight shifts between group and individual attention, but the patterns remain essentially the same.

However, while the *distribution* of interactions remains virtually identical, when we look at the absolute levels of attention which the pupil receives as a class member we do find some significant differences from the 1976 ORACLE pattern. Whereas twenty years ago the teacher's attention generally concerned the task, now it is more equally distributed between *task* and *routine* class activity. This supports the earlier suggestion that the practice of keeping children seated together in a confined space during class instruction tends to create management problems. Observers noted cases of fidgety children being moved to a position adjacent to the teacher, while others were told to sit up or to listen carefully and so on. In contrast to this behaviour when interacting with the *teacher*, there has been a dramatic change in the pattern of communication between the pupils themselves. In 1976, pupil–pupil interactions, within the Pupil Record, accounted for around 19 per cent of all observations. In 1996, this has risen to 27 per cent. However, while twenty years ago most of these interactions were dominated by off-task conversations (5 per cent on-task; 13 per cent off-task), in 1996, three-quarters of the interactions were now on-task (12 per cent on; 3 per cent off). Pupils are not only talking with each other more than they did formerly, but they are now more likely to be talking about their work rather than engaged in social chat about the exploits of the local football team or last night's television programme.

Things have also changed when we examine patterns of interaction between teachers and pupils of differing ability. In 1976, the distribution of pupil–teacher interaction, as described by the Pupil Record, was fairly uniform across the different ability groups. In 1996, the greatest beneficiaries of the teacher's individual attention were the high attainers. In terms of gender, however, there has been little change. Overall, in the 1970s, there was very little difference between boys and girls in the amount of attention they received from the teacher. In 1996 (although both boys and girls get more overall attention because of the decrease in non-interaction time) the distribution is almost identical. Neither the 1976 nor the 1996 data support the argument that boys tend to dominate proceedings in the primary classroom. However, differences do emerge when we begin to look at sub-groups of teachers. In particular, boys seem to gain most in terms of their teachers' individual attention while in the classes of male teachers.

In 1976 there were clear relationships between teaching styles and pupil types. The distinct teaching styles were those of the *individual monitor* and the *class enquirer*. As might be expected from the overall increase in whole class teaching, the proportion of individual monitors has decreased while the identification of the class enquirer as one who engages in higher levels of cognitive challenge is now much clearer. The major change has been within the mixed styles, where the various combinations using group work coupled with individual attention have now largely disappeared, mainly because these were a consequence of certain kinds of curriculum organisation and, with the single subject emphasis of the National Curriculum, such arrangements are no longer regarded as feasible. Instead, there is a link between whole class teaching and *group instructors* where the emphasis is on low order questions of facts and ideas, and on statements which provide information. It seems to represent closely the cycle of direct instruction first identified by Rosenshine (1979), in which a period of questioning designed to reinforce what was learned in the previous lesson precedes a further period of instruction, followed by group or individual practice and concluded by a test or by further questioning to evaluate the learning.

In 1976, these teaching styles were closely identified with certain pupil behaviour. In classes of *individual monitors*, pupils typically worked when observed by the teacher, but when the teacher's attention was elsewhere, they then engaged in off-task activity. Such pupils were called *intermittent workers*. They could be contrasted with groups of pupils who preferred to listen to other children answer the teachers' questions but who, at the same time, remained on-task for lengthy periods. They did this either as *solitary workers*, with *class enquirers*, or as *quiet collaborators*. The latter collectively shared materials but not conversations, chiefly under the style of teaching known as *group instructors*. An interesting group, however, were those who attracted an above average share of the teacher's attention, known as the *attention seekers*. They either solicited the teacher's attention (often because they required reassurance, as when having done the first question in the worksheet they would ask whether they should go on to the second), or they attracted the teacher's attention by their lively behaviour.

In 1996, only some of these patterns remained. *Intermittent workers* can still be found, although given the predominance of the *class* and *group instructors* teaching style, *solitary workers* and *quiet collaborators* have now merged into one group. Attention seeking, however, has almost disappeared. Instead, the analysis produced a small group of pupils who were similar to the *hard grinders* in the analysis of pupils' behaviour in the 1976 secondary transfer schools. These pupils were an even more extreme form of the *solitary worker*. They had comparatively little to do with their peers or with the teacher except as a passive member of the whole class audience. When working individually they rarely left their place or interacted with their neighbours.

The final group of pupils to emerge from the 1996 analysis was characterised by having very little relationship with any of the other pupil types identified two decades earlier. They appeared neither to seek nor to receive the teacher's attention and were not observed to be periodically off-task as were the *intermittent workers*. At the same time they did not demonstrate the same high levels of task engagement as the *solitary workers* or the *hard grinders*. In many respects they were friendly *ghosts*, who for the much of the day remained unnoticed by the teacher. They appeared to have more in common with another type of pupil identified in the 1976 secondary transfer schools called *easy riders*. Easy riders gave the appearance of working but did so more slowly than other pupils. They found ways of extending routine tasks without attracting the teacher's attention. They were often observed sitting and listening to the teacher talking to other pupils as if trying to anticipate and, perhaps, subvert subsequent activity.

Easy riders are a particular problem in that, as argued by Galton (1989), they can create in the teacher low expectations of their ability by slowing down their work rate, particularly at the beginning of the year when the class is new. To the teacher such pupils will often finish only half a page of problems, say in mathematics, while other pupils complete the whole of the page. At the end of the lesson a teacher may conclude that these easy riding pupils have done their best but perhaps lack powers of concentration. By half term, teachers may regard it as satisfactory if an easy rider manages to produce at least half a page of work during a lesson. In our analysis, over a quarter of all pupils engaged in easy riding of one kind or another.

It would seem, therefore, that the shift to whole class teaching, and particularly to the form of whole class teaching known as direct instruction has met a response from some pupils that is characteristic of the secondary school as described in David Hargreaves' book *The Challenge for the Comprehensive School*. Hargreaves (1982: 3) describes an occasion where he followed the progress of two girls of average intellectual capacity with, according to their teacher, a general indifference to school. In seeking to look at the experience from the pupils' point of view, Hargreaves argues that:

> School lessons for them appear to be like seven very dull television programmes which cannot be switched off. They did not want to watch and made little effort to do so; occasionally the volume rose to very high level so that they listened; occasionally a programme became sufficiently interesting to command their attention, but it was never more than a momentary diversion from the general monotony. Part of the problem appeared to be that they were not in fact seven new independent programmes. All of them were serials which demanded some knowledge of the earlier episode. Indeed, most of the teachers generally provided a recapitulation of the earlier episode at the beginning of every lesson. But the girls had lost track of the story a long time ago.

It could be argued, therefore, that the results described in Chapter 6 on pupil attainment reflect this somewhat monotonous diet. There is a decline in language and mathematics scores over the two decades on written tests which were the same shortened form of the *Richmond Tests of Basic Skills* administered to pupils in 1976. Those who formulated the National Curriculum claimed that its introduction would lead to a general raising of standards. Yet in 1996, our tests were administered when the National Curriculum had been fully in operation for six years within these primary schools. In reading, there has been the greatest decline in mean scores. This is readily attributable to the fact that within the National Curriculum there has been, as shown by the observation data, a drop in the amount of time devoted to hearing children read. While in English, the time devoted to listening to children read has, of course, increased, there are now fewer opportunities across the whole curriculum than there were twenty years ago. This appears to be reflected in the performance of the pupils.

The general picture which emerges from these studies, therefore, is one in which there are some positive gains but also some less welcome findings. Hayley's teacher works harder than did Donna's and engages children more often in conversation. But, as in Donna's time, many of these conversations are still dominated by the teacher. There is also an over-reliance on using written materials (worksheets, published schemes, etc.), as the main resource by which the pupils acquire their knowledge and skills. Learning to solve problems is not a noticeable feature of the curriculum any more than it was two decades ago.

Although group work remains the least used strategy, it is now more purposeful. In this atmosphere of increased concentration on set tasks, however, some pupils have reacted by finding ways to convince the teacher that they are not wasting their time, while doing only the minimum amount of work. The majority, however, appear to work through the tasks determinedly with the minimum amount of fuss. Hayley's experiences are similar to those of her mother twenty years ago, except that she now gets to work at the computer on rare occasions. Donna thinks Hayley's work seems harder and that there are fewer opportunities to do fun things than there were in her day. That certainly is the view teachers expressed in Galton and Fogelman's study (1998), where one commented,

> We never have time now to listen to children when they come in in the morning with 'I did this' or 'I did that', or 'Here's a book' or 'I found this twig on the way to school'. It is very hard to make them know that these things are important to us as well and that what they bring to school is important. I feel incredibly sorry here for special needs children, for instance, who always seem to be rushing through it and finding it extremely difficult to finish off pieces of work, without being moved on.

A headteacher in the same study spoke for many when she said,

> Viewing the children in the playground the other day, one of the birds came down to pick up some crisps and to spend five or ten minutes out there just to let the children stand and watch it . . . but it's, 'Come on! Got to get back in because its maths time.'

The future of the National Curriculum

The feelings of frustration, powerlessness and disillusion among primary teachers, expressed in Galton and Fogelman's survey (1998) have been identified by other studies, notably that of Campbell and Neill (1994) and, more recently, Pollard and Broadfoot (1997). Teachers were interviewed by the PACE team during the third year of the study, and it was found that teachers in the upper years of primary school felt that priorities were increasingly being imposed upon them from the outside with a consequent sense of a loss of fulfilment and of autonomy. Older teachers, in particular, found it difficult to reconcile their educational beliefs with the contemporary technocratic approach, where delivery of education to meet national economic goals rather than personal development has become the arbiter of good practice (Osborn 1997: 21).

In such a climate, as we argued in Chapter 2 (p. 52), teachers operate what Doyle and Ponder (1977) called the practicality ethic, with a vengeance. Doyle and Ponder argued that in circumstances where teachers felt power-less in matters determining their practice, the decision to engage in a proposed innovation was largely determined by the results of a personal cost-benefit analysis. The more the innovation was seen to bring about worthwhile change, the more teachers were willing to make personal sacri-fices in terms of the time and effort demanded to bring about a successful outcome. In respect of the National Curriculum, however, while acknowled-ging the benefits in terms of planning and the provision of a broad and balanced curriculum, teachers have been unhappy with the impact at class-room level. They have been reluctant to change their pedagogy as recom-mended in the so called Three Wise Men's 1992 discussion paper (Alexander *et al.* 1992). Instead, they have 'bolted' the new curriculum onto existing practices. In the 1970s primary teaching was dominated by information giving. Within the new National Curriculum the same charac-teristic is dominant, only now the information is more often delivered through whole class teaching rather than through interactions with indivi-dual pupils.

The recent emphasis on numeracy and literacy at a time when the National Curriculum is under review creates further feelings of frustration among some practitioners. We do not dispute the view that without a good grounding in numeracy and literacy children are severely disadvant-aged by the time they move on to secondary school, but we do dispute that this grounding is best achieved by imposing rigid timetables which are applicable in every case. One of the main criticisms by teachers of the exist-ing National Curriculum concerns its inflexibility. In Galton and Fogelman's survey (1998), for example, some KS1 teachers felt the need to devote more time to creating satisfactory classroom relationships, and to instil within the pupils positive feelings towards learning. Such teachers were quite willing to accept that they should have fulfilled the statutory requirements by the end of KS1, but they wished for flexibility in determining how they might best do this, taking into account the particular needs of their pupils. These teachers do not wish to be told to devote a particular number of hours to the 'basics', although as both Galton and Fogelman (1998) and the PACE surveys show, most teachers are already exceeding the new requirements. For example, English now occupies more than five hours a week on average at KS2 (Pollard and Broadfoot 1997). Part of this increase in the time given to English and mathematics beyond the statutory requirements has come about because of the public accountability associated with the Standard Assessment Tasks. Schools now give priority to increasing their SAT scores, mindful that they will be published, even if for many city schools it is social-class features, such as the numbers of pupils on free school meals pre-school experience and so forth, which are limiting factors in raising standards.[1]

The National Curriculum came into being, in part, because of the wide variation in the amount of time given to different subjects, so that the entitlement of one child in a particular school often differed considerably from that of another pupil in a neighbouring school. However, current pressure on teachers to increase the amounts of time given to language and mathematics in an effort to improve SAT scores, has reintroduced variations in curriculum allocation. Although not as great as in the late 1970s and early 1980s, this has resulted in considerable discrepancy in the amount of time devoted to particular subjects in different schools. As one headteacher in Galton and Fogelman's study (1998) remarked,

> We have formulated a curriculum which includes the National Curriculum. However, I do not believe that we fully cover the requirements in practice although our schemes of work show that we should. There is no such thing as discretionary time. However, we operate what I believe is an interesting, challenging curriculum for our children with many opportunities for them to develop the creative and aesthetic elements of a human being. What is left out from the National Curriculum to achieve this is left out.

Even before the introduction of the Literacy and Numeracy Hours there were severe problems with the primary school timetable. Another headteacher in the same study responded to a question about her curriculum allocations by explaining,

> We are feeling pressurised all of the time. I have got to steer a ship and keep everybody sane. For example, we believe that all children should have regular sessions of PE during the week, but we are now having to look at that perhaps to prune back some of the time given over to Maths. But then we are also told that we are not giving enough time to PE and games. Has anyone ever worked out how it is affecting schools? Technology is another case. We find that we have to look at technology and perhaps spend a day at it every so often in order to get something productive done. If I am not careful, I find that some of those foundation subjects are given the push, even though they are down on the teachers' timetables.

The current requirements to devote nearly half of the week to mathematics and language, while at the same time providing adequate coverage of the remainder of the curriculum, including the arts, sharpens the dilemma experienced by headteachers such as the one in the above quotation. There is, of course, a way out of this dilemma, but it requires a return to the pre-1988 position before the National Curriculum Council came into being. In its first attempt at reform, the Council's Interim Primary Committee (NCC

1989) set out to deal with some of the endemic problems associated with the primary curriculum. Noting, for example, the concerns of the Cockcroft Report (1982) that rarely did primary teachers require pupils to apply basic mathematical skills to practical activities in other curriculum areas (paras 247 and 325), members of the Interim Primary Committee set out to design something along the lines of the Humanities Curriculum Project created for the Schools Council in the Humanities by the late Professor Lawrence Stenhouse and his team (HCP 1970). HCP attempted to involve mathematical and scientific knowledge in the study of the human species and its interaction with the environment by outlining schemes of work, providing resource packs, and teacher guides. The latter included advice about the teaching methods to be employed when handling controversial issues in the classroom such as questions involving racial prejudice. In adopting a similar approach, the Interim Primary Committee hoped to move away from the 'potato' style approach to topic work described earlier in this chapter and to provide teachers with clear advice not only on suitable themes but also on appropriate pedagogy.

In the event, as described by Galton (1995: 27), the Committee's deliberations were cut short and its report, *A Framework for the Primary Curriculum: Guidance I*, was drafted by officials from the National Curriculum Council. A decision was taken by the Chief Executive, Duncan Graham, not to proceed with a working group specifically concerned with primary matters.[2] Instead, KS1 and KS2 were entrusted to a group of experts with responsibility for developing the curriculum for each of the core and foundation subjects from ages five to sixteen. A Whole Curriculum Committee was set up, but its concerns were not with integration but with permeation of themes such as citizenship, health and economic awareness into the core and foundation subjects. Even this was too much for Kenneth Baker who 'wrote a two page letter to the Council in which he told it to abandon its investigations into the whole curriculum and get on with the real work' (Graham 1993: 20).

The result of all these decisions at primary level has been a continuing tension, not alleviated by the Dearing (1993b) review, between the need to provide continuity and progression in each specific subject, while at the same time ensuring that all pupils attain adequate standards of literacy and numeracy. It seems obvious that the problem of squeezing a quart of subject matter into a pint curriculum pot can only be solved by returning to a form of integrated curriculum in which a proportion of the statutory time required for the core subjects comes from the inclusion of mathematics, language and science activities within project work. To ensure that these schemes of work do not result in wide variations between what is taught to pupils in one school and what is taught to other children in another, it will be necessary to produce standard approved materials as suggested by Campbell (1997), perhaps using the format adopted by the process-oriented curriculum models of the 1970s. However, before that could happen it would be necessary to overcome the opposition of those such as Her Majesty's Chief Inspector of Schools, who would seem to be totally committed to a primary curriculum based upon discrete subjects.

OFSTED and its Chief Inspector

No one would quarrel with the argument that since children have only one educational opportunity it should be the best that can be provided. This does imply that incompetent teachers should be weeded out from the profession as quickly as possible (or preferably not allowed to enter it). But at issue here is just how many such teachers there are in our primary schools and how we define incompetence. We should certainly be able to agree that such teachers are probably a small minority, in which case it is legitimate to ask what this constant campaign of vilification in the media, described in Chapter 1, has done to the morale of those teachers who are competent, and in some cases exceptionally talented. It is clear that this constant stream of criticism has created considerable stress within the profession (Pollard and Broadfoot 1997). Perhaps more crucial, however, has been the shift away from the culture of primary teaching, described by Campbell and Neill (1994: 215–20) as one of 'conscientiousness'. In the past, primary teachers have regarded the profession 'as a way of life' rather than as a 'job' and been prepared to work long hours provided their professional judgement was respected. Once teachers cease to think of their work in this way there is a danger of it becoming merely a 'technical' activity, in which teachers perform their allotted tasks in ways which require little change to their existing classroom practice. This, as we have demonstrated, appears to have been the typical response to the Chief Inspector's call for an increase in the use of whole class teaching. The proportion of such teaching has increased considerably during his time in office. But what teachers do when they are teaching the class, for the most part, as our study shows, is rarely stimulating. As was the case twenty years ago, teachers talk *at* rather than *with* children during class teaching. Endorsement of 'interactive whole class teaching' and encouragement to choose methods according to 'fitness for purpose' appear to have had little effect, other than to increase the overall proportion of such talk. The pupils, as in the past, respond by finding ways of slowing down the lesson to reduce this flow of information. The difference is that now the use children make of these delaying tactics has increased by nearly two-thirds compared with twenty years ago.

Those advocating these simplistic approaches are guilty of a failure to understand the concept of pedagogy and what it was that Nate Gage (1985) in the United States and Brian Simon (1985) in the United Kingdom intended when they defined pedagogy as the 'science of the art of teaching'. The science part of the definition consists of general principles of teaching which are selected according to certain learning demands, or as Simon described it, 'Starting from what children have in common to establish general principles of teaching and in the light of these principles to determine what moderations of practice are needed to meet specific needs' (Simon 1985: 99). Simon's approach leads to a very different notion of 'fitness for purpose' than that argued for by the present Chief Inspector. In Simon's view, certain methods may be more appropriate for helping children achieve certain learning goals, so that one of the prime responsibilities of a head-teacher is to monitor the teaching strategies used in each class and to provide guidance for teachers in enabling them to become more effective. This is a very different type of approach from the one where teachers are told to use 60 per cent of whole class teaching during mathematics lessons, but are then left to decide which parts of the lesson will be included in this extended period of whole class activity.

The *art* of teaching, according to Gage (1985) comprises the application of these *scientific* pedagogic principles in a flexible manner, according to the characteristics of the particular group of pupils, taking into account the context in which they are working. For example, when teaching concepts it is important to ensure that ideas are mediated through discourse. As Bennett (1992) argues, social interaction is, therefore, important. But whether such discussions (*the pedagogic principle*), should take place with the whole class, a group, or with individuals, is largely determined by the particular classroom context (*the fitness for purpose*). For a variety of reasons suggested by Holt (1984), Measor and Woods (1984) and Pollard (1985), certain pupils respond badly to questioning in whole class situations. Such pupils, in order to save face in front of the teacher and their peers, will employ a number of stratagems to avoid answering the question while giving the appearance that the correct answer is on the 'tip of their tongue'. A teacher with a number of such pupils in the class might, therefore, not engage in whole class questioning but instead look for other ways to stimulate the children's thinking. This is what is meant by the term 'craft knowledge', that is, knowledge of what works and doesn't work in a given context.

At present, we have a situation where the Chief Inspector, and others of similar persuasion, appear to think that the 'pedagogic principle' involves deciding whether to use whole class, group or individual strategies, and the 'fitness for purpose' element is whether to use direct instruction, enquiry or some other teaching method such as brainstorming or role play. A theory of pedagogy, however, works the other way around. It is first necessary to identify the nature of what it is the child is expected to learn, then to decide the most effective pedagogic principle for effecting this learning process. Only then should considerations of class, group or individual approaches come into play. In many cases, there will be obvious links between the use of a teaching method and the most suitable organisational strategy to deliver it. When, for example, seeking the efficient use of direct instruction it is logical to employ the method with the whole class rather than with an individual pupil, although there may be some circumstances when teaching different groups will be considered more effective. What, therefore, needs to be spelt out by those advocating improvements in teaching are not prescriptions of the amounts of whole class and group teaching that should be used, but the links which exist between learning and teaching.

Towards an appropriate theory of pedagogy

In building up a set of pedagogic principles, therefore, we need to start with the nature of children's learning. This first requires that the knowledge demands made upon the learner be identified. A useful start in such analysis is the typology developed by Alexander (Patricia not Robin) and her colleagues. They reviewed a large number of articles in journals of education and psychology, to arrive at a classification of different types of knowledge (Alexander *et al.* 1991). In relation to teaching and learning in the primary school there appear to be three key elements.

The first of these, termed *procedural* knowledge, Alexander *et al.* (1991) define as a general term concerned with the acquisition of information (knowing this or that *about* something) and the rules of acquisition or use of information (knowing how to *use* something). The idea of a procedure, therefore, encompasses not only the knowledge of facts (*declarative* knowledge) but also knowing where such facts would be applicable (*conditional* knowledge).

Such a definition, for example, fits well with the growing use of ICT (Information and Communication Technology) within schools. In a project that was part of the government's Superhighways Initiative, primary-aged children were engaged in various topics and were required not only to locate the relevant information on the pages of the World Wide Web (i.e. knowing about something), but to download it into their own research folders. They edited it to extract relevant information and then made use of the thesaurus within the word processing package on the computer in order to ascribe familiar meanings to unfamiliar words (knowing how to use something). More straightforward examples would include learning and applying various algorithms in mathematics and understanding their application, or the rules of grammar and their use in appropriate language settings.

There is a clear consensus among researchers, both here and in the United States, that teaching explicit procedures of this kind is best done by direct instruction (Rosenshine 1987). This view is echoed by Charles Desforges (1995: 129) who states that 'Direct instruction is best used for knowledge transmission, for showing, telling, modelling and demonstrating. It is never on its own sufficient to ensure deeper understanding, problem solving, creativity or group work capacities.'

The second broad classification in the typology used by Alexander *et al.* is *conceptual* knowledge. This is knowledge of ideas and the understanding of principles, which includes defining elements, or classifying objects, and recognition of instances of belonging and not belonging to given classes. Encompassed within this definition is *domain* and *discipline* knowledge, because in order to process the vast amounts of information which defines a given class, we need to group information into sub-categories or domains. As a concept becomes a part of a formal system of learning or central to a specialised field of study, it develops into a sub-category of a discipline. As well as enabling us to order information, part of this conceptual understanding also includes what Alexander *et al.* (1991) term *discourse* knowledge, that is knowledge about language and its uses. One element of this discourse enables us to convey our understanding of a principle or an idea to another person. To do this, we need to understand how to combine words appropriately to convey meaning in prepositional statements, which Alexander *et al.* call *syntactic* knowledge. The same process also involves *rhetorical* knowledge which has to do with an understanding of the appropriate register for the audience to whom the language is directed or, more simply, the available styles of verbal and written communication.

Constructivist views of learning have tended to concentrate on conceptual understanding and how this is enhanced. It is precisely because the process of construction and reconstruction of ideas is mediated through discourse that, as Bennett (1992) argues, social interaction is so important. Hence, while some more simple concepts can be taught in sequence as a collection of procedures, more complex activities – such as mathematical problem solving, discussion of social issues, hypothesising in science, creative writing – should all involve some degree of co-operative activity, either with adults or with peers. Again, there is strong research support (Slavin 1986; Bennett and Dunne 1992; Galton and Williamson 1992) for the argument that the successful application of co-operative group work in classrooms leads to improved achievement. Moreover, as pupil involvement increases so too does the development of such valued social outcomes as enhancing self-esteem and better understanding between different races and cultures.

The third and final major element in the scheme put forward by Alexander *et al.* (1991) concerns the development of *metacognitive* knowledge, that is knowledge of one's cognitive processes. In the context of the present National Curriculum this mainly involves pupils' understanding of what it is to think, for example, scientifically or historically. In practical terms, it might involve understanding the processes of scientific discovery and, as such, it includes what Shulman (1986) refers to as *strategic* knowledge. This is knowledge which allows us to set the rules for determining what it is legitimate to say in a domain or a discipline and what 'breaks' the rule. For Alexander *et al.* (1991), metacognitive knowledge embodies not only strategic knowledge but *self*-knowledge – that is knowledge of ourselves as learners, including the appropriate control mechanisms required to ensure success, such as the ability to identify our own errors and monitor our own thinking. For example, in group work there is a need to develop mechanisms for evaluating our own and other group members' contributions to the discussion, in terms of, say, keeping to the topic, identifying key issues, and summarising the results.

Because metacognition requires learners to be able to regulate their own thinking, it is essentially an individual process – something that one acquires through experience while being helped and supported in the process by others more knowledgeable than oneself. Various writers, including Ann Brown (1990) in the United States and David Wood (1988) in the UK, refer to this support as *scaffolding*. Where the teacher helps to regulate the pupil's behaviour, the scaffold, or framework, is often a simple set of key elements which allow the student to implement a procedure to solve a problem. Giving the rules for the order of multiplication where brackets are present, to enable students to carry out complex algebraic calculations, would be one example. Helping young pupils to write descriptions of familiar objects by providing cue-cards with *size, shape, colour* printed on each, with an instruction to 'write at least three lines under each heading', provides another instance.

With peer regulation, as within peer tutoring or co-operative group work, the scaffolding will often be in the form of a framework to guide and structure the discussion. In science, for example, a group asked to select the most reasonable explanations of what causes a shadow may well generate a variety of hypotheses during a brainstorming session. Teachers often complain that children waste a lot of time in such discussions attempting to investigate improbable hypotheses. But in teaching children to think as scientists we must apply the same principles as a scientist would in similar circumstances. To begin with scientists are only concerned with hypotheses they can test. If a particular explanation is untestable, it moves to the realms of speculation or philosophy. Second, in many cases, scientists will then go on to consider only those hypotheses which they can test using the available equipment which is relevant to their specialist domain. If they happen to be interested in electro-chemistry, for example, they might pursue a solution to a problem in terms of measuring differences in electrode-potential. If they are crystallographers, they may consider various alternative explanations in terms of the arrangements of atoms and molecules on X-ray pictures. In the same way, children in primary school provided with only a torch, several objects and some card will only be able to investigate a certain number of hypotheses about shadows. The scaffold for the scientific investigation might therefore be, that pupils should first brainstorm their ideas on possible solutions, second, reject all those solutions which are not directly testable, and third, discard some of the remaining solutions which are not testable with the apparatus available.

At metacognitive level, where pupils are learning to regulate their own thinking, the capacity to interrogate and interpret sources of evidence becomes crucial, or to put it in simpler terms, pupils need to be able to ask the right questions. As Ann Brown and her colleague argue, in attempting to reconcile Piagetian and Vygotskyian approaches to conceptual development, the processes involved in this kind of thinking are essentially the same whether the learning is regulated by adults, peers or oneself. When pupils have the capacity to regulate their own thinking they are, therefore, able to solve problems by talking to themselves rather than with a teacher or another pupil (Brown and Palincsar 1986). They learn to engage in the most effective forms of dialogue, particularly questioning, by modelling these internal conversations on those previously held with teachers and peers. Yet as Robin Alexander's (1991) Leeds study clearly demonstrates, there are very few examples in primary classrooms where children ask questions, especially the kind that help them to regulate their own thinking.

Scaffolding this questioning process is a central concern of what Brown and Palincsar refer to as *reciprocal teaching* (Rosenshine and Meister 1994). This is primarily a process of teaching students to use specific cognitive strategies, particularly question generation and summarisation. Reciprocal teaching was first used for improving reading comprehension. In this earlier study, Palincsar and Brown (1984) gave students a passage of exploratory material to read paragraph by paragraph. During this reading the pupils practised the use of four comprehension strategies: generating questions, summarising, clarifying word meanings, and predicting what might appear in the next paragraph. During the early stages of reciprocal teaching, Brown and Palincsar recommend that the teacher assumes the major responsibility for instructing by explicitly modelling the process. The students then practise the strategies on the next section of text, and the teacher supports each student's participation through specific feedback, additional modelling, coaching, hints and explanation. In the early reading programmes reciprocal teaching often took place with individual pupils, but in more recent studies the learning is scaffolded within a co-operative learning framework where peers are invited to initiate discussion and react to other students' statements.

Rosenshine and Meister (1994) cite several examples of investigations involving passages about such topics as the life-cycle of snakes, the role of women in American history, and the nature of energy. In a further meta-analysis, specifically concerned with teaching pupils to generate questions, Rosenshine et al. (1996) identify nine frequently used types of scaffolding, of which six did not figure in conventional studies of teaching effectiveness. Among these missing strategies were the use of cue cards, modelling, and providing pupils with self-evaluation checklists. These supports were found to be essential for teaching higher order cognitive skills.

If standards are to rise, the previous paragraphs suggest that a very different framework is required from that promoted by OFSTED in its current efforts to persuade teachers to engage in greater amounts of whole class teaching. Currently, the distinctions between terms such as 'direct teaching' and 'interactive whole class teaching' are not well defined and teachers appear, therefore, to be responding to OFSTED's pressure by doing more of what they already do, as the research evidence presented in the earlier chapters has demonstrated. Alexander (1995) has distinguished between organisation, discourse and value in extending the idea of what it means to 'teach a class'. The original ORACLE terminology was extended in later studies, such as PRISMS, to define class teaching in terms of *base* (how pupils are expected to sit) and *team* (how pupils are expected to work). We can now build upon Alexander's framework (1995) by subdividing his discourse category into:

- *direct instruction*, which instructs pupils in what to do, how to do it and which checks their progress;
- *enquiry*, which poses problems by asking challenging questions and by offering alternative explanations; and
- *scaffolding*, which is mainly concerned with the development of support for pupils so that they learn to 'think for themselves'.

It can be argued that the reduction of what is a very complex activity into a series of very specific procedures, as in Palincsar and Brown's (1984) example of scaffolding, carries with it the danger that teaching is reduced to a mere technical process. Similar doubts have been raised by Cohen (1994) in her review of co-operative learning and group work, in which she argues that, rather than providing a framework for children to think for themselves, too rigid a scaffolding can become a prison. It is therefore important to emphasise that those seeking to develop a theory of teaching should continually stress Gage's (1985) definition of pedagogy as 'the science of the art of teaching', implying that the effective teacher will always try to ensure that within a given scaffold there are opportunities for children to display their own individuality. In the earlier example, using cue-cards to describe objects, an astute teacher might add a fourth card to those on which s/he has written colour, shape and size, with the question, 'Say what you find interesting about the object'.

The real lessons from the Pacific Rim

The renewed emphasis on whole class teaching has also gained credibility as the result of various international studies which have sought to explain why, compared to countries such as Taiwan, South Korea, Japan, Singapore and Hong Kong, pupils in the UK do less well in mathematics. These studies have been reviewed by Reynolds and Farrell (1996), in work that was supported by OFSTED. They conclude that, although features including the prestige of teachers in countries such as Taiwan are a contributory factor, the main reason why Pacific Rim pupils do better, despite being in larger classes, is that most of their lessons involve what Reynolds and Farrell refer to as 'interactive whole class teaching'. This concept is not well defined but seems to encompass rapid question and answer sessions, as in the process of direct instruction when teachers are finding out what pupils know, followed by slower paced, higher order questioning of the kind which research has suggested contributes to the development of 'higher order' thinking.

Reynolds and Farrell (1996) do, however, acknowledge that there may also be cultural differences, which partly account for the poor performance of English pupils relative to those in countries around the Pacific Rim. For example, Bracey (1991: 113) describes how, in South Korea, the selected group of pupils were clapped all the way to the examination room having been told by their principal that they were representing not only their school, but also their country! While this may be an extreme example of culturally determined behaviour, there are other reservations about such comparisons, mostly emanating from the United States, where there has been a much longer tradition of comparative research, involving pupils in the USA and in Japan. These critics have argued that the systematic differences in attainment between the two countries are reflected in systematic errors within the measurement. For example, Westbury (1993: 23), has suggested that the problem in the United States lies in the relatively poor performance of the lower attaining half of the school population, and similar arguments have been advanced here in the UK. This begs a question, however, of how the population sample was constructed. In both the United States and the United Kingdom the sample would typically consist of the whole year group, but in other countries there can be wide variations in the sampling, notably because weaker students are often held back a year. In some of these international studies the sampling frame was even more skewed because only best students were selected, as in the case of South Korea cited at the beginning of this paragraph.

In the four studies cited by Reynolds and Farrell (1996), most of the mathematics test questions were similar in style to those which were used in this present study. This is not surprising, since for two of the international studies, the tests were devised by the Educational Testing Service (ETS) of the United States; while the Richmond Tests used by ORACLE were originally based upon another American test, the Iowa Test of Basic Skills. Although the simpler number items revolve around subtractions and additions, those which concern problem solving are often quite complicated. For example, in the first study carried out by ETS, the International Assessment of Educational Progress in Mathematics (IAEPM/1), one such mathematical word problem concerned the nutritional values of food. It consisted of a six by four matrix in which six foods, such as milk, eggs and flour, were located and various pieces of information about the quantities, calorific values, protein content and carbohydrate content were listed. It took considerable effort to read the table, but to answer the question students had merely to calculate the protein content of two eggs and half a cup of milk, a simple addition (Keys and Foxman 1989). In items of this kind, it is questionable whether language comprehension or data interpretation is being tested. The fact that items of this type still correlated highly with other straightforward numerical items on the test (the internal consistency was around 0.9), would suggest, therefore, that tests of this type may be of doubtful validity.[3]

Also less than convincing are the arguments advanced by Reynolds and Farrell about the relationship between the high status that Pacific Rim teachers enjoy and their success. What may be true of Taiwan is not necessarily true of Singapore or Hong Kong, whose pupils also do well on the tests. What does distinguish teachers in these countries from our own primary colleagues, however, is that they are not required to teach every period. In some Pacific Rim countries, for example, primary teachers enjoy 25 per cent of the week free from teaching for marking and preparation. There may also be motivational factors involved here, in that in some countries nationalism is closely identified with educational aspiration. Teachers and pupils learn not only for their own satisfaction and personal advancement but also for their country's general prosperity. Another factor is the time devoted to teaching mathematics in different countries. When this is examined on a year to year basis, as Reynolds and Farrell (1996) have done, then English schools come out relatively well, since we devote quite a considerable time to mathematics and, unlike some of our continental European neighbours, children start school in the year they reach their fifth birthday. But if one looks at mathematics over the whole period of schooling, including that of pre-school, then the picture changes. Mathematics is taught at pre-school in countries around the Pacific Rim. The tradition in northern Europe, however, is to teach social skills and to leave academic matters until after entry to the primary school.[4]

Even Reynolds and Farrell (1996), who argue that standards will improve if strategies based on whole class teaching are adopted, concede that social factors such as poverty rates, divorce rates, percentage of single parent households and family occupation, explain sizeable proportions of international achievement variations when compared to schooling factors. As Berliner and Biddle (1995) suggest, families and the communities in which children spend the major proportion of their time must be significant factors in determining school achievement, so that 'the problems of under-achievement will not be easily solved by solely doing something to schools, such as establishing and enforcing high standards of performance' (Maehr and Maehr 1996: 22). Both here and in the United States, the current models of school improvement appear to be based upon the notion that externally imposed standards are needed to provide the will on the part of teachers to pursue excellence and so raise pupils' attainment scores. Failed schools are to be derided in the media, lose their autonomy and even their funds. However, as Maehr and

Maehr (1996) observe, 'behavioural psychologists argue that punishment can be a stimulus to adaptive action if, and only if, an alternative course of activity is available'. In inner city areas, many families now live near the poverty level and are infused with a feeling of hopelessness at their plight. Having their children branded as failures in school only adds to their sense of inadequacy. When failure is added to failure in this way, then, as Dweck and Wortman (1982) argued convincingly a decade ago, the situation leads to a state of learned helplessness and dependence.

A key question raised by Maehr and Maehr (1996) in their critique, therefore, is what should come first in the campaign for school improvement – more whole class teaching, as Professor Reynolds and his supporters, argue, or better support structures for families in need? All governments would no doubt argue that this was a false choice and that we should pursue both initiatives simultaneously. However, the present emphasis appears to be on the use of the *stick* rather than on providing the *carrot*. As we saw in our opening chapter, Donna, as a single parent, already finds it hard to manage and is worried about further threats to her state benefits. She does have aspirations which, if supported and encouraged, may well provide the means by which she and her family could prosper, but changes in the funding of students in higher education also threaten her plans for the future. Donna would like a job but she doesn't wish to be forced to take poorly paid part time work just to survive.

Even if we accept that 'whole class interactive teaching' has a part to play in raising standards, the previous section, in which we looked at the relationship between ways of knowing and ways of teaching, would suggest that Professor Reynolds' formulation is somewhat crude. If, instead of Taiwan, he had based his analyses on visits to Singapore or Hong Kong, where much of the teaching is in English, what he would have observed was not simply the engagement of teachers and pupils in conversation, but a carefully structured series of activities which included examples, not only of direct instruction but also of reciprocal teaching. In Singapore, for example, these forms of instruction are built into a standard curriculum package, so that when the teacher is teaching a certain topic he or she will be given guidance about the pedagogy to adopt. As discussed earlier in this chapter, something similar has been advocated by Campbell (1997) for our own National Curriculum. Furthermore, these pedagogic strategies are clearly articulated within Singapore's initial teacher training programme. Consider, for example, a recent examination paper for the students taking the three-year teaching diploma course at the Singapore Institute of Education. Students were asked to:

- Name the five key steps in direct instruction and explain how they would use the methods for teaching a lesson in either science or mathematics or language.

- Explain how they would organise jigsaw groups, and state the particular advantage that this form of grouping held over other styles of co-operative learning.[5]
- Comment on why a teacher gave her class some wire, a torch bulb and some batteries and asked them to make an electric circuit.

In the third question, the students were told that the whole process took twenty minutes and that the teacher could have demonstrated the process in five minutes. Students were asked to explain why this teacher chose not to demonstrate how to make an electric circuit and in what ways she might have provided a *scaffold* so that the time spent working towards a solution was reduced.

As Biggs (1994) argues, what distinguishes performance in countries such as Hong Kong and other successful countries around the Pacific Rim, is the use of a range of strategies based not upon prejudices about the past, but upon carefully researched evidence. The experience of such countries as Singapore supports his view.

Education in the post-traditional society

At the end of Chapter 1, we promised to return to Donna's daughter Hayley and to consider, in the light of the primary teaching provided in the 1990s, her future prospects in the next millennium. We also saw that this post-traditional society was characterised by uncertainty and for some a sense of helplessness stemming from the capacity for one's actions to have repercussions in other countries many thousands of miles away. At the same time, because of the improvements in information and communications technology, our world is shrinking. In the twenty-first century we will have the capacity to work, shop and be entertained without ever moving outside our home. Both previous and present governments have acknowledged the importance of these amazing advances in communications technology. As mentioned before in Chapter 2, the previous Conservative Government set up the Superhighways Initiative (EDSI) in which schools and industrial partners were encouraged to come together to explore the potential of new technology such as electronic mail, video conferencing and the provision of information through the World Wide Web. Whereas twenty years ago, Donna went to the library to read books about 'food from other lands' as part of her geography project, Hayley will have the potential to link up with children in different countries and to ask them to email her their three favourite foods. Instead of poring over a geography book, or being told by the teacher about the climate, she will be able to send a questionnaire by email asking them about today's weather – whether it is hot, raining or snowing? Further still, she could consult the Web and extract the same charts and satellite picture being used by professional meteorologist to forecast the weather on the TV.

Most politicians appreciate the potential of these new technologies in a general way and indeed the present government has pledged that all schools will be linked to the Web via a National Grid for Learning by the year 2002. The consultation paper for the National Grid initiative, *Connecting the Learning Society* (DfEE 1997b), promised to take 'full account' of the research evidence, including that from the EDSI evaluations (DfEE 1997c). It is to be hoped, therefore, that lessons have been learned from earlier attempts to foster an information revolution in education such as the 'micros for schools' programmes of the 1980s. As we have shown in Chapter 2, for most primary schools at least, this was a revolution that never happened.

Unfortunately, over the years one problem of these successive government initiatives, irrespective of party, is that the thinking behind them tends to be one-dimensional. Politicians are adept at identifying a problem and offering a solution, as for example, the current literacy and numeracy initiatives. Perhaps because their own education has tended to emphasise convergent thinking, they are not very adept at taking a broader view and looking at the ways in which one initiative links or sometimes conflicts with another. The present demand for specific literacy and numeracy hours, while at the same time advocating a broader use of the new information technology, is a case in point. Earlier research, specifically Underwood (1994) together with anecdotal accounts by teachers, supported by the limited amount of systematic research carried out as part of the Superhighways Evaluation, testifies to the effectiveness of the new technology as a motivating force for children with learning difficulties. The computer provides a safer environment in which to make a mistake, since 'getting something wrong' does not lead to a loss of face with the teacher or with peers. It also removes inequalities; a pupil with poor co-ordination, for example, whose handwriting may be illegible, can produce a perfect copy (using word processing software) which is indistinguishable in presentation from that of his more able classmate.

An example of this 'levelling' effect of information technology was observed in a primary school during the evaluation of one of the Superhighways Initiatives, the BEON[6] project. This involved one secondary school and its feeder primaries working with the support of BT and ICL. Each primary school was given thirty networked computers which provided them with access to a wide range of software, email and video-conferencing facilities, and a high-speed link to the Web via BT's *Campus World*. The schools were all situated in an area of the city where general levels of social and economic deprivation were high, with higher than average levels of unemployment. In the school in question, more than 90 per cent of pupils were receiving free meals. Crime was prevalent to the extent that in one of the participating schools, which had an attached residential unit, teachers' cars had to be locked in steel cages to prevent vandalism overnight.

On the day in question at a particular primary school the observer parked his car next to one containing an adult (presumably a parent) and three children who were sharing a packet of chips. The woman was smoking and, on occasion, passed the cigarette to the children in the back of the car who would have been aged between ten and seven. During the course of the afternoon's observation, the following fieldnote was recorded:

> Towards the end of the afternoon, three children, two boys and one girl, knock on the door and enter the classroom, clutching what appears to be their work. Mr Brennan stops the class working and tells them that Damian, Kerry and Kevin have come to show them the story which has won this week's prize. Kerry's story is about a cat and has lots of pictures which she has produced using the software 'Flying Colours'.[7] To produce her story, she must have created a file then switched to the 'Flying Colours' software, made her picture, saved it and then copied it and pasted it into the text. When she comes to show me her story and I ask her whether it was difficult to do all this, she grins and says, 'No, it's easy'. Kevin's story is about a man-eating spider and he tells me proudly that there are no spelling mistakes because he used the spellchecker. All three children clearly savour their moment of glory and bask in their success. Afterwards, Mr Brennan tells me that the computer is the best thing that happened to Damian (one of the children observed in the car at lunchtime, eating chips and smoking). 'He has come on in leaps and bounds. Last year I could hardly get three lines of writing out of him, but now there is no stopping him. And his reading age has shot up too.'

This incident could no doubt be replicated up and down the country in numerous primary schools with children similar to Damian, Kerry and Kevin. A question which needs to be answered is how far such activities are legitimate within the prescriptions of the literacy hour or the suggestion by the Chief Inspector that 60 per cent of the numeracy period should be devoted to whole class teaching. Observing Hayley and her generation working with computers, it is noticeable how much more confident than the adults they are, how prepared they are to take risks in their learning compared to when they are involved in traditional lessons. As Pintrich *et al.* (1993) observed, the problem for most children is not that they do not have sufficient knowledge to solve problems but that they are reluctant to use it in conventional school settings.

The use of the Web as a resource for children's learning also conflicts with another shibboleth of those currently in charge of the educational agenda, namely the emphasis on specialist single subject teaching. Unfortunately for the Chief Inspector of schools and his supporters, when children use the Web as a resource the information is not available in discrete subject packages. It is also rarely presented in some abstract context, but usually situated within a realistic problem-focused context situation, as for example, the study of the effects of global warming. In the BEON project, it was noticeable that some of the primary schools began by placing their thirty computers in a dedicated area so that children could be taught as a class the basic techniques of word processing and the use of different software packages. Gradually, however, as the project progressed, this was seen as an increasingly inefficient use of the machines, partly because pupils who had mastered one aspect of the technology were able, through peer tutoring, to pass it on to less knowledgeable children.

Once the computers were transferred to the classroom, or placed in the corridor so that they could be shared across year groups, it became necessary to ensure the optimum use of machines. At the best, with four machines for a class of thirty, each child during a mathematics lesson could only get six individual minutes' use. If, however, the mathematics was integrated into topic work, then the machines could be used as and when required by children throughout the day, whenever they reached a point in their work where they required information or needed to word process some writing, or construct a picture or diagram. For mainly pragmatic reasons, therefore, teachers increased the amount of integrated subject matter despite the demands of all the National Curriculum. In the BEON project we saw, perhaps, an early glimpse of the future primary school with a link to the secondary school through video conferencing. This enabled the French teacher in the secondary school, for example, to hold conversation lessons with groups of interested pupils from feeder primary schools in the lunch hour.

When the Chief Inspector quoted Matthew Arnold's definition of culture in his lecture to the Royal Society of Arts (Woodhead 1995b) to support his argument for a subject-based curriculum, he did what many do when using the quotation, that is to stop half way, implying that Arnold's objective was to teach the best that was known in art, literature, and philosophy *for its own sake*. In fact, as Williams (1961: 124) makes clear, Arnold's purpose was contained in the second half of the quotation, which goes on to explain that the subject matter is a means to an end, the end being to create thinking individuals by developing all parts of society and all parts of our humanity. In other words, for Arnold, the study of the subjects was the current means available for developing all sides of our personality including our capacity to think. For today's primary teacher the end is still the same – to develop in children like Hayley an understanding of the thought processes required to solve problems within the contemporary context of the post traditional society, such as those discussed in Chapter 1. We need to ask ourselves whether the means to facilitate this process, which were deemed satisfactory in the mid-nineteenth century, are now suitable for beyond the millennium. In this respect, Mr Woodhead and his supporters seem to represent the ultra-nationalist perspective in Giddens' (1994) analysis. Their desire appears to be to 'turn the clock back' and to rely on strong leadership to drive through their reforms. The Chief Inspector seems at times to see himself as the person best equipped to undertake the task of saving the nation state as, like a modern-day Thomas Gradgrind, he regularly warns us of the dangers of progressivism and all he believes it stands for.[8]

If the last paragraph seems somewhat polemical, then it is instructive to examine the contemporary thinking in three of the top-ranking countries in the international mathematics attainment 'league table', Singapore, Hong Kong and Japan, where, if Reynolds and Farrell's (1986) analysis is correct, there should be little incentive to change current practice. Closer examination shows, however, that at a time when we are busy engineering a subject-based, whole class taught, 'back to basics' movement, these countries are transforming their curriculum, moving away from whole class teaching and seeking to use greater amounts of co-operative learning through group work and peer tutoring. At the same time, much attention is being given to the development of children's critical thinking. In a reported speech given to Principals of Singapore primary schools, for example, the Director of Education set out the Government's targets for the next five years. He began by stating that,

> One of the concerns would be to review the present curriculum. There should be time to do more than the content areas. The review might lead to the pruning of the curriculum to enable the acquisition of more process-oriented teaching and learning. The review would also match assessment modes to this changed curriculum.
> (PEC 1997: 1)

It may be that as we advance up the league tables in terms of standardised test scores, we will fall behind on the creative thinking and problem solving which the emerging economies see as the key to successful trading in the new global markets. While not wishing to deny the importance of seeking to raise the standards of literacy and numeracy in our primary schools, it is also important not to give the impression, either to the public or to the teaching profession, that this is the sole aim of primary education.

The problem affecting Hayley and her peers in Year 6 is that most educational change takes several years to work through the school system. During the 1960s when the *Headstart* programme was introduced for disadvantaged children in the United States, the results over the first five years suggested that there was little schools could do to affect improvement in children's intellectual development. The claim at the time was that schools did not matter. It was over two decades latter, when the results of longitudinal studies, such as *Highscope* became available, that the full implications of these early experimental schools began to be evident (Schweinhart and Weikart 1997). The results of the recent decade of experimentation with the National Curriculum, and now the more recent Task Force initiatives, will only be fully evaluated a decade hence, when – we hope – Hayley is about to finish university and enter the workforce. The evidence presented from this replication of the 1976 ORACLE study – particularly that which indicates the pressures on today's teachers to act as transmitters of information rather than to engage in dialogue and enquiry, and the passive response of many of the pupils to this regime – suggests that there may be dangers ahead, especially since rival countries are busily redesigning their education systems by attempting to refashion both curriculum and pedagogy, in ways not dissimilar to those advocated by Lady Plowden and her committee some thirty years ago.

Notes

1 These value-added measures will not be included in future analysis, only prior attainment. Social class, of which variables such as free school meals are in part an indicator, have always been a major determinant of pupils' academic progress (see, for example, Fogelman and Goldstein's analysis (1976) of the social factors associated with attainment between seven and eleven years of age based on findings from the massive National Child Development Study). During the 1980s concerns about educational inequalities of race and gender have tended to push the issue of inequalities of social class from the centre of the debate. This was to the advantage of both central and local government, since charging schools to create a multicultural, anti-racist curriculum was less costly than sustaining educational priority areas. However, there are welcome signs that with the creation of Educational Action Zones this trend could be about to be reversed.

2 A full account of this period is given in Chapter 2 of *Crisis in the Primary Classroom* (Galton 1995). The idea of cross-curriculum themes was not favoured by Kenneth Baker, the then Secretary of State for Education, and it is significant that Duncan Graham in his book, *A Lesson for us All* (Graham 1993) has no reference to the work of the Interim Primary Committee, nor its report!

3 Jean Lave (1992: 76) also suggests that to solve such problems, the learner must be able to abstract features of experience, generalise about them and translate them to novel, unfamiliar situations. As a result, schools become places where children are expected to learn things 'out of context'. Lave further argues this gulf between maths learning in school and everyday experience may be another reason for the poor performance of the weaker students on tests such as those used for international comparisons.

4 One of the present research team, when a consultant to the Council of Europe for its project *Innovation in Primary Education*, observed a session in a Swedish kindergarten (Galton and Blyth 1989). Children were being asked to come out to the blackboard and write capital letters. One child wrote the letter B back to front. The nursery supervisor praised the child and sent him back to his place. When asked about this incident, the supervisor explained that her task was to teach the children to write straight lines on the blackboard, it was not to correct their writing – that was for the teacher in the infant school. Such sentiments would not be condoned in Japanese or Singapore kindergarten schools.

5 Jigsaw grouping was first suggested by Aronson *et al.* (1978). Galton and Williamson (1992: 25) give an example where children are asked to plan a class trip costing £1 per pupil. They form groups of eight and pairs of children in each group are asked to consider: (a) where they should go; (b) what they should eat; (c) how they

should travel; and (d) what they should do when they get to their destination. After a time each pair then joins a new group consisting of the others who have been discussing the same issue (e.g. all those discussing food come together). Finally pupils rejoin their original group, bringing back fresh ideas. Each of the original groups then presents a final plan (as if fitting the different pieces of the jigsaw together) and the group judged the best is given the task of organising the class outing. At the end, because of the group rotation, nobody can be sure who thought of the chosen ideas in the first place, so there is little danger that children risk losing face with the teacher or their fellow pupils. Aronson clearly showed that this way of working led to improved levels of self-esteem among pupils.

6 Bristol Education On-Line Project

7 A graphics package that was used to create various designs to illustrate a story or the covering page of a project and so on.

8 Chapter I of Charles Dickens' novel *Hard Times* begins with Gradgrind explaining his educational philosophy. 'Now, what I want is Facts. Teach these boys and girls nothing but Facts. Facts alone are wanted in life. Plant nothing else, and root out everything else. You can only form the minds of reasoning animals upon Facts: nothing else will ever be of service to them.' To be fair to Mr Woodhead, although he is keen that children 'should suspend their eagerness to criticise and learn something first' (see Chapter 1, footnote 34), he does make it clear that he does not wish this to be done by adopting Gradgrind's teaching methods (Woodhead 1995b: 8).

APPENDIX 1

TRAINING IN SYSTEMATIC OBSERVATION TECHNIQUES

Background

In the ORACLE 1996 study a team of four researchers was involved in systematic observation in the sample of twenty-eight primary classrooms. There is considerable experience in the training of post-graduate students and researchers in systematic observation techniques within the School of Education at Leicester, and a training programme was devised for all of the ORACLE 1996 team.

The Teacher Record and the Pupil Record observation instruments were the focus of much of this training. These two observation systems were devised by Deanne Boydell in the 1970s and used in the original ORACLE studies. Revised manuals in the use of these observation schedules were produced by Anne Jasman in 1983 and were the focus of the training in observational technique for ORACLE 1996.

These manuals were updated during the funding period of the ORACLE 1996 project (1995–7) to take on board coding modifications made as a result of ongoing discussions among the research team. As a consequence, new versions of the Pupil Record User Manual, Teacher Record User Manual and Curriculum User Manual were produced in 1997. Also, Teacher and Pupil 'pocket' manuals were prepared for each observer, which summarised the general observation and coding procedures for each instrument and could be referred to, if necessary, during observation sessions. A Curriculum Manual, which was originally designed by Roger Appleyard and the PRISMS team, was also amended for use by ORACLE 1996 observers.

The ORACLE 1996 Training Programme

The training sequence is outlined below and closely matches that previously described by Anne Jasman in Appendix 1 of *Inside the Primary Classroom*: 166–71.

Teaching

The first step in the training involved the familiarisation of observers with the content of the Pupil Observation Manual. The Teacher Record, as a more complex instrument, was introduced later. The research team read through the Pupil Record manual together, studying and clarifying the category definitions and coding procedures in each section.

Testing

Observers were given written examples to work their way through independently and check their ability to code selected categories correctly. Easier examples were provided at the early stage. At first, the amount and complexity of the information that needed to be retained in order to make coding decisions was daunting, but videotaped extracts of classroom activity enabled the observers to relate text to concrete examples of pupil behaviour and coding parts of the record sheet became easier. As the observers became familiar and more confident with the coding technique it was possible to reduce the time between each observation.

Feedback

Discussions of coding decisions took place after testing. Differences in interpretation of the category system were shared among the research team and particular definitions of codes were clarified. Team meetings continued throughout the observational periods in schools and were essential to ensure the correct interpretation of some of the more complex codes.

Practice

In the Autumn term 1995, practice observation sessions were undertaken in a primary school to enable individual observers to familiarise themselves with observation procedures in the context of a working classroom. There were further feedback sessions before the team spent a day in classrooms in a local junior school, practising their observation techniques. The team was split into two pairs and each pair had a dual earpiece enabling them to link to the same cassette recorder in one classroom. This meant that the pre-recorded time signals for each observation could be co-ordinated and observers could collect data on their record sheets to compare and discuss later in the day. As in Anne Jasman's report on training observers for the original ORACLE study (Galton *et al.* 1980, Appendix 1) coding live events proved easier than coding from video extracts or written examples. Since these practice observations occurred in 'real time', the sequence of events was not being stopped and played back for discussion and interpretation at regular intervals.

Retesting

The live-practice records were compared and, at the end of the training period, agreement trials were held using further videotaped extracts from classroom events. This ensured that observers viewing the same event were coding it in the same way. Tests of reliability produced coefficients of between 0.7 and 0.79. These are of the same order as in the original ORACLE (see Appendix 2: 174 of Galton *et al.* 1980: 174).

In addition to the training in how to use the two main observational instruments – the Teacher Record and the Pupil Record – written guidance was also given on the procedure for randomly selecting target pupils and observing them in a pre-arranged order. There was also a range of summary sheets that needed to be completed alongside the Teacher and Pupil Records, which located each record of data within a description of the session in which it was collected and the curricular activities for that day. Table 1A1 shows when these instruments were completed and describes their main focus.

ORACLE 1996: general observation procedure

The Pupil Record observation schedule was developed to provide a detailed picture of pupil activity in the classroom. The observer recorded a sample of the behaviour and activities of a series of target pupils on Pupil Record sheets. Each 'target' child was pre-selected at random from the class. He or she was observed for ten time signals and at each of these the observer always recorded three pupil activity codes, and, when applicable, four pupil–adult interaction codes and five pupil–pupil interaction codes. The signal, or 'bleep', was emitted from a cassette recorder via an earpiece at twenty-five-second intervals. Each Pupil Record, therefore, took about four and a half minutes to complete and contained coded records of ten successive observations of one pupil (referred to as a 'set'). An observation period involved six sets of pupil observations (alternating between boy and girl) and one set of teacher observations.

Once the set of observations had been recorded and the front of the Pupil Record schedule completed, the observer made a brief note about Curriculum Content for that period. At the end of the session these were coded into columns under the six category headings of curriculum, task activity, media, cognitive demand, resources, and equipment. Up to three values could be coded for each of these categories, depending on their order of importance in the child's task. The first value coded was referred to as 'dominant' for that set of observations (for example see Appendix 5, Table 5A1).

Observations were done in an uninterrupted period of approximately one hour. This gave time to observe the six targets (in ORACLE 1976 eight pupils were observed per session), complete the administration details on

Table 1A1 Instruments used in data collection (Spring and Summer terms 1996)[a]

Title	When completed	Focus
School Summary sheet	Headteachers/class teachers completed this with the observer during an 'acclimatisation visit' in the Spring term 1996.	Whole school information and details of two KS2 classes. Recording of classroom layouts.
Pupil Record	Six 'target' pupils were observed in each of three observation sessions per class per term. Observations were made in the Spring and Summer terms 1995–6.	The target's activities and interactions with other pupils and the teacher; curricular activity during the observation session.
Teacher Record	Each teacher was observed once during each of the three observation sessions per class per term	Teacher questions and statements, silent interaction, no interaction, teacher's audience and curricular activity.
Session Summary sheet	Completed at the end of each observation session.	Pupils' seating, outline of curricular content and methods used; apparatus, and incidents. Order of teacher and pupil observations.
Daily Summary sheet	Completed at the end of each full day of observations (one per class per term).	Day timetable for the class and outline of organisation. To include observed and unobserved activity.
Descriptive account	Completed for each class at the end of three observation sessions(Spring term and Summer term 1996).	Observer's impressionistic account of the pupils, teacher, classroom organisation, etc.

Note
a This table is adapted from Table 1.3 in Galton et al. (1980).

the Record schedules, and have some leeway to reorientate oneself to new targets between observations. There was also sufficient time left to observe the teacher.

The teacher was observed by coding a sample of his or her interactions with class members and the curriculum activity that they were engaged in. The teacher was observed at different times during the day: at the beginning of a session, in the middle of a session and at the end of a session. For example:

P^1 (boy), P^2 (girl), P^3 (boy), P^4 (girl), P^5 (boy), P^6 (girl), Teacher.

The teacher was observed for about nineteen minutes, that is for forty-five time signals at twenty-five-second intervals. Up to four codes were entered on each time signal.

APPENDIX 2

REVISIONS TO THE TEACHER AND PUPIL RECORDS SINCE ORACLE 1976

The ORACLE Teacher and Pupil Records were the principal means of data collection for this new ORACLE study, twenty years on, and the observation categories listed on the instruments were, with the exception of the few revisions shown in Table 2A1 (for the Teacher Record), essentially those developed for the original 1976 study. The main changes to the instruments concern more detail in the recording of the curriculum on both records and substantial re-formatting of the schedules. The latter was necessary due to the different, and more economic, procedure used to record observations in ORACLE 1996: while the original ORACLE 1976 system required the observer to record information by ticking boxes, the 1996 team were able to select the appropriate pre-coded description of the pupil's or teacher's behaviour from a list and directly insert codes into the boxes. This meant that coded data could be entered directly on to the computer from completed observation records.

The User Manuals for observers

The procedures for using the Pupil Record and Teacher Record observation instruments are fully described in the 1997 versions of the ORACLE Teacher Record and ORACLE Pupil Record User Manuals which contain the ground-rules for the application of all coding categories. These manuals are substantively based on the 1983 manuals for observers, which in turn were originally devised by Deanne Boydell (1974). A number of minor alterations, extensions of coding categories and additional ground-rules have been incorporated into the main body of the revised manuals to reflect the changes in the ORACLE 1996 programme outlined above and described in more detail below.

Differences in the Teacher and Pupil Records 1976–96

At the end of Chapter 1 we touched upon the similarity of research methodology used in ORACLE 1976 and ORACLE 1996 and how both the

Teacher Record and Pupil Record, originally designed by Deane Boydell, were used to record our observations of the class teacher and pupils in the sample of primary schools. There were some additions and revisions made to the original instruments, however, mostly as a result of changes brought about by the implementation of the National Curriculum.

Changes made to both observation schedules were:

• Revisions in the layout of the Teacher and Pupil records.
• Use of pre-coded categories instead of ticks to record observations.
• The recorded curriculum was expanded to include National Curriculum definitions of subject areas.

In ORACLE 1976, information on the nature of the curricular area(s) on which teacher and pupil(s) were engaged during a period of observation was written under the ACTIVITY category on the Teacher Record, and under TOPIC on the Pupil Record. The coding system for the curriculum covered four major categories: mathematics, language, general studies, and art and craft. Mathematics and language were subdivided into minor categories: mathematics into basic number work, practical mathematics and abstract mathematics; and language work into reading, formal written English, spoken English and creative writing. General studies included science, history, geography, topic and project work.

The present ORACLE study has analysed the curriculum in much more detail than the original project. The revised teacher and pupil records include sixteen codes for curricular activity. These cover not only all of the statutory subjects taught under the National Curriculum, but also personal and social education, cross-curricular themes, rapid change in curriculum and routine activity observed in the primary classroom.

Teacher Record changes

The following section focuses on the changes made to the original ORACLE Teacher Record instrument for the 1996 project and should be read alongside Table 2A1 which lists the Teacher Record observation categories for the 1976 and 1996 ORACLE studies. The table shows that, besides the expansion of 'curriculum' highlighted above, additions were made to the following categories: Silent Interaction, No Interaction and Teacher's Audience. Amendments were also made to some of the Conversation Categories relating to statements about task supervision and routine.

Additions to the ORACLE 1976 Teacher Record categories were:

Silent Interaction. The addition of a Listening and Watching sub-category (codes 20, 21, 22) to denote when the teacher listened to a pupil report back, explain or read, or watched them work for an extended period of ten seconds or more. In ORACLE, extended listening would have been coded as

No Interaction on the Teacher Record. However, the present team felt that a teacher attending to a pupil in this sustained way was actively engaged in non-verbal interaction, and therefore silent interaction would be a more appropriate code.

No Interaction. Watching a child work (code 22 on the Teacher Record) can be distinguished from an addition to the No Interaction category: 'general monitoring'(code 26). While the former referred to a teacher focusing on an individual, pair or group for an extended period (e.g. looking over a pupil's shoulder at their work), the latter category was devised to cover periods when the teacher generally surveyed the whole class with no focus on particular individuals or groups.

Teacher's Audience. The original ORACLE schedule had three Audience codes: private individual attention, group, and class. These sub-categories were increased to ten for ORACLE 1996, primarily to account for possible gender differences in teacher–pupil interaction. Gender differences in teacher–pupil interaction could only be reported through analysis of pupil record data in *Inside the Primary Classroom* (Table 4.5, p. 66) since this variable was not monitored on the Teacher Record.

A *sustained interaction* category was also included in the Teacher's Audience to denote when the teacher interacted with the same individual or group into the next time signal, for example, when the teacher listened to a child read for a sustained uninterrupted period, perhaps pausing occasionally to ask questions and discuss the text.

A *pair* category was added after the first round of observations to record the teacher's interactions with children working with partners. In the subsequent analyses of the 1996 Teacher Record data, 'pair' was subsumed under 'group,' as it was in the original ORACLE project.

Amendments to the ORACLE 1976 Teacher Record categories

As Table 2A1 shows, the only amendments made to the Teacher Record categories of the original ORACLE observation schedule were changes to three codes in the sub-categories of Task Supervision and Routine, under the major conversational category of (teacher's) Statement.

Statement–Task Supervision; Statement–Routine. Changes to these categories were made in order to separate value judgements about the child's work or behaviour from informational, constructive feedback on the child's work or behaviour, and to identify clearly positive and negative feedback from the teacher.

S4 (praising work or effort) on the original Teacher Record allowed for positive approval of the pupil's work or effort under task supervision, and S5 (feedback on work or effort) for both neutral and critical feedback on the pupil's work or effort under task supervision. Judgements made by the teacher could be accompanied by directives which told the child how to

Table 2A1 Comparing ORACLE 1996 and ORACLE 1976 Teacher Record categories

1996	1976
QUESTIONS	**QUESTIONS**
TASK	**TASK**
1 recalling facts	Q1 recalling facts
2 offering ideas, solns (closed)	Q2 offering ideas, solns (closed)
3 offering ideas, solns (open)	Q3 offering ideas, solns (open)
TASK SUPERVISION	TASK SUPERVISION
4 referring to task supervision	Q4 referring to task supervision
ROUTINE	ROUTINE
5 referring to routine matter	Q5 referring to routine matter
STATEMENTS	**STATEMENTS**
TASK	TASK
6 of facts	S1 of facts
7 of ideas, problems	S2 of ideas, problems
TASK SUPERVISION	TASK SUPERVISION
8 telling child what to do	S3 telling child what to do
9 praise/crit. of work/effort (+/− if strong)	S4 praising work or effort
10 informational feedback re work/effort	S5 feedback on work or effort
ROUTINE	ROUTINE
11 providing information, directions	S6 providing information, directions
12 praise/crit of rtn/behvr (+/− if strong)	S7 providing feedback
13 informational feedback re routine/behvr	S8 of critical control
14 of small talk	S9 of small talk
SILENT INTERACTION	**SILENCE**
	SILENT INTERACTION
15 gesturing (+non-verbal/material i/actn)	gesturing
16 showing/demonstrating/participating	showing
17 marking	marking
18 waiting	reading
19 reading or telling a story	not observed
	not coded
LISTENING/WATCHING	
20 listening to report/explntn	
21 listening to child read	
22 watching child/chn work	
NO INTERACTION	**NO INTERACTION**
23 adult interaction	adult interaction
24 visiting pupil	visiting pupil
25 housekeeping (or not i/act'g)	not interacting
26 general monitoring	out of room
27 out of room	
28 not observed	
29 not listed	**AUDIENCE**
30 HELP! (+ note)	**COMPOSITION**
	ACTIVITY
TEACHER'S AUDIENCE	
1 boy individual	
2 girl individual	
3 boy for group	
4 girl for group	
5 boy for class	
6 girl for class	
7 sustained interaction	
8 group	
9 class	
10 pair	

CURRICULUM
1 Eng., 2 Math., 3 Sci., 4 Hist., 5 Geog., 6 RE, 7 Art, 8 Music, 9 PE, 10 IT, 11 Tech., 12 PSE, 13 X-curric., 14 rapd ch., 15 routn., 16 other.

correct or improve their work. One of the difficulties in coding, which was raised during the training of observers for ORACLE 1996, was that value judgement feedback without accompanying informational comment could be coded, in effect, as neutral feedback.

The schedule was therefore amended so that feedback categories clearly differentiated between feedback as the teacher's value judgement and feedback as neutral information from the teacher. Two feedback codes were used to refer to value judgements about the pupil's work/effort (code 9) or routine/behaviour (code 12), with the particular stress on praising or criticising indicated, where appropriate, by use of positive and negative signs inserted beside the recorded code. The other two feedback codes were used when the teacher commented about the child's work/effort (code 10) or routine/behaviour (code 13) in a neutral tone of voice, which could be accompanied by a mild statement of approval or disapproval.

Pupil Record changes

Besides an expanded Curriculum section, few changes were made to the ORACLE 1976 categories on the new version of the schedule. No codes were amended, but some new codes were added to existing major categories.

Base (pupils' seating arrangements). In the earlier schedule there were five bases which identified where the target was seated during the observation: Alone, two same sex (2SS – target and one other same sex pupil) two opposite sex (2OS – target and one other opposite sex pupil) several same sex (SSS) and several opposite sex (SOS). On the ORACLE 1996 pupil schedule we added 'class' to this list in order to differentiate between seating arrangements where the target and two or more children (i.e. group) were together, and arrangements where the target was either standing or sitting with the rest of the class. For example, when the children were sitting together in the carpet area listening to a story; or when the children were standing around the teacher's desk watching a science demonstration.

Team (pupils' working). In ORACLE 1976, it was observed that children's seating groups were not necessarily their working groups for class activities. The PRISMS project on curriculum provision in small primary schools (Galton and Patrick 1990: Appendix III) took this finding on board and devised the Team category upon which the ORACLE 1996 category is based. Team is divided into individual, pair, group and class, and describes the level of collaboration of pupils with each other as they work. Team composition is decided with reference to the teacher's intention for the activity; if the pupil is interacting with another pupil but is not required to work with a partner, the team is individual and not pair.

In the PRISMS project, class was defined as the whole class co-ordinating their actions, such as singing in unison. This is not comparable with the ORACLE 1996 definition of class, which was broadened to include situations such as when the teacher addressed the whole class, and the children were expected to listen actively as if to be ready to answer a question, for example, when the class were expected to collaborate together by employing 'listening behaviour' while the teacher read a story. This definition conforms to the definition used by Pollard *et al.* in the PACE studies.

Additions to the ORACLE 1976 Pupil Record categories

Other changes to the Pupil Record since the original ORACLE were made in the category *Pupil–Adult Interaction*. This is the middle of three coding boxes on the Pupil Record sheet (Pupil Activity, Pupil–Adult Interaction and Pupil–Pupil Interaction) and is coded when the target pupil is involved in attempted or ongoing verbal or non-verbal interaction with an adult.

Pupil–Adult Interaction. Within the Pupil–Adult Interaction Category, the *Interacting Adult* codes were extended beyond the three ORACLE 1976 categories of 'teacher', 'observer' and 'other', to include the following adults who were observed working in class with the teacher: team teacher, parent, classroom assistant, SEN teacher and student teacher. 'Other' then denoted another visiting adult, for example the school secretary or headteacher. The research team were, therefore, able to collect more detailed information about the roles occupied by other adults who interacted with pupils in class during the observation periods.

Also, within the Pupil–Adult Interaction Category, finer detail of the *Adult's Communication Setting* was obtained by extending the initial ORACLE codes of 'individual attention', 'group' 'class' and 'other' to include individual for group and individual for class. This enabled the collection of data on when the teacher interacted individually with a child while requiring a group or the class to attend to the conversation.

Changes to curriculum content on the Pupil Record

As stated earlier, there was much more detail in the recording of curriculum in the 1996 ORACLE project (see also Appendix 5: Table 5A1).

- Curriculum content was divided into six areas based on those originally devised for the PRISMS project.
- National Curriculum Attainment Targets were used, where applicable, as a means of describing task activity.

Discussion following the first round of systematic observation in classrooms resulted in minor amendments to the Pupil Record for the second round of primary school observations. These were made in the curriculum categories of cognitive demand and resources and do not affect the data included in this publication, which are focused on teacher–pupil and pupil–pupil interaction rather on the detailed analysis of curriculum.

Table 2A2a Definitions of ORACLE 1996 Pupil Record categories (pupil activity)

Pupil activity		
Category	Item	Brief definition of item
8 Target's activity	1 COOP TK	Fully involved and co-operating on approved task work (e.g. reading)
	2 COOP R	Fully involved and co-operating on approved routine work (e.g. sharpening a pencil)
	3 DSTR	Non-involved and totally distracted from all work
	4 DSTR OB	Non-involved and totally distracted from all work by the observer
	5 DSRP	Non-involved and aggressively disrupting work of other pupil(s)
	6 HPLY	Non-involved and engaging in horseplay with other pupil(s)
	7 WAIT T	Waiting to interact with the teacher
	8 CODS	Partially co-operating and partially distracted from approved work
	9 INSTRST T	Interested in teacher's activity or private interaction with other pupil(s)
	10 INTRST P	Interested in the work of other pupil(s)
	11 WOA	Working on an alternative activity which is not approved work
	12 RIS	The target is responding to internal stimuli
	13 NOT OB	Not coded because the target is not observed for some reason
	14 NOT LIST	The target's activity is not listed
9 Target's location	1 P IN	Target in base
	2 P OUT	Target out of base but not mobile
	3 P MOB	Target out of base and mobile
	4 P OUT RM	Target out of room
10 Teacher activity and location	1 T PRES	Teacher present with target through interaction or physical proximity
	2 T ELSE	Teacher privately interacting elsewhere with other pupil(s) or visitor
	3 T MNTR	Teacher not interacting but monitoring classroom activities
	4 T HSKP	Teacher not interacting but housekeeping
	5 T OUT	Teacher out of room

Table 2A2b Definitions of ORACLE 1996 Pupil Record categories (pupil–adult interaction)

Pupil–adult interaction			
	Category	*Item*	*Brief definition of item*
1	Target's role	1 INIT	Target attempts to become focus of attention (not focus at previous signal)
		2 STAR	Target is focus of attention
		3 PART	Target in audience (no child is focus)
		4 LSWT	Target in audience (another child is focus)
2	Interacting adult	1 TCHR	Target interacts with teacher
		2 OBSR	Target interacts with observer
		3 OTHER	Target interacts with another visiting adult (not listed)
		4 TM TCHR	Target interacts with team teacher
		5 PARENT	Target interacts with parent
		6 CRM ASST	Target interacts with classroom assistant
		7 SEN TCHR	Target interacts with Special Needs teacher
		8 STUDENT	Target interacts with student teacher
3	Adult's content	1 TK WK	Adult interacts about task work (task content or supervision)
		2 ROUT	Adult interacts about routine matter (classroom management and control)
		3 POS	Adult reacts positively to task work/behaviour, etc. (praises)
		4 NEG	Adult reacts negatively to task work behaviour etc. (criticises)
		5 IGN	Adult ignores attempted initiation
4	Adult's communication setting	1 TGT IND ATTN	Adult gives private individual attention to target pupil
		2 IND for GRP	Individual attention: GROUP required to attend
		3 GROUP	Adult gives private attention to target's group
		4 IND for CLS	Individual attention: CLASS required to attend
		5 CLASS	Adult interacts with whole class
		6 OTHER	Adult gives private attention to another child or group or does not interact.

Table 2A2c Definitions of ORACLE 1996 Pupil Record categories (pupil–pupil interaction)

Pupil activity		
Category	Item	Brief definition of item
5 Target's role	1 BGNS	Target successfully begins a new contact
	2 RSPNDS	Target co-operates by responding to an initiation
	3 TRIES	Target unsuccessfully tries to initiate
	4 IGN	Target ignores attempted initiation
	5 SUST	Target sustains interaction
6 Mode of interaction	1 MTL	Non-verbal, mediated solely by materials
	2 CNTC	Non-verbal, mediated by physical contact or gesture (with or without materials)
	3 VRBL	Verbal (with or without materials, physical contact or gesture)
7a Other pupil's task	1 S TK	Same as target's task
	2 D TK	Different to target's task
7b Other pupil's no. and sex	1 SS	Target interacts privately with one pupil of the same sex
	2 OS	Target interacts privately with one pupil of opposite sex
	3 SSS	Target interacts publicly with two or more pupils having the same sex as target
	4 SOS	Target interacts publicly with two or more pupils, of whom one at least is of the opposite sex to target
7c Other pupil's base	1 OWN BS	From target's own base
	2 OTH BS	From another base.

APPENDIX 3

TEACHER STYLES 1976 AND 1996

ORACLE 1976 and teacher styles

The original ORACLE study investigated variations between groups of teachers in order to develop an understanding of a teaching style that was somewhat different from that used by Bennett (1975). Initially, the style was defined solely in terms of the teaching tactics which consisted of all observations recorded during lessons. These styles were then related to the organisational strategies that teachers employed in the classroom. From this initial analysis, four teaching styles emerged, three of which were clearly linked to a particular organisational strategy. Of these four styles, almost half were classified as 'style changers' because they tended to adopt a modified version of the various patterns of interaction associated with different degrees of emphasis placed upon individual class and group organisation. A further analysis broke these style changers down into three further clusters or groups. In retrospect, the emphasis given to the organisational strategy for these three styles tended to divert attention from the important differences within the tactics which were used by each of the groups. The descriptions of each of these teaching styles are given below.

ORACLE 1996: six types of teacher

Group instructors

These spend about a fifth of their time working with groups of pupils – three times more than any other style. When doing it they concentrate more on giving pupils instructions and routine information than engaging in more interesting discussion of ideas. But they give pupils plenty of verbal feedback, and ask a fair number of open questions. Children mostly work on their own, and very few demand attention from the teacher.

Most group instructors were in their thirties. Their pupils made good progress on language skills, but did less well on mathematics and reading. The pupils were also good at listening and at acquiring information from

214

tapes and pictures but did not shine at mapping, block graphs or original drawings.

Class enquirers

These are highly organised teachers who use class teaching for 31 per cent of the time. They are clear and lucid when explaining the work, saving a lot of time for questions and – this style's speciality – statements of ideas. Children worked individually when not part of the whole class, with the teacher helping and questioning them one-to-one.

Half the class enquirers were over forty, and the ratio of men to women was two-to-one. The majority of children in their classes were 'solitary workers', avoiding as far as possible personal contact with the teacher or other children. The pupils of the class enquirers made most progress of any style on mathematics and language tests, but significantly less progress on reading than some others. These particular pupils were good at posing questions, less good at mapping and block graphs, and low on originality.

Infrequent changers

These are the 'Plowden superteachers' who, by efficient organisation and hard work, interact with children for 90 per cent of the time and achieve a high level of individualisation. They make occasional and carefully planned switches in classroom organisation – between class and individual work – depending on the needs of a particular class. They ask children more questions than any other teachers, and more interesting questions. They like children to learn to sort out their own tasks, and seem to encourage children to ask for attention.

Many Infrequent changers were over thirty. Their pupils made more progress than any other group on reading, and progressed well on mathematics and language tests. The pupils also did well on mapping, but less well on other study skills.

Individual monitors

These teachers work mainly one-to-one with children, using lower levels of group and class teaching than the other teaching styles. They spend a lot of time briefly telling children what to do, rather than discussing ideas that come out of the work. In fact, they talk less than other teachers, tending to mark silently and hand back work. Nearly half the children in their classes are 'intermittent workers' who mix work with social chat.

Individual monitors were mostly young teachers. Their pupils made good progress on reading, but came out among the worst in progress on mathematics and language tests. Pupils of individual monitors also did well on

Table 3A1 Cluster characteristics of the 1976 teacher styles as a percentage of all observations[a]

Teacher Record 1976	1 indiv. montr	2 class enquir.	3 group instruct.	4 style changr	4a[b] infreq. changr	4b[b] rotat. changr	4c[b] habitl changr
QUESTIONS							
Q1 recalling facts	3.9	4.1	2.4	3.4	3.8	3.2	3.6
Q2 offering ideas, solns (closed)	1.1	3.3	2.0	2.4	4.1	2.5	1.7
Q3 offering ideas, solns (open)	0.3	1.0	0.9	0.6	1.4	0.4	0.4
All task questions	5.3	8.4	5.3	6.4	9.3	6.1	5.7
Q4 task supervision	2.9	4.1	3.2	4.5	4.1	6.5	3.4
Q5 routine matter	1.3	2.2	1.5	2.0	2.4	2.0	1.8
All other questions	4.2	6.3	4.7	6.5	6.5	8.5	5.2
STATEMENTS							
S1 of facts	5.6	8.0	11.9	6.0	6.5	4.9	6.5
S2 of ideas	2.1	4.2	1.0	2.6	3.2	2.5	2.4
All task statements	7.7	12.2	12.9	8.6	9.7	7.4	8.9
TASK SUPERVISION							
S3 telling	15.8	11.2	11.6	11.8	13.3	12.0	10.9
S4 praising	1.0	1.3	0.6	1.1	0.9	1.4	1.0
S5 feedback	8.7	10.9	15.9	8.7	12.1	7.2	6.8
ROUTINE							
S6 information	5.6	7.0	6.7	6.8	8.0	7.5	5.8
S7 feedback	1.8	2.3	2.3	2.0	3.1	1.9	1.5
S8 critical control	2.0	1.5	2.4	2.6	2.7	3.4	2.1
S9 small talk	1.3	1.7	0.6	1.4	0.9	1.0	1.9
All other statements	36.2	35.9	40.1	34.4	41.0	34.4	30.0
SILENT INTERACTION							
Gesturing	1.8	0.9	3.7	1.8	1.5	0.6	2.8
Showing	2.4	3.3	2.0	2.6	2.1	2.3	3.0
Marking	16.4	5.7	7.4	9.4	10.3	7.4	10.2
Waiting	1.7	1.6	2.1	2.0	1.9	1.7	2.2
Story	0.6	1.8	1.0	0.7	0.4	1.4	0.4
Reading	3.0	3.4	2.2	3.8	2.9	5.5	3.0
All other interactions	25.9	16.7	18.4	20.3	19.1	18.9	21.6
N =	13.0	9.0	7.0	29.0	6.0	9.0	14.0

Notes

a These data are reproduced from Table 6.1. and Table 6.2. of Galton *et al.* (1980) *Inside the Primary Classroom.*

b Please note that 4a, 4b and 4c are sub-groups within Style 4.

Table 3A2 Cluster characteristics of the 1996 teacher styles as a percentage of all observations

Teacher Record 1996	All	Cluster A class enquirer	B indiv. montr	C group superv.	D cls-grp instructor
QUESTIONS					
1 recalling facts	4.1	4.7	2.5	2.1	4.9
2 offering ideas, solns (closed)	6.2	9.4	3.8	4.5	6.1
3 offering ideas, solns (open)	1.5[a]	3.3	0.2	2.8	0.9
4 task supervision	2.8	2.5	3.3	4.3	2.4
5 routine matter	2.1	1.8	2.4	2.1	2.1
STATEMENTS					
6 of fact	8.5	6.7	8.0	6.6	9.9
7 of ideas, problems	4.9	4.6	3.4	4.8	5.5
Task supervision					
8 telling	13.4[a]	9.7[c]	15.1	10.4	14.9
9 praise/crit. of work/effort	2.8	3.4	3.03	2.8	2.5
10 feedback	10.3	10.8	13.4	12.5	8.7
Routine					
11 information	10.2	9.7	9.3	12.4	10.4
12 praise/crit of rtn/behvr	2.0	2.8	2.5	1.1	1.7
13 feedback	4.6	5.0	5.9	3.7	4.1
14 small talk	1.5	1.7	1.4	1.0	1.5
SILENT INTERACTION					
15 Gesturing	1.2	0.9	1.3	1.9	1.2
16 Showing	2.7[b]	2.1	1.3[d]	7.1[d]	2.5
17 Marking	2.4	2.4	4.8	4.0	1.4
18 Waiting	0.9	1.1	0.5	0.3	1.0
19 Story	2.1	7.8[d]	0.4	0.0[c]	0.9
20 Reading (listening/ watching)	4.2	4.7	2.8	4.07	4.5
Composite variables					
Low cognitive (1+6)	12.7	11.4	10.5	8.7	14.7
High cognitive (2+3+7)	12.6	17.3	7.4[c]	12.1	12.5
Challenging questions (2+3)	7.7	12.7[d]	4.0[c]	7.3	7.0
All questions (1+2+3+4+5)	16.7	21.7[d]	12.2[c]	15.8	16.3
All task (1+2+3+6+7)	25.3	28.7	17.8[c]	20.9	27.2
Task statements (6+7)	13.4	11.3	11.7	11.4	15.4
All task supervision (4+8+9+10)	29.2	26.4	34.8	29.9	28.4
All routine (5+11+12+13+14)	20.3	21.0	21.5	20.3	19.8
N =	29.0	6.0	5.0	3.0	15.0

Notes
a= 5% significant variation across clusters (ANOVA).
b= 1% significant variation across clusters.
c= a cluster score at least one standard deviation *below* the overall mean for 29 teachers.
d= a cluster score at least one standard deviation *above* the overall mean for 29 teachers.

block graphs, and produced the most original drawings of all, but were bad at mapping and posing questions.

Habitual changers

These teachers switch about unpredictably from class teaching to individual work as a response to the behaviour of the class. They use the fewest open questions and statements of ideas of any style, and are the most likely to go in for small talk with children. They believe in topic work, and spend the least time directly on the basics.

Habitual changers were mostly in their twenties, and women. Their pupils made among the least progress at reading and mathematics. Although not among the worst at language skills, their progress was still significantly worse than the three of the other styles. However, the pupils of the habitual changers did best overall on the study skills, particularly block graphs, mapping and sequencing a story.

Rotating changers

These teachers organise their classrooms so that different groups of pupils work on different curriculum areas at the same time. When the teacher gives the signal, they all change over – with groups either physically swapping places, or swapping curriculum materials. One result can be discipline problems, and rotating changers go in for more criticism of children, and verbal attempts to control them, than other styles.

Rotating changers were mainly in their twenties. Their children came out among the worst on every test of progress on basic skills, and on every study skill except one – and even for that, they did significantly worse than the most successful style. The ORACLE 1976 research team's comment was that this is 'the one style that overall has little to commend it' (*Progress and Performance in the Primary Classroom*, Galton and Simon 1980: 193).

APPENDIX 4

PUPIL STYLES 1976

Table 4A1 Characteristics of the four pupil clusters (pupil record, 1976)[a]

Pupil Record 1976	% total observations				
	All pupils	Attention seekers	Intermitttent workers	Solitary workers	Quiet collaborators
PUPIL ACTIVITY					
Target activity					
coop tk	58.1	54.8	52.4	65.7	59.1
coop r	11.9	11.8	12.0	11.4	13.5
dstr	15.9	16.7	20.5	10.8	14.5
wait teacher	4.3	6.4	3.8	3.3	5.5
cods	1.9	2.1	2.4	1.5	1.4
intrst teacher	1.7	1.6	1.8	1.9	1.4
intrst pup	3.4	2.8	4.3	3.3	2.3
Target location					
P in	86.1	78.4	87.0	89.6	85.8
P out	9.9	16.0	9.0	7.3	10.2
P mob	2.7	3.4	2.9	2.0	2.7
Teacher activity					
T pres	22.2	24.2	15.1	24.8	32.9
Telse	67.2	67.7	71.7	64.9	58.5
Tmntr	3.2	2.6	3.3	3.9	1.6
T hskp	4.1	1.7	5.9	4.3	2.5
T out rm	2.7	2.8	3.4	1.4	3.8
PUPIL–ADULT INTERACTION					
Target's role					
init	1.2	2.3	0.7	1.1	1.4
star	1.6	4.1	0.9	0.9	1.5
part	11.0	9.6	6.8	14.6	16.3
lswt	2.3	2.2	1.1	3.3	3.5
Interctng ad					
teacher	15.9	17.9	9.3	19.6	22.5
Ad's content					
tk wk	13.2	14.3	7.3	17.1	18.6
rout	2.4	3.0	1.8	2.4	3.4

Ad's comun setng					
target indiv attention	2.2	5.5	1.3	1.4	2.0
group	1.5	1.1	0.7	0.7	7.1
class	11.8	11.3	6.9	16.9	13.5
Target's role					
bgns	5.4	5.3	7.0	3.7	5.4
rspnds(coop)	6.2	6.7	7.6	4.9	5.0
sust	6.3	6.6	8.2	3.3	8.1
Mode of inter'n					
vrbl	16.2	17.3	20.2	11.1	15.6
Other pup. task					
s tk	14.1	13.5	17.5	9.5	16.7
d tk	4.3	5.4	5.7	2.8	2.4
Other pup. no. & sex					
SS	13.1	12.9	16.7	8.9	13.1
OS	2.2	2.7	2.4	1.6	2.2
SevSS	2.1	1.8	3.0	1.2	2.6
SevOS	1.1	1.6	1.1	0.7	1.0
Other pup. base					
own base	14.8	13.7	19.4	9.9	16.3
oth base	3.6	5.4	3.9	2.4	2.7

Note

a This table is based on Table 3A2, Appendix 3 and Table 5A1, Appendix 5 of Galton *et al.*
(1980) *Inside the Primary Classroom.* Individual coding categories which constitute less
than 1% of observations have been excluded.

APPENDIX 5

CURRICULUM

Table 5A1 Comparing percentage figures for Pupil Record observations of *dominant* subject, 1976 (equivalent) and 1996[a] (see Table 4.15)

% of ORACLE 1996 observations

Subject	All ORACLE 1996	ORACLE 1976-equivalent
English	28.2	29.8
mathematics	22.4	23.7
science	11.7	12.4
art	11.3	11.9
history	5.5	5.8
geography	7.1	7.5
RE	0.3	0.4
music	0.3	0.4
cross-curricular	3.0	3.2
IT	0.9	no category
technology	3.8	no category
PSE	0.1	no category
routine	2.5	no category
PE	1.6	not recorded
other	1.3	not recorded
total	100.0	95.1

Note
a Comparing % observations with those calculated using a restricted dataset based on ORACLE 1976-equivalent categories

APPENDIX 6

PUPIL PERFORMANCE IN BASIC SKILLS

Appendix 6.1: ORACLE 1996 Test Items: content and correspondence with National Curriculum Programmes of Study

Table 6A1a Mathematics skills test items

Mathematics concepts

Item no.	RTBS[a] no.	Item content	National Curriculum Mathematics: Key Stage 2[b] Programmes of Study[c]
1	1	Whole nos.: relative values	2.2a[d]
2	3	Numeration: ordinal numbers	2.2a
3	6	Place value & expanded notation	2.2a
4	8	Measurement: quantity	3.4a (KS1)
5	18	Currency: relative values of coins	2.4a, b (24a at KS1)
6	23	Whole nos.: rounding	2.2a
7	30	Geometry: recog kinds of geom. figures	3.2b (KS1)
8	36	Whole nos.: number fact	2.3c
9	39	Properties of numeration	2.3c
10	47	Ratio (time)	2.3d, 2.4a, 3.4a
End of Year 4 Items			
11	53	Fractions: equivalence	2.2c
12	56	Whole nos.: fundamental operations: terms	1.3a, 2.3c
13	64	Fractions: relative values	2.2c
14	73	Decimals: reading and writing	2.2b, c
15	77	Equations	2.3g, 2b
16	84	Equations inequalities and number sentences	2.3a
17	90	Decimals: fundamental operations estimating results	2.2b, c
18	94	Geometry: angles and triangles	3.2a, 3c

Mathematics problem solving

19	1	Whole nos: subtraction	2.2c, 4a
20	2	Whole nos: addition	2.2a, 4a
21	18	Fractions: subtraction (metres)	2.2a, 3.4a
22	19	Currency: multiplication	2.2b, 4a
23	23	Whole nos: division	2.4a
24	32	Measurements: addition (time)	3.4a
25	36	Whole nos: multiplication	2, 3a, 3d, 4a
End of Year 4 Items			

26	43	Fractions: multiplication/division; (area)	2.3g; 3.4a
27	49	Measurements: subtraction (time)	2.4a, b; 3.4a
28	53	Currency: multiplication; addition	2.4a, b
29	59	Ratio	2.2c, 4a
30	62	Decimals: subtraction (currency)	2.4a, 4b

Notes
a RTBS: Richmond Tests of Basic Skills.
b All Key Stage 2 (KS2) unless otherwise stated.
c Mathematics Programmes of Study (PoS): (1) Using and applying mathematics; (2) Numbers; (3) Shape, space and measures; (4) Handling data.
d '2.2a' means PoS2 (Numbers), point 2a which begins, 'Read, write and order whole numbers...'.

Table 6A1b Language skills test items

Language skills

Item no.	RTBS no.	Item content (RTBS manual)	National Curriculum English at Key Stage 2 Programme of Study
		CAPITAL LETTERS[a]	WRITING
1	1	First word of sentence	2c (KS1)
2	14	Countries or continents	2c (KS1)
3	27	Title of respect, honour, rank	2c (KS1)
4	43[b]	Over-use of capital letters	2c (KS1)
End of Y4 Items			
5	55	Names of specific organisations	2c (KS1)
6	64	Over-use of capital letters	2c (KS1)
7	80	First word in quotation	2c (KS1)
		PUNCTUATION[c]	WRITING
8	1	Full stop at end of complete sentence	2c
9	12	(No mistakes)	2c
10	22	Use of question mark	2c
11	44	Over-use of comma	2c
12	47	Double quotation marks	2c
End of Y4 Items			
13	32[d]	Over-use of comma	2c
14	67	Exclamation mark	2c
15	79	Comma to separate quote from sentence	2c
		USAGE[e]	WRITING
16	1	Verbs: past tense	3b
17	14	First person pronouns	3b
18	27	Avoidance of redundancies	3b
19	39	Pronouns: case forms	3b
End of Y4 Items			
20	53	Adjectives and adverbs	3b
21	62	Miscellaneous modifying forms	3b
	L-1	SPELLING[f]	WRITING
22	1	w, u, ou, ue substitutions 'abel'	2d
23	12	(No mistakes)	2d

24	22	Vowel substitution – I 'radeo'	2d
25	31	Interchanged letters 'feild'	2d
26	43	Final e 'tast'	2d
27	52	Double letter 'allthough'	2d
End of Y4 Items			
28	84	Omitted letters 'enormus'	2d
29	96	y, ey, i substitutions 'gloomey'	2d
30	104	Vowel substitution – a 'intrupted'	2d

Notes

a Writing: Key Stage 1. 2c: In punctuation...Pupils should be taught to punctuate their writing, be consistent in their use of capital letters, full stops and question marks, and begin to use commas (DfEE 1995).

b ORACLE 1976 used item 41

c Writing: Key Stage 2. In punctuation, pupils should be taught to use punctuation marks correctly in their writing, including full stops, question and exclamation marks, commas, inverted commas, and apostrophes to mark possession (DfEE 1995).

d Item 32 in 1975 RTBS became Item 61 in 1988 RTBS

e Writing: Key Stage 2. Standard English and Language Study: 3a: Pupils should be given opportunities to reflect on their use of language, beginning to differentiate between spoken and written forms. 3b: Pupils should be given opportunities to develop their understanding of the grammar of complex sentences including clauses and phrases. They should be taught to use the standard written forms of nouns, pronouns, verbs, adjectives, adverbs, prepositions, conjunctions and verb tenses.

f Writing: Key Stage 2. 2d: In spelling...pupils should be taught to:

- Spell complex, polysyllabic words that conform to regular patterns, and to break long and complex words into more manageable units, by using their knowledge of meaning and words structure.
- Memorise the visual patterns of words, including those that are irregular.
- Recognise silent letters.

Table 6A1c Vocabulary and Reading Comprehension test items

Item no.	RTBS no.	Item content (RTBS manual)	National Curriculum English at Key Stage 2 Programmes of Study	
Vocabulary[a]		Recognise meaning of the following words:	Writing	Speaking & Listening
1	1	final	3c	3b
2	4	even	3c	3b
3	8	healed	3c	3b
4	15	destroy	3c	3b
5	23	weed	3c	3b
6	31	fairly	3c	3b
7	39	explain	3c	3b
8	46	knit	3c	3b
End of Y4 Items				
9	54	individual	3c	3b
10	62	antique	3c	3b
11	69	suburb	3c	3b

| 12 | 77 | situated | 3c | 3b |
| 13 | 85 | leisure | 3c | 3b |

Reading Comprehension[b]

Narrative passage

Programme of Study: Reading

14	6	Details – implied facts & relationships	2b; 2c
15	7	Details – implied facts & relationships	2b; 2c
16	8	Evaluation: generalisation from a selection	2b; 2c
17	9	Recog. & undstd important facts and details	2b; 2c
18	10	Organisation – time sequence	2b; 2c
19	11	Details – implied facts and relationships	2b; 2c
20	37	Details – implied facts and relationships	2b; 2c

Information Passage

21	38	Details – important facts and details	2b; 2c
22	39	Details – important facts and details	2b; 2c
23	40	Details – implied facts and relationships	2b; 2c
24	41	Details – important facts and details	2b; 2c
25	42	Detect main purpose of paragraph	2b; 2c

End of Y4 Items

Poem

26	132	Recognise main idea or topic of paragraph	2b; 2c
27	133	Details – deduce meaning of words	2b; 2c
28	134	Details – deduce meaning of words	2b; 2c
29	135	Details – deduce meaning of words	2b; 2c
30	136	Evaluation – generalisations from a selection	2b; 2c

Notes

a Writing Key Stage 2. Standard English and Language Study: 3c: Pupils should be taught to distinguish between words of similar meaning, to explain the meanings of words, and to experiment with choices of vocabulary. Their interest in words should be extended by the discussion of language use and choices.

b Reading Key Stage 2. Range: 1c: Pupils' reading should include texts:

- with more complex narrative structures and sustained ideas;
- that include figurative language, both in poetry and prose;
- with a variety of structural and organisational features.

Key Skills: 2b:

Pupils should be taught to consider in detail the quality and depth of what they read. They should be encouraged to respond imaginatively to the plot, characters, ideas, vocabulary and organisation of language in literature. They should be taught to use inference and deduction. Pupils should be taught to evaluate the texts they read, and to refer to relevant passages or episodes to support their opinions.

2c: [extracts]

Pupils should be taught to:

- identify the precise information they wish to know;
- distinguish between fact and opinion;
- consider an argument critically;
- note the meaning and use of newly encountered words.

Appendix 6.2 ORACLE 1996 item facilities by year group and sex

Table 6A2a: Mathematics skills item facilities: percentage of children who answered item correctly

Item no.	RTBS no.	Item Type	Y4 (%) boys	girls	Y5 (%) boys	girls	Y6 (%) boys	girls
MATHEMATICS CONCEPTS								
1	1	Whole nos: relative values	91	83	93	93	86	90
2	3	Numeration: ordinal numbers	87*	75	82	88	85	89
3	6	Place value & expanded notation	69**	50	74	72	64	78*
4	8	Measurement: quantity	66*	54	81	72	79	79
5	18	Currency: relative values of coins	52	47	70	77	83	76
6	23	Whole nos: rounding	56**	30	66	55	84*	70
7	30	Geometry: recog kinds/parts of geom figures	67	79*	79	86	93	90
8	36	Whole nos: number fact	41	38	56	56	65	69
9	39	Properties of numeration	40	38	46	48	53	64
10	47	Ratio (time)	41	42	66	60	64	71
11	53	Fractions: equivalence			72	81	64	77*
12	56	Whole nos: fundamental operations: terms			42	34	46	50
13	64	Fractions: relative values			38	34	51	44
14	73	Decimals reading and writing			13	9	18	26
15	77	Equations			75	76	75	84
16	84	Equations: inequalities and number sentences			20	16	15	26
17	90	Decimals: fundamental operations: estimating results			27*	14	32	23
18	94	Geometry: angles and triangles			56	57	73	64
MATHEMATICS PROBLEM SOLVING								
19	1	Whole nos: subtraction	72	70	77	80	80	88
20	2	Whole nos: addition	73	79	78	81	87	79
21	18	Fractions: subtraction (metres)	73**	56	73	63	80	79
22	19	Currency: multiplication	49	41	61	67	63	68
23	23	Whole nos: division	34**	18	42	51	68	60
24	32	Measurements: addition (time)	56**	37	62	60	64	81**
25	36	Whole nos: multiplication	29*	16	49**	30	51	52
26	43	Fractions: multiplication			34	35	47	40
27	49	Measurements: subtraction (time)			46	42	69	67
28	53	Currency: multiplication: addition			20	17	29*	17
29	59	Ratio			31	23	31	29
30	62	Decimals: subtraction			37	33	47	46

Notes
* p < 0.05.
** p < 0.01 (sex difference within year group).

Table 6A2b Language skills item facilities: percentage of children who answered item correctly

Item no.	RTBS no.	Item content	Y4 (%) boys	Y4 (%) girls	Y5 (%) boys	Y5 (%) girls	Y6 (%) boys	Y6 (%) girls
	L-2	CAPITAL LETTERS						
1	1	First word of sentence	58	59	61	72*	78	80
2	14	Countries or continents	34	41	53	63	57	61
3	27	Title of respect, honour, rank	22	25	24	23	22	20
4	43[a]	Over-use of capital letters	35	38	49	45	38	46
5	55	Names of specific organisations			26	26	31	33
6	64	Over-use of capital letters			56	59	56	61
7	80	First word in quotation			28	47**	32	37
	L-3	PUNCTUATION						
8	1	Full stop at end of complete sentence	69	72	71	81	73	77
9	12	No mistakes	61	69	58	67	65	72
10	22	Use of question mark	35	28	36	53*	28	42*
11	44	Over-use of comma	44	34	34	42	48	63*
12	47	Double quotation marks	35	29	40	40	45	61*
13	32[b]	Over-use of comma			14	17	13	08
14	67	Exclamation mark			24	23	20	27
15	79	Comma, separating quote from sentence			18	13	15	13
	L-4	USAGE						
16	1	Verbs: past tense	53	57	58	66	57	76**
17	14	First person pronouns	59	61	63	71	65	92**
18	27	Avoidance of redundancies	43	54	53	60	49	68**
19	39	Pronouns: case forms	20	22	30	31	34	45
20	53	Adjectives and adverbs			20	40**	32	40
21	62	Misc. modifying forms			26	31	39	29
	L-1	SPELLING						
22	1	w, u, ou, ue substitutions 'abel'	55	55	47	58	69	80
23	12	(No mistakes)	54	66	44	55	59	80**
24	22	Vowel substitution – I 'radeo'	55	67	50	60	67	83*
25	31	Interchanged letters 'feild'	36	44	36	45	49	61
26	43	Final e 'tast'	28	37	29	35	46	56
27	52	Double letter 'allthough'			32	28	27	40
28	84	Omitted letters 'enormus'			15	19	29	27
29	96	y, ey, i substitutions 'gloomey'			19	26	24	33
30	104	Vowel substitution – a 'intrupted'			10	14	25	18

Notes
* $p < 0.05$.
a ORACLE 1976 used item 41.
** $p < 0.01$ (sex differences within year group).
b Relocated as item 32 from 1975 edition.

Table 6A2c Vocabulary and Reading item facilities: percentage of children in each group who answered correctly

Item no.	RTBS no.	Item content	Y4 (%) boys	girls	Y5 (%) boys	girls	Y6 (%) boys	girls
VOCABULARY								
Recognise meaning of:								
1	1	final	80	86	80	92*	93	93
2	4	even	78	78	81	88	82	83
3	8	healed	67	74	74	82	84	90
4	15	destroy	83	83	83	81	91	93
5	23	weed	50	54	48	68**	60	76*
6	31	fairly	15	24	27	18	36	41
7	39	explain	21	28	17	27	27	31
8	46	knit	59	66	43	55	60	69
9	54	individual			69	79	79	82
10	62	antique			58	58	69	74
11	69	suburb			34	25	34	35
12	77	situated			44	40	47	55
13	85	leisure			37	58**	28	33
READING COMPREHENSION								
Narrative passage								
14	6	Details – implied facts & relationships	73	78	75	82	82	87
15	7	Details – implied facts & relationships	68	65	63	82**	86	89
16	8	Evaluation: generalisation from a selection	77	83	80	92*	88	93
17	9	Recognise & understand important facts and details	62	70	76	86	91	88
18	10	Organisation – time sequence	38	43	63	76*	77	83
19	11	Details – implied facts & relationships	43	49	61	67	64	71
20	37	Details – implied facts and relationships	30	36	36	33	42	41
Information passage								
21	38	Details – important facts and details	46*	34	44	48	63*	48
22	39	Details – important facts and details	53	44	56	55	62	65
23	40	Details – implied facts and relationships	43	52	48	51	71	73
24	41	Details – important facts and details	42	38	44	56	62	61
25	42	Detect main purpose of para.	38	34	31	45*	28	46*
Poem								
26	132	Recognise main idea or topic of para.			13	20	16	22

27	133	Details – deduce meaning of words	14	24	28	22
28	134	Details – deduce meaning of words	48	41	57	58
29	135	Details – deduce meaning of words	36	27	44	37
30	136	Evaluation – devel generalisations from a selection	44	33	35	36

Notes
* p < 0.05.
** p < 0.01 (sex difference within year group).

Appendix 6.3 ORACLE test reliabilities

Table 6A3 ORACLE 1996 test and sub-test reliabilities

ORACLE test	Short form 1996 (Y4 only)	Long form 1996 (Y5, 6)	Short form 1996 (Y4, 5, 6)
LANGUAGE SKILLS			
Total	0.74	0.80	0.76
Spelling	0.72	0.79	0.77
Use of capitals	0.41	0.33	0.36
Punctuation	0.34	0.36	0.38
Usage	0.61	0.62	0.61
N (language)	238	394	632
MATHEMATICS			
Total	0.71	0.83	0.80
Concept mastery	0.55	0.72	0.66
Problem solving	0.65	0.74	0.73
N (maths)	234	389	623
READING			
Total	0.69	0.74	0.80
Vocabulary	0.60	0.64	0.60
Comprehension	0.68	0.73	0.74
N (reading)	242	387	629

Appendix 6.4 Tables of comparisons between the 1976 and 1996 cohorts' performance in the tests of basic skills

Table 6A4a Overall comparison of raw scores based on the total number of ORACLE 1996 pupils who took any of the tests

	ORACLE 1976 %[a]	s.d.	N	ORACLE 1996 %[b]	s.d.	N[c]
Mathematics	16.8	5.3	409	14.4[d]	6.2	624
Language skills	13.0	5.3	410	11.3[d]	5.3	630
Reading/vocabulary	18.8	6.0	410	14.8[d]	5.7	627

Table 6A4b Overall comparison of raw score test results for pupils of all three age groups in 1976 and 1996

	ORACLE 1976 %[a]	s.d	N	ORACLE 1996 %[b]	s.d.	N
Mathematics	16.8	5.3	409	13.5[d]	4.4	516
Language skills	13.0	5.3	410	10.8[d]	4.6	520
Reading/vocabulary	18.8	6.0	410	14.1[d]	5.9	519

Table 6A4c Comparison of 1996 and 1976 cohorts by year group including 'as if' scores

	ORACLE 1976[e] 8/9[f] mean percentage scores (s.d.)[g]	9/10	10/11	ORACLE 1996 Y4[f] mean percentage scores (s.d.)[g]	Y5	Y6
Mathematics skills	42 (13)	62 (22)	75 (22)	31 (11)[d]	55 (18)[d]	62 (17)[d]
N *children*	580	306	315	235	193	196
Language skills	31 (13)	49 (21)	55 (21)	28 (12)[d]	41 (14)[d]	47 (17)[d]
N *children*	580	306	315	238	194	200
Vocabulary & reading comprehension	50 (16)	74 (24)	86 (24)	36 (12)[d]	53 (18)[d]	61 (16)[d]
N *children*	580	306	315	242	189	198

Notes for Tables 6A4a, 6A4b and 6A4c

a Cell values derived from post-test scores, shown in Tables 4.1, 4.2 and 4.3 of 'Progress and Performance in the Primary Classroom'.

b 1996 pooled scores have been calculated by weighting the Y4, Y5 and Y6 means in the ORACLE 1976 ratio of 580:306:315 (Galton and Simon 1980: Table 3.3). Unweighted calculation of the means has a very small effect on the values and no effect on the significance of the result.

c These large numbers include all children in the ORACLE schools who took any of the tests of basic skills. In subsequent analyses, the numbers are much smaller because these include only those children about whom we have other forms of quantitative data.

d $p < 0.01$ (1976/1996 difference).

e Extrapolated from beginning of year 1976 figures in Table 3.3 (Galton and Croll 1980).

f 8/9 year olds and Y4 took shorter tests but their scores are taken as a percentage of the total items (30) for ease of comparability.

g Percentages rounded to nearest whole number.

Appendix 6.5 Girls' and boys' performance on the tests of basic skills in 1976 and 1996

Table 6A5 Girls' and boys' performance on tests of basic skills, 1976 and 1996

	Y4boys[a] %	Y4 girls [a] %	Y5 boys %	Y5 girls %	Y6 boys %	Y6 girls %
LANGUAGE SKILLS						
Spelling	45.7 (3.1)	53.9 (3.0)	31.4 (2.8)	37.7 (3.3)	43.9 (2.6)	53.1 (2.2)[b]
Capitals	37.3 (2.6)	40.6 (2.6)	42.5 (1.5)	48.7 (2.1)[c]	44.8 (2.2)	48.3 (2.1)

Punctuation	49.0 (2.4)	46.4 (2.1)	36.9 (1.7)	43.2 (2.1)[c]	38.5 (2.0)	45.3 (1.8)[c]
Usage	43.8 (2.9)	48.8 (3.1)	41.7 (2.7)	50.0 (2.7)[c]	46.1 (2.9)	57.0 (2.4)[b]
Language Total	44.3 (2.0)	47.7 (1.8)	37.5 (1.6)	44.2 (1.9)[c]	43.1 (1.8)	50.6 (1.5)[b]
N	116	122	108	86	97	103
READING AND VOCABULARY						
Vocabulary	56.6 (2.0)	61.5 (2.0)	53.4 (2.1)	59.3 (1.8)[c]	60.8 (1.8)	65.8 (1.7)[c]
Comprehension	51.1 (2.2)	52.1 (1.9)	48.9 (2.1)	54.0 (2.0)	58.6 (1.8)	60.0 (1.8)
Reading Total	53.3 (1.8)	55.9 (1.7)	50.9 (1.9)	56.3 (1.8)[c]	59.6 (1.6)	62.5 (1.6)
N	117	125	104	85	95	103
MATHAMATICS SKILLS						
Maths concepts	61.0 (2.0)[b]	53.5 (1.8)	58.8 (1.9)	57.1 (1.8)	62.8 (1.8)	65.1 (1.8)
Problem solving	55.2 (2.7)[b]	45.4 (1.5)	50.6 (2.3)	48.6 (2.5)	59.8 (2.4)	58.9 (2.1)
Mathematics Total	58.6 (2.0)[b]	50.2 (1.5)	55.5 (1.9)	53.7 (1.9)	61.6 (1.8)	62.6 (1.7)
N	116	119	107	86	95	101

Notes

a percentage means based on the short form of the tests. Standard errors in brackets.

b $p < 0.01$ (sex difference within year group).

c $p < 0.05$ (sex difference within year group).

Appendix 6.6 Adjustments to test scores for comparative purposes: calculating the 'as if' scores

Adjustments have been made to the ORACLE 1976 scores in order to facilitate comparison with the 1996 results, as follows:

1   We have estimated what we can call 'year progress factors', which have been calculated and added to what the original ORACLE report termed the 1976 pre-test scores (see note 9, Chapter 6) to render them 'as if' the children had taken the tests at the end of the school years in question: i.e. as if they had taken the tests in June 1977 as opposed to September 1976.

The 'year progress factors' are the ratio of the mean raw-score gains for each subject area to the pre-test raw-score means scores as shown in Tables 4.1, 4.2 and 4.3 of Galton and Simon (1980) for Mathematics, Language and Reading respectively. These ratios have then been expressed as percentages. To obtain the 'as if' score these percentages of the pre-test percentage scores were calculated using Table 3.3 (Galton and Simon 1980: 50), and the amount added to the pre-test value in Table 3.3. This provides some measure of what the 1976 children's scores would have been if we had detailed breakdowns of the 1976 post-test scores. For example, in Mathematics, the mean raw-score gain was +5.1 (Table 4.1, Galton and Simon 1980) and the pre-test mean was 11.7. The ratio 5.1:11.7 is 0.436. Expressed as a percentage this is 43.6 per cent. Moving to Table 3.3 the mean percentage mathematics score for eight-year-olds is 29 per cent, which, rounded, becomes 42 per cent when increased by 43.6 per cent.

Expressed as percentages, the 'year progress factors' are: 43.6% for Mathematics; 47.7% for Language Skills; 48.0% for Reading.

An alternative approach, which is more generous as far as the 1996 children are concerned, is to use the ratio of the mean raw-score gains to the total number of items in the test. In the case of mathematics, this would be 5.1:30, which gives a value of 0.17 or 17 per cent. In this case the eight-year-olds' mean mathematics score would be 29 plus 17 per cent of 29, which rounded to the nearest whole number is 34 per cent. Thus, we could say that the 'as if' score allowing for expected progress in the course of the school year in mathematics concepts for eight-year-olds would be between 34 and 42 per cent, or the equivalent of answering four or five more items correctly. Any comparisons based on gender or age group are shown using these 'as if' values. They do not allow for any differential progress in the different sub-skills according to sex or age group in the 1976 cohort, however. This method implies a longitudinal sample between year groups, which was not the case.

2   The ORACLE 1976 sample contained almost twice as many eight-year-olds (N = 580) as nine- (N = 306) and ten-year-olds (N = 315). The younger children would obtain lower scores in the tests by virtue of their ages, but also because they took shorter tests which were subsequently given percentage scores based on the number of items in the longer tests taken by the older children. This would have the effect of lowering the 1976 overall mean. In order to make a fair comparison the 1996 sample has been weighted and randomly sampled to provide a 1996 sample which reflects the age balance of the 1976 sample in each table where the pooled test results have been used.

3   No variance measures are given for the ORACLE 1976 pre-test scores. Post-test (Summer 1977) standard deviations have therefore been calculated on the basis of statistics provided in the tables of covariance analyses in Appendix C of *Progress and Performance in the Primary Classroom* (Galton and Simon 1980). These have then been used as estimates for the standard deviations for the pre-test scores.

REFERENCES

Abbot, D. with Broadfoot, P., Croll, P., Osborn, M. and Pollard, A. (1994) 'Some Sink, Some Float: National Curriculum Assessment and Accountability', *British Education Research Journal* 29 (20): 155–74.

Aitken, M., Bennett, S. and Heskett, J. (1981) 'Teaching Styles and Pupil Progress: A Reanalysis', *British Journal of Educational Psychology* 51: 170–86.

Alexander, P., Schallert, D. and Hare, V. (1991) 'Coming to Terms: How Researchers in Learning and Literacy Talk About Knowledge', *Review of Educational Research* 61 (3): 315–43.

Alexander, R. (1991) *Primary Education in Leeds*, twelfth and final report from the Primary Needs Independent Evaluation Project: University of Leeds.

Alexander, R. (1994) *Innocence and Experience: Reconstructing Primary Education*, APSE Paper No.5, Stoke: Trentham Books Ltd.

Alexander, R. (1995) *Versions of Primary Education*, London: Routledge.

Alexander, R. (1996) *Other Schools and Ours: Hazards of International Comparison*, University of Warwick: Centre for Research in Elementary and Primary Education (CREPE) Occasional Paper.

Alexander, R. (1997) *Policy and Practice in Primary Education*, 2nd edition, London: Routledge.

Alexander, R., Willcocks, J. and Kinder, K. (1989) *Changing Primary Practice*, Basingstoke: Falmer Press.

Alexander, R., Rose, J. and Woodhead, C. (1992) *Curriculum Organisation and Classroom Practice in Primary Schools*, London: Department of Education and Science.

APU (1989) *Science at 13: Review of APU Survey Findings*, London: HMSO.

Aronson, E., Blaney, N., Stephen, C., Sikes, J. and Snapp, M. (1978) *The Jig Saw Classroom*, London: Sage.

Ashton, P., Kneen, P., Davies, F. and Holley, B. J. (1975) *The Aims of Primary Education: A Study of Teachers' Opinions*, Schools Council Research Studies, London: Macmillan Education.

Askew, M., Brown, M., Rhodes, V., Johnson, D. and Wiliam, D. (1997) *Effective Teachers of Numeracy*, Final Report for the TTA 1995–6, London: King's College School of Education.

ATL (1996a) *Doing Our Level Best: An Evaluation of Statutory Assessment in 1995*, London: Association of Teachers and Lecturers.

REFERENCES

ATL (1996b) *Level Best Revisited: An Evaluation of Statutory Assessment in 1996*, London: Association of Teachers and Lecturers.

Auld, R. (1976) *The William Tyndale Junior and Infants Schools*, a report of the Public Inquiry, London: ILEA.

Baker, K. (1993) *The Turbulent Years*, London: Faber & Faber.

Ball, S. (1990) *Policies and Policy Making in Education*, London: Routledge.

Barker Lunn, J. (1970) *Streaming in the Primary School*, Slough: NFER.

Barrett, G. (1986) *Starting School: An Evaluation of the Experience*, final report to the AMMA, CARE, University of East Anglia.

Bassey, M. (1978) *Nine Hundred Primary School Teachers*, Slough: NFER.

Bealing, D. (1971) 'The Organization of Junior School Classrooms', *Educational Research* 14 (1): 231–5.

Beggs, D. and Hieronymous, A. (1968) 'Uniformity of Growth in the Basic Skills throughout the School Year and during the Summer', *Educational Measurement* 5: 91–7.

Bennett, N. (1975) 'Teaching Styles: A Typological Approach', in Chanan, G. and Delamont, S. (eds) *Frontiers of Classroom Research*, Slough: NFER.

Bennett, N. (1976) *Teaching Styles and Pupil Progress*, London: Open Books.

Bennett, N. (1988) 'The Effective Primary School Teacher: The Search for a Theory of Pedagogy', *Teaching and Teacher Education* 4 (1): 19–30.

Bennett, N. (1992) *Managing Learning in the Primary School*, Association for the Study of Primary Education, Chester: Trentham Books.

Bennett, N., Andreae, J., Hegarty, P. and Wade, B. (1980) *Open Plan Schools*, Slough: NFER.

Bennett, N., Desforges, C., Cockburn, A. and Wilkinson, B. (1984) *The Quality of Pupil Learning Experience*, London: Lawrence Erlbaum.

Bennett, N. and Dunne, E. (1992) *Managing Classroom Groups*, Hemel Hampstead: Simon & Schuster.

Berliner, D. (1979) 'Tempus Educare', in Peterson, P. and Walberg, H. (eds) *Research on Teaching: Concepts, Findings and Implications*, Berkeley, California: McCutchan.

Berliner, D. and Biddle, B. (1995) *The Manufactured Crisis: Myths, Fraud and the Attack on America's Public Schools*, New York: Addison Wesley.

Best, S. (1996) 'What can be Made of Some Complex Concepts in the Writings of Anthony Giddens: The Far Side of Modernity', *Social Science Teacher* 25(3): 9–13.

Biggs, J. (1994) 'What are Effective Schools? Lessons from East and West', *Australian Educational Researcher* 21(1): 19–40.

Blatchford, P. (1992) 'Childrens' Attitude to Work at 11 Years', *Educational Studies*, 18 (1): 107–18.

Blyth, W. (1984) *Development and Experience in Primary Education*, London: Routledge.

Borko, H. and Livingston, C. (1989) 'Cognition and Improvisation: Differences in Mathematics Instruction by Expert and Novice Teachers', *American Educational Research Journal* 26(4): 473–98.

Boydell, D. (1974) 'Teacher Pupil Contact in Junior Classrooms', *British Journal of Educational Psychology* 44: 313–18.

Boydell, D. (1975) 'Pupil Behaviour in Junior Classrooms', *British Journal of Educational Psychology* 45: 122–9.

Boydell, D. (1978) *The Primary Teacher in Action*, London: Open Books.

234

Bracey, G. (1991) 'Why Can't They Be Like We Were? '*Phi Delta Kappa* 73, 105–7.

Brighouse, T. (1997) 'Leading and Managing Primary Schools: The Changing World of the Local Education Authority', in Cullingford, C. (ed.) *The Politics of Primary Education*, Buckingham: Open University Press.

Brogden, M. (1986) 'Open Plan Primary Schools: Rhetoric and Reality', in Cohen, A. and Cohen, L. (eds) *Primary Education : A Sourcebook for Teachers*, London: Harper & Row.

Brooks, G., Foxman, D. and Gorman, T. (1995) *Standards in Literacy and Numeracy: 1948–1994*, National Commission on Education Briefing, new series 7, Slough: NFER.

Brophy, J. E. and Good, T. L. (1986) 'Teacher Behaviour and Student Achievement', in Wittrock, M. C. (ed.) *Handbook of Research on Teaching*, 3rd edition, New York: Macmillan.

Brown, A. (1990) 'Domain-specific Principles Affect Learning and Transfer in Pupils', *Cognitive Science* 14 (1): 107–33.

Brown, A. and Palincsar, A. (1986) *Guided Cooperative Learning and Individual Knowledge Acquisition*, Technical Report 372, Cambridge (Mass): Bolt, Beranak & Newham Inc.

Brown, G. and Desforges, C. (1979) *Piaget's Theory: A Psychological Critique*, London: Routledge & Kegan Paul.

Bruner, J. and Haste, H. (1987) *Making Sense: The Child's Construction of the World*, London: Methuen.

Bullock Report (1975) *A Language for Life*, Report of the Committee of Inquiry appointed by the Secretary of State for Education and Science under the chairmanship of Sir Alan Bullock, London: HMSO.

Burstall, C. and Kay, B. (1978) *Assessment: The American Experience*, London: Department of Education and Science.

Byers, S. (1998) 'Keynote Address to XIth International Congress for School Effectiveness and Improvement', *Reaching Out to All Learners*, 5 January, University of Manchester: ICSEI.

Callaghan, J. (1976) 'Towards a National Debate – The Prime Minister's Ruskin Speech', *Education*, 22 October, 332–3.

Callaghan, J. (1992) 'The Educational Debate 1', in Williams, M., Daugherty, R. and Banks, F. (eds) *Continuing the Education Debate*, London: Cassell Education.

Campbell, J. (1993a) 'The Broad and Balanced Curriculum in Primary Schools: Some Limitations on Reform', *The Curriculum Journal* 4 (2): 215–29.

Campbell, J. (1993b) 'A Dream at Conception: A Nightmare at Delivery', in Campbell (ed.) *Breadth and Balance in the Primary Curriculum*, London: Falmer Press.

Campbell, J. (1994) 'Managing the Primary Curriculum: The Issue of Time Allocation', *Education* 22(1) 3–13.

Campbell, J. (1997) 'Towards Curriculum Subsidiarity', in *Developing the Primary School Curriculum: The Next Steps*, Papers from an invitational conference held by the Schools Curriculum and Assessment Authority, June 1997, London: SCAA.

Campbell, J. and Neill, S. (1994) *Primary Teachers at Work*, London: Routledge.

Chanan, G. and Delamont, S. (eds) (1975) *Frontiers of Classroom Research*, Windsor: NFER.

Chew, J. (1990) Letter to the *Times Educational Supplement*, 22 June 1990, cited in Turner, M. (1990) *Sponsored Reading Failure*, IPSET.

235

Clarkson, M. (ed) (1988) *Emerging Issues in Primary Education*, Lewes: Falmer Press.

Clarricoates, K. (1980) 'The Importance of Being Ernest...Emma...Tom... Jane: The Perception and Categorisation of Gender Conformity and Gender Deviation', in Deem, R., *Schooling for Women's Work*, London: Routledge & Kegan Paul.

Cockcroft Report (1982) *Mathematics Counts*, Report of the Committee of Inquiry into the Teaching of Mathematics in Schools under the Chairmanship of Dr W. H. Cockcroft, London: HMSO.

Cohen, E. (1994) 'Restructuring Classrooms: Conditions for Productive Small Groups', *Review of Educational Research* (64): 1–35.

Cohen, A. and Cohen, L. (eds) (1986) *Primary Education: A Sourcebook for Teachers*, London: Harper & Row Ltd.

Cohen, L., Manion, L. and Morrison, K. (1996) *A Guide to Teaching Practice* (4th edition), London: Routledge.

Connell, R. (1989) 'Cool Guys, Swots and Wimps: The Interplay of Masculinity and Education', *Oxford Review of Education* 15(3): 291–303.

Cooper, H., Nye, B., Charlton, K., Lindsay, J. and Greathouse, S. (1996) 'The Effects of Summer Vacation on Achievement Test Scores: A Narrative and Meta-analytic Review', *Review of Education Research* 66(3): 227–68.

Cox, C. and Dyson, A. (eds) (1969) *Fight for Education: A Black Paper*, London: The Critical Quarterly Society.

Creemers, B. (1994) 'The History, Value and Purpose of School Effectiveness Studies', in Reynolds, D., Creemers, B., Nesselradt, P., Schaffer, E., Stringfield, S. and Teddlie, C. (eds) *Advances in School Effectiveness Research and Practice*, Oxford: Pergamon Press.

Croll, P. (ed.) (1996a) *Teachers, Pupils and Primary Schooling*, London: Cassell.

Croll, P. (1996b) 'Teacher–Pupil Interaction in the Classroom', in Croll, P. and Hastings, N. (eds) *Effective Primary Teaching: Research Based Classroom Strategies*, London: David Fulton.

Croll, P. and Moses, D. (1985) *One in Five: The Assessment and Incidence of Special Educational Needs*, London: Routledge & Kegan Paul.

Croll, P. and Moses, D. (1990) 'Perspectives on the National Curriculum in Primary and Secondary Schools', *Educational Studies* 16: 187–8.

Cuban, L. (1984) *How Teachers Taught: Constancy and Change in American Classrooms, 1890–1980*, New York: Longman.

Cullingford, C. (1996) *Parents, Education and the State*, Aldershot: Arena Press.

Cullingford, C. (1997a) 'Children's Experience of Primary Education: Has it Changed?', in Cullingford, C. (ed.) *The Politics of Primary Education*, Milton Keynes: Open University Press.

Cullingford, C. (ed) (1997b) *The Politics of Primary Education*, Milton Keynes: Open University Press.

Cunningham, P. (1987) 'Open Plan Schooling: Last Stand of the Progressives?' in Lowe, R. *The Changing Primary School*, Lewes: Falmer Press.

Dadds, M. (1992) 'Monty Python and the Three Wise Men', *Cambridge Journal of Education* 22(2): 129–41.

Daugherty, R. (1997) 'Consistency in Teachers' Assessment: Defining the Problem, Finding the Answers', *British Journal of Curriculum and Assessment* 8(1): 32–8.

Davies, J. and Brember, I. (1997) 'Monitoring Reading Standards in Year 6: A Seven Year Cross-sectional Study', *British Educational Research Journal* 23(5): 615–22.

Dean, J. (1992) *Organising Learning in the Primary School Classroom* (2nd edition), London: Routledge.

Dearing, R. (1993a) *The National Curriculum and its Assessment*, an Interim Report, York: National Curriculum Council; London: School Examinations and Assessment Council.

Dearing, R. (1993b) *The National Curriculum and its Assessment*, Final Report, London: Schools Curriculum and Assessment Authority.

Delamont, S. and Galton, M. (1986) *Inside the Secondary Classroom*, London: Routledge & Kegan Paul.

Denham, C. and Lieberman, A. (1980) (eds) *Time to Learn*, report of the Beginning Teacher Education Studies, Washington, DC: National Institute of Education.

DES (1972) *Open-Plan Primary Schools*, London: HMSO.

DES (1980a) *A Framework for the School Curriculum*, London: HMSO.

DES (1980b) *A View of the Curriculum*, London: HMSO.

DES (1983) *Curriculum 11–16: Towards a Statement of Entitlement: Curricular Reappraisal in Action*, London: HMSO.

DES (1985a) *The Curriculum from 5–16*, London: HMSO.

DES (1985b) *Better Schools*, Cmnd 9469, London: HMSO.

Desforges, C. (1982) 'In Place of Piaget: Recent Research on Children's Learning', *Educational Analysis* 4(2): 27–42.

Desforges, C. (1995) *An Introduction to Teaching*, Oxford: Blackwell.

Dewhurst, J. (1996) 'Differentiation in Primary Teaching', *Education 3–13* 24(3): 27–36.

DfEE (1992) *Choice and Diversity*, London: Department for Education and Employment.

DfEE (1995) *Key Stages 1 and 2 of the National Curriculum*, London: Department for Education and Employment.

DfEE (1996) 'Statistics of Schools in England', *News*, January edition, London: Department for Education and Employment.

DfEE (1997a) *Excellence in Schools*, presented to Parliament by the Secretary of State for Education and Employment by command of her Majesty, London: Department of Education and Employment.

DfEE (1997b) *Connecting the Learning Society: National Grid for Learning, The Government's Consultation Paper*, London: Department for Education and Employment.

DfEE (1997c) *Preparing for the Information Age*, Synoptic Report of the Education Departments Superhighways Initiative (EDSI), London: Department for Education and Employment.

DfEE (1998a) 'Byers Welcomes Teaching Improvements', Press Release 56/98: 3 February.

DfEE (1998b) 'Councils Get Tough New English Test Targets', Press Release 005/98: 7 January.

DfEE (1998c) 'National Curriculum Assessments of 7, 11 and 14 Year Olds by Local Education Authority, 1997', Press Release, 2 February.

DfEE (1998d) 'Byers Outlines Co-ordinated Action to Tackle Boys' Underachievement', Press Release 002/98: 5 January.

DfEE (1998e) *Numeracy Matters: The Preliminary Report of the Numeracy Task Force* (published for consultation January 1998), London: Department for Education and Employment.

Dickinson, C. and Wright, J. (1993) *Differentiation: A Practical Handbook of Strategies*, Coventry: NCET.

Donaldson, M. (1978) *Children's Minds*, London: Fontana.

Donneau, S. (1985) 'Soliciting in the Classroom', in Husen, T. and Postlethwaite, T. (eds) *The International Encyclopedia of Education: Research and Studies*, Oxford: Pergamon Press.

Doyle, W. and Ponder, G. (1977) 'The Practicality Ethic and Teacher Decision Making', *Interchange* (8): 1–12.

Driver, R. (1983) *The Pupil as Scientist*, Milton Keynes: The Open University.

Dweck, C. and Wortman, C. (1982) 'Learned Helplessness, Anxiety and Achievement: Neglected Parallels in Cognitive, Affective and Coping Responses', in Krohne, H. and Laux, L. (eds) *Achievement, Stress and Anxiety*, Washington, DC: Hemisphere.

Edwards, A. and Westgate, D. (1987) *Investigating Classroom Talk*, Lewes: Falmer Press.

Elwood J. and Comber, C. (1996) 'Gender and A Level Examinations: New Complexities or Old Stereotypes?', *British Journal of Curriculum and Assessment* 6(2): 24–8.

Everitt, B. (1994) 'Cluster Analysis', in Husen, T. and Postlethwaite, N. (eds) *International Encyclopedia of Education*, 2nd Edition, Volume 2, Oxford: Pergamon.

Flanders, N. A. (1964) 'Some Relationships Among Teacher Influence, Pupil Attitudes and Achievement', in Biddle, B. J. and Ellena, W. J. (eds) *Contemporary Research on Teacher Effectiveness*, New York: Holt, Rinehart & Winston.

Fogelman, K. and Goldstein, H. (1976) 'Social Factors Associated with Changes in Educational Attainment between 7 and 11 Years of Age', *Educational Studies* 2(2) 95–105.

France, N. (1981) *The Primary Reading Test*, Windsor: NFER-Nelson.

France, N. and Fraser, I. (1975) *Richmond Tests of Basic Skills*, Windsor: NFER-Nelson.

French, J. and French, P. (1984) 'Gender Imbalances in the Primary Classroom: An Interactional Account', *Educational Research* 26(2):127–36.

Gage, N. (1985) *Hard Gains in the Soft Sciences, The Case for Pedagogy*, CEDR Monograph, Bloomington, Indiana: Phi Delta Kappa.

Galton, M. (1989) *Teaching in the Primary School*, London: David Fulton Publishers.

Galton, M. (1995) *Crisis in the Primary Classroom*, London: David Fulton Publishers.

Galton, M. (1997) 'Primary Culture and Classroom Teaching', in Kitson, N. and Merry, R. (eds) *Teaching in the Primary School*, London: Routledge.

Galton, M. and Simon, B. (eds) (1980) *Progress and Performance in the Primary Classroom*, London: Routledge & Kegan Paul.

Galton, M., Simon, B. and Croll, P. (1980) *Inside the Primary Classroom*, London: Routledge & Kegan Paul.

Galton, M. and Willcocks, J. (eds) (1983) *Moving from the Primary Classroom*, London: Routledge & Kegan Paul.

Galton, M., Bernbaum, G., Patrick, K. and Appleyard, R. (1987) *Educational Provision in Small Primary Schools*, Final Report to the Department of Education and Science (DES) Leicester: School of Education, University of Leicester.

Galton, M. and Blyth, A. (eds) (1989) *Handbook of Primary Education in Europe*, London: David Fulton Publishers for the Council of Europe.

Galton, M. and Patrick, H. (1990) *Curriculum Provision in the Small Primary School*, London: Routledge.

Galton, M., Fogelman, K., Hargreaves, L. and Cavendish, S. (1991) *The Rural Schools Curriculum Enhancement National Evaluation (SCENE) Project: Final Report*, London: Department of Education and Science.

Galton, M. and Williamson, J. (1992) *Group Work in the Primary Classroom*, London: Routledge.

Galton, M. and Hargreaves, L. (1996) 'Today I felt I Was Actually Teaching: The Effects of Class Size on Pupils' Behaviour', *Education Review* 10(2): 26–33.

Galton, M. and Fogelman, K. (1998) 'The Use of Discretionary Time in the Primary School', *Research Papers in Education*.

Galton, M., Hargreaves, L. and Comber, C. (1998) 'Classroom Practice and the National Curriculum in Small Rural Primary Schools', *British Educational Research Journal* 24(1): 43–61.

Gardner, H. (1983) *Frames of Mind*, New York: Basic Books.

Giddens, A. (1994) 'Living in Post-Traditionalist Society', in Beck, U., Giddens, A., and Lash, S. (eds) *Reflexive Modernization: Politics, Tradition and Aesthetics in the Modern Social Order*, Cambridge: Polity Press.

Gipps, C. V. (1992a) *What Do We Know about Effective Primary Teaching?*, London: Tufnell Press.

Gipps, C. V. (1992b) 'National Curriculum Assessment: A Research Agenda', *British Educational Research Journal* 18(3): 277–86.

Gipps, C. V. (1994) *Beyond Testing: Towards a Theory of Educational Assessment*, London: Falmer Press.

Gipps, C. V. and Goldstein, H. (1983) *Monitoring Children: An Evaluation of the Assessment of Performance Unit*, London: Heinemann.

Gipps, C.V. and Murphy, P. (1994) *A Fair Test? Assessment, Achievement and Equity*, Buckingham: Open University Press.

Gipps, C. V., Brown, M., McCallum, B. and McManus, S. (1995) *Intuition or Evidence? Teachers and National Assessment of Seven-Year-Olds*, Buckingham: Open University Press.

Gipps, C.V., Steadman, S., Blackstone, T., and Stierer, B. (1983) *Testing Children: Standardised Testing in LEAs and Schools*, London: Heinemann.

Golby, M. (1988) 'Traditions in Primary Education', in Clarkson, M. (ed.) (1988) *Emerging Issues in Primary Education*, Lewes: Falmer Press.

Graham, D. (with Tyler, D.) (1993) *A Lesson For Us All: The Making of the National Curriculum*, London: Routledge.

Gray, J. (1980) 'How Good Were the Tests?', *Times Educational Supplement*, 7 November: 17.

Hagues, N. and Courtenay, D., with Patilla, P. (1994) *Mathematics 7*, Teacher's Guide, Windsor: NFER-Nelson.

Hall, N. (1987) *The Emergence of Literacy*, London: Hodder & Stoughton.

Hammersley, M. and Scarth, J. (1993) 'Beware of Wise Men Bearing Gifts: A Case Study in the Issue of Educational Research', *British Educational Research Journal* 19(5): 489–98.

Hargreaves, D. H. (1982) *The Challenge for the Comprehensive School*, London: Routledge & Kegan Paul.

Hargreaves, D. H. (1997) 'In Defence of Research for Evidence-based Teaching: A Rejoinder to Martyn Hammersley', *British Educational Research Journal* 23(4): 405–20.

Hargreaves, L. (1990) 'Teachers and Pupils in Small Schools', in Galton, M. and Patrick, H. (eds) *Curriculum Provision in the Small Primary School*, 75–103.

Hargreaves, A. and Dawe, R. (1990) 'Paths of Professional Development: Contrived Collegiality, Collaborative Culture and the Case of Peer Coaching', *Teaching and Teacher Education* 6(3): 227–41.

Harlen, W. (1985) *Teaching and Learning in Primary Science*, London: Harper Education Series.

Harlen, W. (1992) *The Teaching of Science*, London: David Fulton.

Hartley, J. (1997) 'Where Shall We Sit?', *Psychology Review* 4(1): 17–19.

Hastings, N. (1995) 'Seats of Learning?', *Support for Learning* 10(1): 8–11.

Hastings, N. and Schwieso, J. (1995) 'Tasks and Tables: The Effects of Seating Arrangements on Task Engagement in Primary Classrooms', *Educational Research* 37(3): 279–291.

Hastings, N., Schwieso, J. and Wheldall, K. (1996) 'A Place for Learning', in Croll, P. and Hastings, N. (eds), *Effective Primary Teaching: Research Based Classroom Strategies*, London: David Fulton.

HCP (Humanities Curriculum Project) (1970) *The Humanities Curriculum Project: An Introduction*, London: Heinemann.

Hieronymous, A. N., Lindquist, E. F. and France, N. (1988) *Richmond Tests of Basic Skills: Administration Manual*, Windsor: NFER-Nelson.

HMI (1980) *Education 5–9*, London: HMSO.

Holt, J. (1984) *How Children Fail*, London: Penguin.

Hughes, M., Wikeley, F. and Nash, T. (1994) *Parents and their Children's Schools*, Oxford: Blackwell.

Hunter, P. (1997) 'The Market Experiment', in Cullingford, C. (ed.) *The Politics of Primary Education*, Buckingham: Open University Press.

Jeffery, B. and Woods, P. (1996) 'Feeling Deprofessionalised: The Social Construction of Emotions During an OFSTED Inspection', *Cambridge Journal of Education* 26(3): 325–43.

Keys, W. and Foxman, D. (1989) *A World of Difference: A United Kingdom Perspective on an International Assessment of Mathematics and Science*, Slough: NFER.

Keys, W., Harris, S. and Fernandes, C. (1996) *Third International Mathematics and Science Study: First National Report: Part 1*, Slough: NFER.

Kliebard, H. (l986) *The Struggle for the American Curriculum 1893–1958*, New York: Methuen.

Klinzing-Eurich, G. (1987) 'Teacher Questioning', *Questioning Exchange* 3: 1–16.

Lave, J. (1992) 'Word Problems: A Microcosm of Theories of Learning', in Light, P. and Butterworth, G. (eds) *Content and Cognition: Ways of Knowing*, Hillsdale, New Jersey: LEA.

Lawlor, S. (1988) *The Correct Core*, London: Centre for Policy Studies.

Lawlor, S. (1990) *Teachers Mistaught: Training in Theories or Education in Subjects*, Policy Study No. 116, London: Centre for Policy Studies.

Lawton, D. (1975) *Class, Culture and the Curriculum*, London: Routledge & Kegan Paul.

Maehr, M. and Maehr, J. (1996) 'Schools Aren't as Good as They Used to Be; They Never Were', *Educational Researcher* 25(8): 21–4.

McClelland, D. (1963) 'On the Psychodynamics of Creative Physical Scientists', in Gruber, M., Terrell, H. E. and Wertheimer, M. (eds) *Contemporary Approaches to Creative Thinking*, New York: Atherton.

McKinsey & Company (1997) *The Future of Information Technology in U.K. Schools*, London: McKinsey & Company.

McNamara, D. and Waugh, D. (1993) 'Classroom Organisation: A Discussion of Grouping Strategies in the Light of the "3 Wise Men's' Report"', *School Organisation* 13(1): 41–50.

Measor, L. and Woods, P. (1984) *Changing Schools: Pupils' Perspectives on Transfer to a Comprehensive*, Milton Keynes: Open University Press.

Mortimore, P., Sammons, P., Stoll, L., Lewis, D. and Ecob, R. (1988) *School Matters: The Junior Years*, Wells: Open Books.

Mortimore, P. and Goldstein, H. (1996) *The Teaching of Reading in 45 Inner London Primary Schools: A Critical Examination of OFSTED Research*, London: Institute of Education.

Moyles, J. (ed.) (1995) *Beginning Teaching: Beginning Learning*, Buckingham: Open University Press.

Moyles, J and Hargreaves, L. (eds) (1998) *The Primary Curriculum: Learning from International Perspectives*, London: Routledge.

Murphy, P. (1982) 'Sex Differences in Objective Test Performance', *British Journal of Educational Psychology* 52: 213–19.

Murphy, P. (1989) 'Gender and Assessment', in Murphy, P. and Moon, B., *Developments in Learning and Assessment*, London: Hodder & Stoughton.

Murphy, R. and Broadfoot, P. (1995) *Effective Assessment and the Improvement of Education: A Tribute to Desmond Nuttall*, London: Falmer Press.

NCC (1989) *A Framework for the Primary Curriculum*, York: National Curriculum Council.

Nias, J., Southworth, G. and Yeomans, R. (1989) *Staff Relationships in the Primary School*, London: Cassell.

Nisbet, J. and Shucksmith, J. (1984) *Learning Strategies*, London: Routledge & Kegan Paul.

Nuttall, D. (1980) 'Will the APU Rule the Curriculum?', supplement to *Education*, 155, 21: ix–x. Reprinted in Murphy, R. and Broadfoot, P. (1995) *Effective Assessment and the Improvement of Education: A Tribute to Desmond Nuttall*, London: Falmer Press.

Nuttall, D. (1989) 'National Assessment – Will Reality Match Aspirations?', *British Psychological Society Education Section Review* 13(1/2): 6–9.

Nuttall, D. (1991) *Assessment in England*, report prepared for Pelavin Associates. Reprinted in Murphy and Broadfoot (1995).

Nuttall, D. (1993) Presentation at Centre for Policy Studies Conference, reprinted in Murphy, R. and Broadfoot, P. (eds) *Effective Assessment in the Improvment of Education: A Tribute to Desmond Nuttall*, London: Falmer Press.

241

OFSTED (1993) *Curriculum Organisation and Classroom Practice in Primary Schools: A Follow-up Report*, London: Office for Standards in Education.

OFSTED (1994) *Primary Matters: A Discussion on Teaching and Learning in Primary Schools*, London: Office for Standards in Education.

OFSTED (1995) *Teaching Quality: The Primary Debate*, London: Office for Standards in Education.

OFSTED (1996a) *The Annual Report of Her Majesty's Chief Inspector of Schools: Standards and Quality in Education 1994–95*, London: HMSO.

OFSTED (1996b) *The Teaching of Reading in 45 London Primary Schools*, London: HMSO.

OFSTED (1996c) *The Gender Divide: Performance Differences Between Boys and Girls at School*, EOC/OFSTED London: HMSO.

OFSTED (1997) *The Annual Report of Her Majesty's Chief Inspector of Schools: Standards and Quality in Education 1995–96*, London: HMSO.

Osborn, M. (1996) 'Teachers Mediating Change: Key Stage 1 Revisited', in Croll, P. (ed.) *Teachers, Pupils and Primary Schooling*, London: Cassell.

Osborn, M. (1997) 'Teachers' Work, Professional Identity and Change', in Pollard, A. and Broadfoot, P. (1997) (eds) *PACE: Primary Assessment, Curriculum and Experience*, Symposium Papers for Annual Conference of British Educational Research Association (BERA), York, 11–14 September; Bristol: Researching Culture and Learning on Organisations (CLIO) University of Bristol.

Osborn, M., McNess, E., Broadfoot, P., with Pollard, A. and Triggs, P. (forthcoming) *Policy, Practice and Teacher Experience: Changing English Primary Schools?*, London: Cassell.

Palincsar, A. and Brown, A. (1984) 'Reciprocal Teaching of Comprehension-fostering and Comprehension-monitoring Activities', *Cognition and Instruction* 2: 117–75.

Paynter, J. (1982) *Music in the Secondary School Curriculum*, Cambridge: Cambridge University Press.

PEC (1997) 'Future Directions for Singapore Education: Special Interview with the Director of Education, Mr Wee Heng Tin', *Principals' Executive Centre (PEC) Bulletin* (3): 1–2.

Phillips, M. (1996) *All Must Have Prizes*, London: Little, Brown & Co.

Pintrich, P., Marx, R. and Boyle, R. (1993) 'Beyond Cold Conceptual Change: The Role of Motivational Beliefs and Classroom Contextual Factors in the Process of Conceptual Change', *Review of Educational Research* 63(2): 167–200.

Plowden Report (1967) *Children and their Primary Schools*, report of the Central Advisory Council for Education in England, London: HMSO.

Plunkett, D. (1996) 'Snapshot in the Dark', *Education* 1 March: 12–13.

Pollard, A. (1985) *The Social World of the Primary School*, London: Holt, Rinehart & Winston.

Pollard, A., Broadfoot, P., Croll, P., Osborn, M., and Abbott, D. (1994) *Changing English Primary Schools*, London: Cassell.

Pollard, A. and Broadfoot, P. (1997) (eds) *PACE: Primary Assessment, Curriculum and Experience*, Symposium Papers for Annual Conference of British Educational Research Association (BERA), York, 11–14 September; Bristol: Researching Culture and Learning on Organisations (CLIO) University of Bristol.

Pollard, A. and Tann, S. (1987) *Reflective Teaching in the Primary Classroom: A Handbook for the Classroom* (2nd edition), London: Cassell.

Popham, J. (1987) 'The Merits of Measurement-driven Instruction', *Phi Delta Kappa* May: 679–82.

Reynolds, D., Creemers, B., Nesselradt, P., Schaffer, E., Stringfield, S. and Teddlie, C. (eds) (1994) *Advances in School Effectiveness Research and Practice*, Oxford: Pergamon Press.

Reynolds, D. and Cuttance, P. (eds) (1992) *School Effectiveness: Research, Policy and Practice*, London: Cassell.

Reynolds, D. and Farrell, S. (1996) *Office for Standards in Education (OFSTED) Reviews of Research*, London: HMSO.

Richards, C. (1988) 'Primary Education in England: An Analysis of Some Recent Developments', *Cambridge Journal of Education*, 17(3): 197–201.

Richards, C. (1997) *Primary Education, Standards and OFSTED: Towards a More Authentic Conversation*, University of Warwick: Centre of Research in Elementary and Primary Education (CREPE) Occasional Paper.

Richards, C. (1998) 'Changing Primary/Elementary School Curricula: An Analysis of the English Experience 1862–2012', in Moyles, J. and Hargreaves, L. (eds) *The Primary Curriculum: Learning from an International Perspective*, London: Routledge.

Ridley, K. and Trembath, D. (1986) 'Primary School Organisation: Some Rhetoric and Some Reason', in Cohen, A. and Cohen, L, (eds) *Primary Education; A Sourcebook for Teachers*, London: Harper Rowe Ltd.

Rosenshine, B. (1979) 'Content, Time and Direct Instruction', in Peterson, P. and Walberg, H. (eds) *Research on Teaching Concepts, Findings and Implications*, California, Berkeley: McCutchan.

Rosenshine, B. (1987) 'Direct Instruction', in Dunkin, M. (ed.) *Teaching and Teacher Education*, Oxford: Pergamon.

Rosenshine, B. and Meister, C. (1994) 'Reciprocal Teaching: A Review of Research', *Review of Educational Research* 64(4): 479–530.

Rosenshine, B., Meister, C. and Chapman, S. (1996) 'Teaching Students to Generate Questions: A Review of Intervention Studies', *Review of Educational Research* 66(2): 181–221.

Rutter, M., Maughan, B., Mortimore, P. and Ouston, J., with Smith, A. (1979) *Fifteen Thousand Hours: Secondary Schools and their Effects on Children*, London: Open Books.

Sainsbury, M. (ed.) (1996) *SATs: The Inside Story: the Development of the First National Assessment for Seven Year Olds 1989–1995*, Slough: NFER.

Sammons, P., Hillman, J. and Mortimore, P. (1995) *Key Characteristics of Effective Schools: A Review of School Effectiveness Research*, London: Office for Standards in Education (OFSTED).

Samson, G., Strykowski, B., Weinstein, T. and Walberg, H. (1987) 'The Effects of Teacher Questioning Levels on Student Achievement: A Quantitative Synthesis', *Journal of Educational Research* 80(5): 290–95.

SCAA (1996) *Standards in Public Examinations 1975 to 1995*, SCAA/OFSTED London: SCAA Publications.

SCAA (1997) *Standards at Key Stage 2 English, Mathematics and Science: Report on the 1996 National Curriculum Assessments for 11 Year Olds*, London: SCAA.

Scarth, J. and Hammersley, M. (1986) 'Questioning ORACLE: An Assessment of ORACLE's Analysis of Teachers' Questions', *Educational Research* 28(3): 174–84.

Scarth, J. and Hammersley, M. (1987) 'More Questioning of ORACLE: A Reply to Croll and Galton', *Educational Research* 29 (1): 37–46.

Schmitt, A.P., Mazzeo, J. and Bleistein, C. (1991) *Are Gender Differences Between Placement Multiple-choice and Constructed Response Sections a Function of Multiple-choice DIF?*, Princeton, NJ, Educational Testing Service.

Schweinhart, L. and Weikart, D. (1997) *Lasting Differences: The Highscope Pre-School Curriculum Comparisons Study through Age 23*, Ypsilanti, Michigan: Highscope Press.

Shorrocks, D., Daniels, S., Frobisher, L., Nelson, N. and Waterson, A. (1992) *Evaluation of National Curriculum Assessment at Key Stage 1*, London: Schools Examination and Assessment Council.

Shulman, L. (1986) 'Those who Understand: Knowledge Growth in Teaching', *Educational Research* 15: 4–14.

Simon, B. (1964) *Non-streaming in the Junior School*, Leicester: PSW (Educational) Publications Forum.

Simon, B. (1966) 'The Junior School: Anatomy of the Non-streamed Classroom', *Forum* 8: 79–85.

Simon, B. (1981a) 'The Primary School Revolution: Myth or Reality?' in Simon, B. and Willcocks, J. (eds) *Research and Practice in the Primary Classroom*, London: Routledge & Kegan Paul.

Simon, B. (1981b) 'Why no Pedagogy in England?', in Simon, B. and Taylor, W. (eds) *Education in the Eighties, The Central Issues*, London: Batsford.

Simon, B. (1985) *Does Education Matter?*, London: Lawrence & Wishart.

Simon, B. (1993) 'Primary Education', *Education Today and Tommorrow* 44(3): 13–14.

Simon, B. (1994) *The State and Educational Change: Essays in the History of Education and Pedagogy*, London: Lawrence & Wishart.

Sirotnik, K. (1983) 'What You See is What You Get – Consistency, Persistency and Mediocrity in Classrooms', *Harvard Educational Review* 53(1): 16–31.

Slavin, R. (1986) 'Small Group Methods', in Dunkin, M. (ed.) *The International Encyclopedia of Teaching and Teacher Education*, London: Pergamon.

Somekh, B. and Davis, N. (eds) (1997) *Using Information Technology Effectively in Teaching and Learning: Studies in Pre-service and In-service Teacher Education*, London: Routledge.

Southgate, V., Arnold, H. and Johnson, S. (1981) *Extending Beginning Reading*, London: Heinemann for the Schools' Council.

Spender, D. (1982) *Invisible Women: The Schooling Scandal*, London: Writers & Readers Publishing Cooperative.

Stannard, J. (1995) 'Managing the Primary Curriculum after Dearing: A Rationale', *Education 3 –13* 23(1) March: 3–13.

Sternberg, R. and Wagner, R. (1986) *Practical Intelligence: Nature and Origins of Competence in the Everyday World*, Cambridge: Cambridge University Press.

Stevenson, D. (1997) *Information and Communications Technology in UK Schools*, An Independent Inquiry (The Stevenson Report), The Independent ICT in Schools Commission.

Stobart, G., Elwood, J. and Quinlan, M. (1992) 'Gender Bias in Examinations: How Equal are the Opportunities?', *British Educational Research Journal*, 18(3): 261–76.

244

Stobart, G., White, J., Elwood, J., Hayden, M. and Mason, K. (1992) *Differential Performance at 16+: English and Mathematics*, London: SEAC.

Terwilliger, J. (1997) 'Semantics, Psychometrics and Assessment Reform: A Close Look at Authentic Assessments', *Educational Researcher* 26(8): 24–7.

TGAT (Task Group on Assessment and Testing) (1988) *National Curriculum: A Report of the Task Group on Assessment and Testing*, London: DES and Welsh Office.

Thomas, N. (1990) *Primary Education from Plowden to the 1990s*, London: Falmer.

Tizard, B. and Hughes, M. (1984) *Young Children Learning: Talking and Thinking at Home and School*, London: Fontana.

Tizard, B., Blatchford, D., Burke, J., Farquhar. C. and Plewis, I. (1988) *Young Children at School in the Inner City*, Hove: Lawrence Erlbaum.

Tomlinson, J. (1992) 'Retrospect on Ruskin: Prospect on the 1990s', in Williams, M., Dougherty, R. and Banks, F. (eds) *Continuing the Education Debate*, London: Cassell.

Torrance, H. (1992) 'Research in Assessment: A Response to Caroline Gipps', *British Educational Research Journal* 18(4): 343–50.

Turner, M. (1990) *Sponsored Reading: Failure of an Object Lesson*, Warlingham, Surrey: IPSET Education Unit.

Turner, M. (1992) 'Organised Inferiority? Reading and the National Curriculum', *British Psychological Society Education Section Review* 16(1), 1–8, 23–5; *Peer Review* 16(1): 9–22.

Underwood, J. (1994) (ed.) *Computer Based Learning: Potential into Practice*, London: David Fulton.

Vygotsky, L. (1978) *Mind in Society: The Development of Higher Psychological Processes*, Cambridge, Mass.: Harvard University Press.

Waterland, L. (1985) *Read with Me: An Apprenticeship Approach to Reading*, Stroud: Thimble Press.

Watkins, P. (1993) book review: 'A Lesson For Us All', *Headlines* (Journal of Secondary Headteachers Association, SHA), No.11: 65–6.

Webb, R. (1993a) *Eating the Elephant Bit by Bit: The National Curriculum at Key Stage 2*, Final Report of research Commissioned by the Association of Teachers and Lecturers (ATL), London: ATL Publishers.

Webb, R. (1993b) 'The National Curriculum and the Changing Nature of Topic Work', *The Curriculum Journal* 4(2): 239–51.

Webb, R. and Vulliamy, G. (1996) *Roles and Responsibilities in the Primary School: Changing Demands, Changing Practices*, Buckingham: Open University Press.

Wells, G., Chang, G. and Maher, A. (1990) 'Creating Classroom Communities of Literate Thinkers', in Sharan, S. (ed.) *Cooperative Learning*, New York: Praeger.

Westbury, I. (1993) 'American and Japanese Achievement – Again', *Educational Researcher* 22(3): 21–5.

Wheldall, K. and Congreve, S. (1981) 'Teachers and Behaviour Modification: What Do They Think of it So Far?', in Wheldall, K. (ed.) *The Behaviourist in the Classroom*, Birmingham: Educational Review Publications.

Wheldall, K. and Lam, Y. (1987) 'Rows versus Tables II: The Effects of Two Classroom Seating Arrangements on Disruption Rate, On-task Behaviour and Teacher Behaviour in Three Special School Classes', *Educational Psychology* 7(4): 303–12.

Wheldall, K. and Olds, D. (1987) 'Of Sex and Seating: The Effects of Mixed and Same-sex Seating Arrangements in Junior Classrooms', *New Zealand Journal of Educational Studies* 22(1): 71–85.

Wiliam, D. (1992) 'Value-added Attacks: Technical Issues in Reporting National Curriculum Assessments', in *British Educational Research Journal* 18(4): 329–41.

Williams, R. (1961) *Culture and Society*, London: Penguin Books.

Wood, D. (1988) *How Children Think and Learn*, Oxford: Blackwell.

Woodhead, C. (1995a) 'Teaching Quality: The Issues and the Evidence', in OFSTED *Teaching Quality: The Primary Debate*, London: Office for Standards in Education.

Woodhead, C. (1995b) *Education: The Elusive Engagement and the Continuing Frustration*, Annual HMCI Lecture, Royal Society of Arts, London: Office for Standards in Education.

Wroe, M. A. *Thoughts on the Training of Children*, London: National Society's Depository (early twentieth century – undated).

Yeomans, J. (1989) 'Changing Seating: The Use of Antecedent Control to Increase On-task Behaviour', *Behavioural Approaches with Children* 13(3): 151–60.

INDEX

secondary school, transition to 51; lack
of continuity between the primary
feeder and the secondary transfer
schools 132; Moving from the
Primary School: 20 Years On 38
self-confidence: pupils' levels of 139
SEN 51
sex of the teacher 98–9
silent marking 60, 67
small talk 66 (see also conversations)
social reconstructionists 11; common
culture 11
society: 'globalisation': process of 30;
post-traditional 6, 30 (education
in 193; state of manufactured
uncertainty 30)
specialised subject knowledge (see also
National Curriculum) 31;
specialisation 42; specialisms 173
spelling (see also punctuation) 145, 166;
performance 153; punctuation, usage
and reading vocabulary 163
standards 135–6; fallen 137, 159;
improved educational standards 168;
national standards 136; significant
drop in performance 149; small
schools did no worse 160
statement: of 'fact' 74; of 'ideas' 75;
routine 75
storage space 48–9 (see also layout)
superhighways: evaluation 194;
initiative (EDSI) 193
supervisors: group 118, 121, 129
sustained: contact 88; conversations 88;
interaction 72

Task Group on Assessment and Testing
(TGAT) 140
tasks 139: related activities 89;
statements: a proportion of all
observations 66; statements:
critical 66; supervision 76–7
(feedback 66, 76; questioning 64;
statements 64, 66)
teacher: aims 144–5; assessment
(TA) 142; expectations 139; and
pupil record 58; record 66, 70 (see
also ORACLE); response to
demands placed upon them 41;
statements 64, 69; statements,
percentage of uniformity across all
subjects 74

teacher's desk (see also layout) 47;
a 'base' 42; centrally positioned 39;
'housekeeping' 42, 67; location 42;
position of 42; symbol of
authority 42; traditional centre-front
position 42
teaching: art of 184; direct 189;
organisation across subjects 70;
reciprocal 188; secondary
approach 131; team teaching 50–51,
86–7; theory of 190; 'transmission
teaching' 169
teaching styles 109–12, 123, 132;
combined 118; distribution of pupil
types across 129; front of class style
of delivery 42; mixed 113–14; of the
1990s are not as distinct as those of
the 1970s 130; pupil types:
relationships between 128
teaching methods: traditional 24;
trendy 24
technology: room 50; sessions 51
tests 139, 143; mathematics 146;
multiple-choice, favour boys 57;
reliabilities 146; Richmond Tests 190
(of basic skills 178, 'criterion
referenced' 144, 'domain referenced'
144); scores 161; spelling,
reading 144; vocabulary 167
TGAT 143
Third International Mathematics
Studies 135 (see also mathematics)
time 'on-task' 81, 90, 172; level of 47
traditional-progressive dichotomy 24
Turner, Martin 136
tutoring: peer 187, 197
TVEI (Technical and Vocational
Education Initiative) 12
typical: 'average lesson' 107; primary
aged pupil: life of 79; pupil: point of
view 79; pupil, teacher, lesson 107;
teacher: then and now 78; teacher:
working even harder 78

validity: content 145
value-added 135
Victorian building 41, 48
Vygotsky (see also conceptual
development) 141

whole class 42, 79, 105; activity 89;
exposition 79; and group

252

teaching 184; interaction 46, 130;
settings 69–70, 99; situations 184;
teaching 42, 43, 50, 59, 63, 72, 83–4,
93, 130–1, 160, 168, 173 (emphasis
on 71, endorsement of
interactive 183, specialist subject
matter 24, increased use of 52, 175,
188; interactive 189; the major
vehicle for enquiry 60; the norm 127;
on-task supervision 63; the shift
to 178)
wild men of the classroom 4, 34
William Tyndale School 8, 15
Woodhead, C. 16–17, 20, 31–2, 34,
38; 'a very unpleasant
atmosphere' 35; criticisms of
contemporary primary teaching 31;
critics such as 58; HM Chief

Inspector of Schools 4, 23, 27;
resistance to the use of whole class
teaching 33; supporters, ultra-
nationalist perspective 196
workers: collaborative 124;
intermittent 121, 123–4, 128–9,
176–7; solitary 122–4, 128, 177
working: consensus 109, 128;
intermittent 130–1; styles, individual,
group and whole class 47
world wide web: provision of
information 193; resource for
children's learning 195

year progress factors (see also
comparison; ORACLE) 148 'as
if' 148 (correction factor 151,
estimated scores 150)